Enjoy the Adven...

Bri & Peggy

The Adventure
of
Two Lifetimes

by Peggy Newland Goetz & Brian Goetz
with June Meyer Newland

ANACUS
PRESS INC.

The Adventure of Two Lifetimes

Cover: *Jean Sullivan*
Maps: *Richard Widhu*

ISBN: 0-933855-23-0
Library of Congress Control Number: 2001 132005

www.TheAdventureBook.com

Published by

PRESS INC.

P.O. Box 156, Liberty Corner, New Jersey 07938

www.anacus.com

Printed in the United States of America

for Haley June-Marie

Prologue

Peggy

Forty years ago, two Girl Scout leaders from New York City rode their three-speed Schwinns across the country. One of these women was my mother, June Meyer Newland. She was almost 24 years old at the time. She wore saddle shoes and Bermuda shorts and, if it was hot, she just rode in her bathing suit. Schwinn donated three-speed bikes for the trip, "ultra sleek" Traveler models that weighed nearly 50 pounds. Her saddle bags were filled with the following: a cocktail dress, high-heel shoes, pantyhose, a pearl necklace, extra shorts and camp shirts, one towel, a bathing suit, a sleeping bag, a journal, some toiletry items, "just a little bit of makeup for the evening," and a bible. She strapped a camera around her waist along with a canteen bottle and off she went on the road to California.

My mother was not only a pedaling pioneer, but a counterculture pioneer. She protested conformity and blandness and instead searched for the freedom to do as she pleased. She went against the prevailing tide of materialism and suburban living and pushed herself cross-country on a three-speed, strapping on a few possessions, just going. She was a female Jack Kerouac, wanting to soak up the world and escape the mundane—*On the Road*. But while Kerouac cruised through his experience at 50 miles an hour, my mother was content to let the country pass at 50 miles a day. I would argue that her trip went more to the core of experience because she relied on herself and her own ingenuity, not on pushing a gas pedal behind wind-shielding glass, the radio blaring.

As a child, I listened as my mother told and retold her stories about "the adventure of a lifetime." She'd describe how she stayed at farmers' houses and slept in barns, how police officers would guard the city parks for them so that they could camp out, how they had to get jobs as chamber maids in the Grand Canyon because they were low on money, how farmboys took them out on dates ("Before I met your father, of course"), and how people were "so kind and generous, giving us dinner, taking us on city tours, fixing our bikes and trying to give us money."

Ever since I was around three years old, riding my tricycle behind my mother on her rusting (but still working) Schwinn, I wanted to go on that adventure—a cross-country bike tour where I could sleep in farmers' houses and in city parks and be a maid in the Grand Canyon. *How exciting*, I thought. I decided that I would eventually follow my mother's lead.

But I couldn't find anyone to ride across the country with me. After graduating from college in 1985, I moved to Portland, Maine, and became a social worker at Mercy Hospital. I'd ride to work from South Portland over the Million Dollar Bridge and on the weekends I'd join the charity rides organized by the Multiple Sclerosis Society and various other bike tours around Maine. Still, no one wanted to ride with me across America. My friends already knew to say "No!" whenever I'd ask them if they'd like to do the ride with me.

I had almost forgotten about my dream, when, in 1992, on a visit to my brother's place in Chicago, I met Brian. We discussed our graduate degrees—his from Indiana University in environmental policy, mine in social work from the University of Utah—where we had grown up and where we had lived, and most importantly, how we loved to ride bikes. When Brian told me that his dream was to ride his bike across the country but that he could not find anyone to ride with him, my dream was rekindled. Of course, we had to get married. Five months later we did just that, and began planning our trip.

My mother finalized her trip plans in just 10 days after Schwinn decided to donate bikes for the ride. She trained by riding around her block a couple of times. She figured she would get in shape by taking the trip. Her philosophy was simply to "just do it," years before such a phrase became synonymous with the '90s and Generation X. She just wanted to have something to do over the summer. Because she couldn't afford a plane ticket and didn't have a car, biking seemed the best way to see the nation and get to California to bask in the sun, see Hollywood, and maybe, "get jobs and start all over." She didn't even know how to change her tire.

In the '50s, life seemed full of limitless opportunity and technology was seen as a way for social advancement. Families were moving out of the cities and buying single-family homes filled with all the newest innovations like refrigerators and electric appliances. Parents sat down together for dinner every evening with their children. The economy was booming after the despair of the Depression and the World Wars. Moms stayed home while Dads commuted to the city in new Chevrolets. Peace and prosperity were apparently available for all. My mother went into her trip trusting the goodness of it all; she saw no danger in the world. Not worrying about bills ("They'll take care of themselves"), she quit her job as a school teacher and just took off.

On the other hand, Brian and I were the "just plan it" kind of people. We read through my mother's old journal from the bike trip so that we could stay on her actual route. We stared at maps and figured out routes that would keep us off the busy roads. We worried about things that could go wrong. The world in the '90s was quite different from that of the '50s: drive-by shootings, interstate highways, cable television, fast-paced workplaces directed by e-mail, modems, faxes, pagers, cellular phones, and voice-mail, and homes with every convenience under the sun.

When Brian and I decided to do this trip, we were going against the tide of technology. We were planning to cover 65 miles per day on average as opposed to 65 miles per hour. We weren't pushing ourselves to "get there" as fast as we could, racing across America for time, for speed. We had had enough of racing through life with our 40-hour-a-week jobs, the car repairs, the alarm clocks, the traffic jams, paying bills, and bosses demanding more time at work. Now, our effort was put into the experience of allowing time its place, and letting it slow to levels we could understand.

Even though our friends and co-workers were concerned with our trip—warning that we'd lose our jobs, get run off the road, grow tired of one another—we knew our only choice was to simply go. To take a risk, leave our routine, jump into the unknown— these reasons spoke louder than the warnings. But no louder than the echoes of my mother's endless talk of her trip and all the wondrous experiences and memories she took away from it.

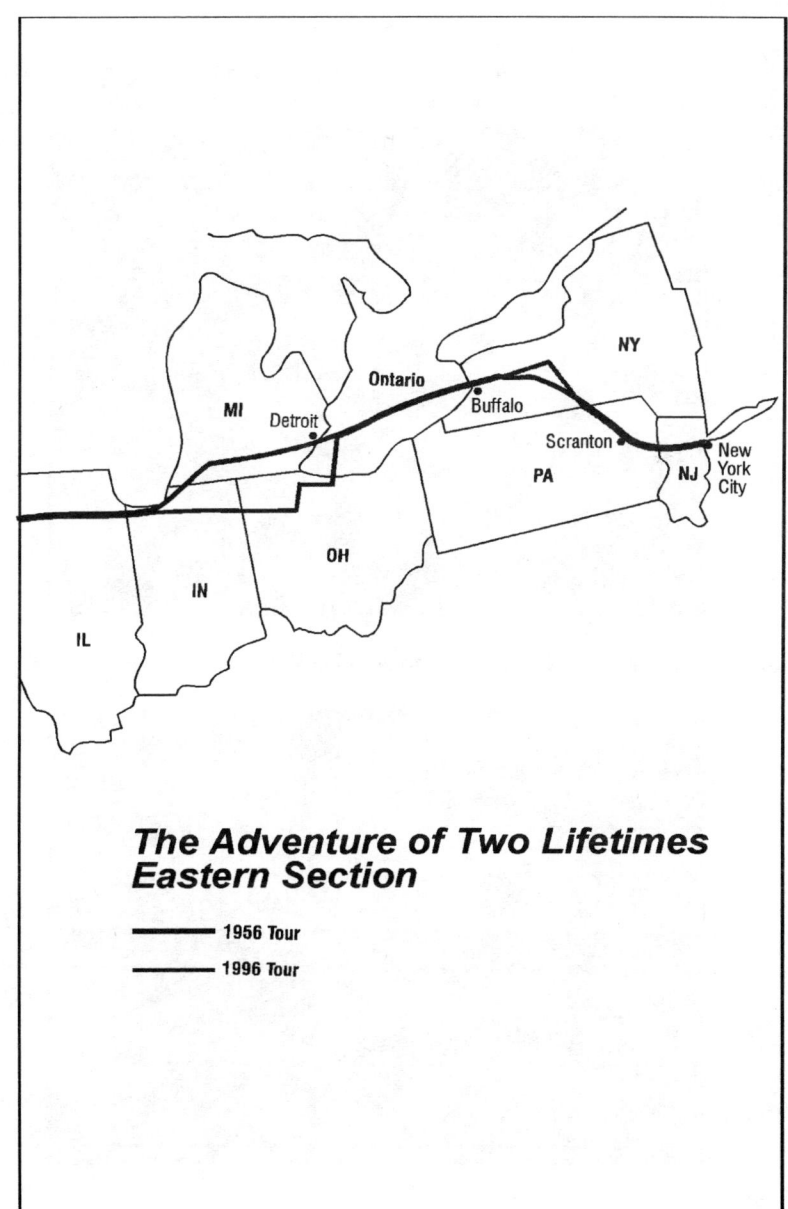

The Adventure of Two Lifetimes
Eastern Section

—— 1956 Tour

—— 1996 Tour

The Today Shows - 1956 and 1996

1

"Once a journey is designed, equipped, and put in process, a new factor enters and takes over. A trip, a safari, an exploration, is an entity, different from all other journeys. It has personality, temperament, individuality, and uniqueness. A journey is a person in itself; no two are alike. We find after years of struggle that we do not take a trip; a trip takes us."
—John Steinbeck, *Travels with Charley*

Peggy

"So, what time is the limousine picking you up tomorrow?" Mom asks me. We're on the phone to figure out when we'll meet for *The Today Show*.

"We're not taking a limo Mom ... " I try to answer back. Mom doesn't let me finish. In fact, my mother likes to finish my sentences, inserting her words for mine. I've gotten used to it. I roll my eyes at Brian and he laughs as I cup the telephone in the palm of my hand.

"Well, why not? *The Today Show* will pay for it, you know. They're sending us a limo at 5:30 and they'll probably have a mini-bar and television in the back for us. Don't you want to watch TV and drink orange juice?"

"We're two blocks away from the studios and we're going to ride our bikes there."

"Why ride your bikes there if *The Today Show* will pick you up in a limo?"

"We don't need a limo!" Good lord, this woman never stops. She wants everyone to live life like she does. Getting what you can get when you can get it. Living life with a two-for-one coupon in hand. I start to doubt why I am doing this bicycle trip; I'll be spending all 3,000 miles across the country riding in her shadow.

"It's too dangerous to ride on these New York City roads," she tells me.

"But, Mom, you rode your bike in New York City 40 years ago. That's why we're doing this anyway—remember?"

"Of course I remember." Mom has that tone to her voice, the one that reminds me not to mess with her memories. "But that was 40 years ago. People go too fast and they don't care anymore."

"But *The Today Show* wants us to have our bicycles with us. What good will it be for us to talk about our bicycle trip without bicycles?"

"Bring the bikes on the limo."

She never stops. I sigh into the phone and she continues.

"Oh, that's right. You've got those fancy new bicycles, you probably won't want them to get scratched up. How many speeds do they have anyway?"

"Twenty-four."

"Twenty-four! What do you need with all those gears?"

"All the bicycles are like that now, Mom."

"Well, three worked just fine for us. Third gear was for going fast on the flat parts, second was for the in-between parts and first was for climbing the mountains. I'd be all confused with what you've got."

I'm suddenly ready to go down to the hotel bar and have a shot of tequila.

Mom changes the subject. "I've got a whole box of my books to bring on the show. I'm going to sell one to Katie Couric when she interviews us and then I'll find ... "

"You can't bring a box of books with you when we're being interviewed."

Mom just finished self-publishing her memoir about her 1956 bicycle trip and filled it with poetry, pictures, and photocopied journal entries. She has been trying to sell her books at church bazaars,

AARP meetings, and in front of the house, but she mainly gives them to friends and family as birthday gifts. I think Brian and I have three copies so far—and my birthday is coming up.

"Mom, we're being interviewed by Bryant Gumbel, not Katie Couric. She's on vacation."

"Oh, no. I autographed a copy to Katie. Now, I'll have to sign another one for Bryant. Do you think Bryant will buy my book?"

"I don't think it's a good idea to bring a box of books with you on *The Today Show*. Who's going to carry that box for you? I'm not and neither is Brian."

"I'll find a nice assistant to carry it for me, or maybe our limo driver ... "

I listen as Mom rambles on about how she's going to take pictures of all the staff at *The Today Show*, how she's ripped out magazine pictures of hairstyles she wants the show's beautician to create for her, how she's wearing blue because "blue is best on television—I read about it in *People*," and why it's important to wear low heels when being interviewed because she has "funny" knees. I wonder to myself: *Will I be like my mother in 40 years, rambling on like this?* Will I be selling my story at AARP meetings and at church when I'm in my 70s? What if Brian and I have a daughter—will she ride her bike across the country as I worry about low heels and my hair?

I suddenly smile. Life seems circular. I'm following my mother, yet at the same time I'm turning away.

Brian

I was up most of the night dealing with our equipment and making sure that everything was oiled and running smoothly. I made Peg get her bags packed the night before, even though she thought she could get it done in the morning. Just like her to not be organized and then rush around in the morning being late as usual. I hate being late and unorganized. Peggy laughs at me and calls me "Mr.

Organization," but at the same time thanks me for getting everything in order for this trip.

"Brian, without you, I don't think I'd have the follow-through to do all of this. Getting the bikes into bike boxes at the airport, disassembling and reassembling, packing all the water bottles and oil for gears and making sure that we have tools for breakdowns..." Peggy says, talking in her usual stream-of-consciousness manner, "...and sunscreen and maps. Good God! Maps! All those maps you ordered way ahead of time, and thinking about what we need to pack and mail off to Denver for the mountainous roads and getting a cell phone—it all just gives me a headache!"

We leave the hotel on our bikes for the NBC Studios with plenty of time to spare. As luck would have it at a time like this, I notice that one of Peggy's tires is low on air. Our trip hasn't even started yet as I find myself assuming my role of trip mechanic, only this time on the streets of Manhattan with horns blaring, Peggy worrying, and my tools packed deeply in our bags. Luckily, the tire is only low on air, not flat. After a few strokes of the bike pump we are back on our way.

"Maybe this is Karma," Peg says to me. "Life giving you practice at disorganizing your organization." Peggy just loves to smooth out every dramatic situation with her own touch of ironic insight.

We meet my brother, Phil, just outside the entrance to *The Today Show* and he starts documenting our every move on video as the doorman checks his guest list and lets us inside. A couple of assistants grab our bicycles and take them out to the street for the cameras. We board the elevator and head up to meet the show's producer.

When we get upstairs, she asks us if we ran into June on our way up. "No," we respond as we start to look for her in one of the two places she'd probably be: the "Green Room"—a waiting room that's filled with food and beverages—or the smoking room. We discover her in the corner eating grapes with a few of the members of Liza Minelli's band.

"Now, is it Leeza or Liza?" We overhear June ask the horn player. June is a sharp and well-groomed lady in her pantsuit; all her hair is combed and curled. I almost don't recognize her out of her regular outfit, a loose-fitting and comfortable Hawaiian muumuu.

"June, it's Liza," I answer, since the horn player ignores her.

"Oh, I just love that Leeza. She's going to sing for us downstairs after we're on the air. Isn't that exciting? I'm going to see if she'll buy one of my books. Excuse me, do you know where Leeza is?" June asks the drummer, who ignores her too. So much for our bicycle trip when "Leeza" Minelli is in the vicinity.

Peggy

It is a little strange starting our cross-country adventure in pancake makeup and hair spray. "Fix her up natural-like," the producer says between conversations on his cell phone, walkie-talkie, and a regular telephone, "We've got 15 before it's time for the street!" I only have 15 minutes left for Katie Couric's makeup assistant to blush my cheeks to highlight a healthy glow, open my eyes with mascara, and put sparkle in my smile with rose-colored lipstick. Brian has already "been done," as they say in show business, and I must say he does look quite athletic with his makeup and blush.

"Your eyebrows are too square; we must round them out and soften you a bit," the makeup woman says to me. Before I can say, "I really can't afford to soften up a bit—I need all the hardness I can get for this bike trip," I'm whisked into a chair for hair. I sit in the "hair chair" as the hairdresser ponders what to do with me. She sighs then rolls her eyes. "Athletic, how can I do athletic with this?" she says to the television; it's 10 minutes and counting. She starts sticking large round brushes all over my head ("for body") as I watch the television monitor and see my cousin Kris and Aunt Adelaide waving at the camera. I can even hear my Aunt Adelaide laughing before they cut to a commercial about Prell shampoo, complete with a bouncy-haired model. The hairdresser starts pulling all the brushes out and spraying out my "first day on a cross-country bicycle trip" hairstyle. "There you go," she says, and to tell you the truth, I think it looks the same as when I first sat down in the hair chair. No bouncy hair for me today.

A loudspeaker calls in to us, "Street in eight minutes!" All I know is that I suddenly have to go to the bathroom. Rather urgently. Unfortunately, I'm all hooked up, with my microphone wired down my bike shorts and up my shirt, through my jog bra. I whisper to Brian that I have to go to the bathroom, and even though he is enjoying a muffin in the Green Room with my Dad and Liza Minelli's band, he finds the beepered, headphoned, clip-boarded producer who quickly disconnects me so I can go. The producer is sweating, probably because it's only five minutes until we have to be on the street, holding our bicycles.

In the bathroom, a production assistant or writer wonders if the padding in my pants feels like a diaper. Luckily, I got to the bathroom in time so I wouldn't have to carry the diaper analogy any further during our interview with Bryant Gumbel.

In the elevator, my mother looks as calm as can be, singing show tunes with Al Roker and asking, "How's show business these days, Al?" I wonder what we've gotten ourselves into as we get out of the elevator and go into the street to our bikes. Mom waves to the crowd, a queen bee, with her self-published memoir under her arm. I notice that the hairdresser gave her an Ann Landers/Betty Crocker kind of look (quite different and becoming on a woman who asked for an ax for a wedding present because she loves to chop wood) and she's wearing dark blue eye shadow. Normally, when Mom gets dressed up she wears her lime green eye shadow that she's had since the '70s, no matter what her outfit. I tell Mom that she looks gorgeous and she says that she has to if she's going to sell her book on national TV.

We stand three in a row, Mom, Brian, and me, as the lights are tested on our complexions and people click light monitors in our faces. I'm suddenly worried about the clipless pedals that I am still getting used to. You have to step into the pedal with your shoe and wiggle your foot around until the shoe locks into place and twist out when you stop. It still feels like a torture device even though Brian, the guys at Bingham Cyclery in Salt Lake City, and most of my friends say, "It's great. You'll love it. Just remember to clip out before you stop." Great. Now I'm in the middle of New York City on national television and the last few times I rode my bike in Salt Lake I forgot I had my shoes clipped in and I just sort of keeled over in the middle of the street in front of various cars stopped at traffic lights. *What am I doing? I'm going to smash into traffic or, worse yet, fall on top of Bryant Gumbel on my way out of the show.* "Oh, God, oh God, oh God," I'm saying over and over again, like a mantra. The crowd screams as Bryant Gumbel strolls nonchalantly over to us. *Go away, Bryant Gumbel! Go away! I'm going to crash into you with my clipless pedals and you'll sue me for ruining your career. Go away!* To make matters worse, my eye starts to twitch. It's the kind of twitch that starts underneath your eye and quickly consumes the rest of your face in uncontrollable spasms.

"We've got three minutes before live feed," a cameraman says to us and I really feel like I will be live feed to the public watching us at home over their Wheaties because I'll be such a twitching, crashing fool.

We hear a roar from the crowd and notice that Bryant is coming out to the street. He knows our names and we chitchat for less than a minute before a cameraman starts doing the countdown. Bryant is definitely a professional, because he doesn't flinch or smirk or roll his eyes at my twitching face. Then again, he looks over the top of my head as he asks pleasant questions. He is smart, too, because his lack of eye contact relaxes me and my spasms subside as the *five, four, three* becomes *two, one* and we are *Live on The Today Show.*

It's all a blur, and I don't remember much other than flailing my hands, giggling too much, and forgetting to put my helmet on as we simulate the start of our trip by riding away at the end of the questions. Brian and Mom handle it pretty well, though. Mom stands confidently with her memoirs in hand, telling Bryant how great it is "to be back on the show again," while Brian reels off the technical details about the bikes, their gears, and how much they weigh. He even tries to get a plug in for our web site, but Bryant just says "Uh huh," and moves on to the next question in his slick, newsman way.

And then it is over. The lights go off, they cut to commercials, and Bryant disappears back into the confines of the indoor studio as assistants unhook Brian and me from our microphones.

Andy Warhol once said that we would all have 15 minutes of fame. Unfortunately, we were only famous for five minutes. But after the successful clipping and unclipping of my pedals and our simulated exit down the street (we had to stop around the corner and give our microphones back to the producers after the show), we're quite exuberant. Almost giddy. Then again, my giddiness might be due to the excessive amount of coffee I drank before the show (which could also explain the urgency for the bathroom and/or the twitching eye phenomenon). Because this is a momentous occasion, we are in the picture-taking mood. Brian's brother, Phil, and his best friend/assistant, Andy, have Brian and I waving and wheeling around the courtyard of *The Today Show* as Liza Minelli sings "New York, New York." For a while, we're on top of the world, our stars are shining, nothing can be finer with the universe—at least until the security guard comes and explodes our celebrity balloon.

He's a rather burly man in his 50s, with deep creases furrowed into his brow and a blue security suit. He has the look of a man who gets angry a lot.

"Take off out of here now!" he barks. Certain that he can't be talking to us, we ignore him and continue to smile at the camera as we ride in circles while Liza croons.

"Now, wave, look up at the same time, smile!" Phil and Andy say, their cameras clicking, the video camera catching our every move. It's so wonderful being celebrities—I even like the way the pancake makeup holds my face up.

"I said, get on out of here!" He's a little sterner now, and as he gets closer, it becomes apparent that he is talking to us. *To us!*

I clip out of my clipless pedals with an ease that comes from being a television natural, a newfound star. Brian still hasn't really heard him and continues to circle, cycling and waving.

I look at this man—this fan of ours—and smile at him. He frowns back.

"Go on, this is private property. Take off!" This man is relentless. I decide to be kind with him and explain quietly who we are.

"We were just on *The Today Show*. We're the bicyclists riding across the country, following my mother's route, and ... "

He cuts me off in mid-sentence. "You've had your five minutes—now *move along* out of here!" It's as if my bicycle became a pumpkin and I was back to being a psychiatric worker instead of the newest cycling sensation.

Meekly, we wheel our bicycles away from the street we once called home, the place that held us so safely in front of the cameras for the public to cherish. We've been banished. Our newfound glory, no more.

Somewhere we still have 10 more minutes of fame.

Brian
A major hurdle in planning our trip was getting the time off. We really couldn't just quit our jobs with the expectation of getting new ones quickly upon return. Perhaps we were fearful of the unknown; what with our bills and mortgage and car payments and

college repayments, it would have been a lot of stress to deal with on the trip. Fortunately, Peg got a three-month leave of absence from the University of Utah and I can do my work from the road via cellular telephone, calling cards, and Federal Express mailings.

Peg and I trained extensively in the months before the trip by climbing and riding nearly 1,000 miles up and down the Wasatch Mountains surrounding Salt Lake. Basically, our plans are to cross the country in about 55 days, following nearly the same route as June took in 1956. However, it only takes one day—or more specifically, only about 20 miles—for us to realize that this trip might be tougher than we anticipated.

Back at the Crown Plaza Hotel we bid Peggy's mother, father, aunt, and cousin good-bye. After a blessing by Peggy's father Bob, we load our gear into our friend Andy Pollock's Honda Accord. Phil and Andy then shuttle us out of the traffic of Manhattan to Morristown, New Jersey—our starting point. Before we leave, June tells Peg to call her every day with all the "news of the road." Peg, of course, rolls her eyes at her mother and says that she'll try to keep in touch before the trip ends.

"I'll call you in a couple of months, Mom," she says. "Anyway, you can read all about us on our web site like everyone else."

"Web site. *Web* site!" exclaims June. "I don't want to talk to a computer, I want to talk to you, so you better call."

"Okay Mom," Peggy replies with a grin, giving her a hug as she gets into the car. "But you really should try to keep up with us on the Internet. It will be fun."

"You know I don't know anything about computers and those spider webs, Peggy," June adds. "Anyway, I did just fine without them on my bicycle trip. Why, back then, we just … "

June continues to ramble as Andy starts to drive away from the hotel. We wave our good-byes from the backseat as she fades into the distance and we break from the past. I turn to Peggy, kiss her smiling face and tell her it's our ride now.

We finally get on the bicycles around 12:30 and hit the open road from the parking lot of the Morristown Diner. There's a bit of traffic to deal with, but that isn't much of a problem compared with the heat. For today—August 23, 1996—just happens to be the hottest day of the summer. Lucky us. My trusty watch/thermometer/altimeter says that it is 96 degrees out. The heat is coupled with very humid air—a miserable combination.

We are definitely used to heat, often training in 90-degree temperatures back in Utah. But we don't have to struggle with humidity, because it is so dry out west. Back east, there is no escaping the hazy, sweltering moisture that always accompanies the heat. I comment to Peggy that maybe I should have trained for a month by riding a stationary bicycle in a steam bath or something. Soon, I am hurting.

As we pull into Long Valley, New Jersey, at about 2pm, we have gone about 20 miles. I am sweating buckets and look like I just rode my bike through a car wash. Everything on me is soaked.

Ahead of us is Schooley's Mountain, two miles of winding road with 500 feet of elevation gain—a five percent grade. As we start up, Peggy is handling things much better than I am, spinning her pedals in low gears. She's a better climber than I am anyway, and fortunately, she isn't as affected by the heat as much as I am. Soon my legs start cramping and I begin to fall back. She looks over her shoulder now and then to see how I'm doing. Finally, I pull over into a driveway and wave her on, saying, "I'll meet you at the top."

Setting my bike down I reach for my right calf. It's one big knot. I sit down on the driveway and try to stretch and massage it. Not only am I working on my legs, but I'm massaging my ego too, for my spirits are quite low. I'm thinking to myself, *How can this be, only 20 miles into the ride?* I have visions of failure before we've even begun. I had expected that we might run into physical problems sometime during the trip, but I figured that it would probably be somewhere in Colorado, at 10,000 feet, not in New Jersey, and certainly not on the first day!

Get a hold of yourself Brian, I tell myself. *One day at a time, one mile at a time. We don't have to get to California today.* I take a few deep breaths and a few more gulps of water and clip myself back into the pedals. Ten minutes later, still sweating like a pig and cramping a bit more, I crest the hill and see Peggy, Phil, and Andy waiting for me in a church parking lot. They're playing catch with an empty water bottle.

"Don't worry, I'm gonna make it," I assure them as I take a break in the shade of a tree. "This has happened before. Heat and I just don't get along." As I'm saying this I'm wringing out my socks and dumping the water out of my shoes. In my mind I conjure worse images, like only making it as far as Ohio or something like that. I try to tell myself that things can only get better. Fortunately, they do.

Following a late-day thunderstorm (a common occurrence in this kind of weather) we arrive at our hotel in Stroudsburg, Pennsylvania, at about 6:30pm. Peggy and I jump into the pool, still in our bicycle clothes. I follow the swim with a warm bath. Sitting there experiencing a few more cramps, I have more time to contemplate things. Again, I fight hard against self-doubts.

I'm pretty upset with myself. Here I am soaking in some damn motel bathtub, spasming, and outside Peg is floating around in the pool, drinking beer with Phil and Andy, without a care in the world. I can see ruining this entire trip for both of us because my body is giving out on me. I wonder how I am going to handle the days ahead, especially if it stays hot like the weather reports predict. I have visions of ending the trip before it even starts.

Just then, Peg came into the bathroom and started massaging my shoulders and leg. "We can get through this, Booley." Peg has called me "Booley" as a nickname since we met. It's strange, I know, but I kind of like it. "It's our trip and we'll take it as it comes. I'm sure there will be days when I'll be flopping out too."

"Yeah, but this is the beginning of your golden opportunity and I'm wrecking it for you."

"This is the beginning of *our* golden opportunity and I'm in it for the adventure. Whatever happens, happens for a reason. We'll be okay."

I know she is right. Looking into her eyes gives me all the reassurance I need.

June and Teri Shake hands with Miller More,
President of American Youth Hostels

2

"This is news, big news—unusual news! When in this day and age has such a journey on a bicycle ever been contrived? Especially in an era when automobiles blaze the trails—East, West, North, South."

—*Montclair* (New Jersey) *Times* article about
June and Teri, June 24, 1956

June

My idea of riding across the country was really just a lark. It came up one night when Teri Foster, a professional Girl Scout worker, and I were sitting around a campfire during summer camp in 1956. We both talked of our goals and dreams and how we wanted to see California. Neither one of us had a car and we didn't have much money to take trains or a plane. But we were young and healthy. One of us said that we should just ride bicycles, rationalizing that we had all the time in the world, and besides, we'd get to see a lot of the country between Long Island, New York, and Los Angeles. When I told my very best friend, Anne Finnegan, that I was planning a cross-country bicycle trip to California, she just laughed at me and said, "Oh, June, not another one of your crazy ideas!" It seemed that the more "Oh Junes" I got from friends and family, the more I had to follow through on this silly trip.

I remember being very bored back then. And sad. My father, Pierpont Meyer, had died two years before and Mother had remarried fairly quickly—to Charlie. He was a very bossy man who wanted me to call him Daddy. I wouldn't do it and I wouldn't listen to him either. He'd tell me when I had to be home from dates and he'd criticize me for reading newspapers at the breakfast table and he'd tell me to brush my hair. Here I was, a 23-year-old professional schoolteacher, and I had this stepfather telling me what to do! So I just ignored him and went up into my room to look out over the Baldwin Harbor and wonder how Daddy was doing up in Heaven.

Daddy was always my best friend. He understood me and we'd cry together over symphonies and sad movies. We both loved Greta Garbo. When he died, I think a part of me died too. Maybe the bicycle trip was a way to search for pieces of Daddy out in the world. Maybe if I saw a rainbow after a storm, it would be Daddy saying it's okay, I'm here with you. Or maybe if I actually finished the trip, if I got to California, then my heart would be healed and I'd feel happy again. I wouldn't have to cry anymore and I'd have a place in the world. But in all honesty, I really did the trip to be adventuresome.

For our ride, Teri and I were sponsored by the American Youth Hostels (AYH). The AYH helped us plan our itinerary and arranged places for us to stay along the way. It was nice but kind of cramped my style. I had plans in my head that I would be a good will ambassador on this trip and that I would knock on people's doors and ask to sleep in their barns or on their front lawns. I really just wanted to depend on the hospitality of others and trust that the people I met along the way would take us in. But I went along with the AYH itinerary because Teri reassured me that it would be nice to have lodging if we got tired of sleeping on the dirt. I figured if we ran out of money along the way and we wanted to stay in some ritzy motel then we could just find jobs for a few days and maybe pick grapes or clean some toilets. I was a pretty industrious gal and could really have done almost anything to make some cash.

I knew that we would have miles and miles of unknown road ahead of us, but being a Girl Scout prepared me for things like that. In my little duffel bag I had some maps showing good roads throughout the United States. I knew that these maps would point me to my girlfriends' houses and Girl Scout camps—the really fun places to go like Elmira, New York (Teri's hometown), Buffalo, Detroit (for the Girl Scout Jamboree), Chicago, Nebraska, and Denver to visit my brother. Our agenda allowed us approximately three to four months. I wanted to keep it flexible because I had quit my boring school teaching job and was planning on getting a new job in California—or even Hawaii—at the end of our trip. I could picture myself doing the hula for tourists on famous Waikiki Beach or maybe even teaching canoeing camps in California. Outdoors! I decided that I needed to work and be outdoors from then on, so I guess that, except for all the pedaling and sweating I'd be doing, bicycling out in the open fit me to a "T."

Mother and Charlie drove Teri and me into the city the day our trip was to start, June 22, 1956. It was very hazy and all my curls came down per usual. My hair has always misbehaved, and I remember wishing that it would just stay curly enough to look good on television. Charlie got my bike from the Schwinn Company in the city and rode it out to the car at Penn Station. But we couldn't fit it into the car so I had to ride it over to the 49th Street NBC studios. I must say I was nervous, riding it full-pack in the city with all the cars and trucks, but, as always, I survived.

We met the TV men and they set us up on the street. We stood at the corner of 52nd Street and 5th Avenue in the heart of New York City. Cameras swung toward us as microphones were placed around our necks. Before we knew it we looked at the television monitor inside and saw ourselves giggling. Dave Garroway, host of *The Today Show*, came out and interviewed us at 7:25am. I remember grinning when I nudged Teri right before we went on the air, saying, "Don't you think we've taken this thing far enough?" Just then the red light went on and we were live on *The Today Show* and officially off on our bicycle trip. I don't remember a word I said during the interview and before I knew it we were off the air. Then we went downstairs and had coffee. It sure didn't seem like we were on a nationwide TV hookup.

Ray Owen met us and interviewed us on the Bill Cullen radio show on the street from his red Thunderbird. At 9:30 we were interviewed again by Dave Garroway (there were no tape delays in those days, so they did the show twice each day—once for the eastern time zones and a second time for the western half of the nation). There were six photographers there and they had us riding down the sidewalk waving to the crowd gathered around us. People were everywhere, staring and getting close. I wavered and nearly fell into a camera.

Then the cameras stopped flashing, the spectators went their own ways, and we were off the air; I realized that it was up to Teri and I to actually ride our bikes now. I put a big smile on my face, hoping to look confident, and we hopped on our bikes and rode down the street as the people stepped back to make room for us. We had just started our 3,000-mile bicycle trip that would take us across plains, over mountains and through deserts to Los Angeles, California!

Boy, was I scared. But excited. Always excited!

It has been years since I really thought about my cross-country trip. So much happened after that; I was just too busy. I got married to Robert Newland and moved out to California where he was working with Proctor and Gamble. Then, we moved back east when he decided to become a minister and attended Episcopal Divinity School in Cambridge, Massachusetts. That's where Peggy was born. Then I went on to graduate school and got my master's degree in social work. After his ordination, Bob was given various church assignments in Portsmouth and Virginia Beach, Virginia, Augusta and Lewiston, Maine, and Sayville, New York. In between, our son

Paul was born. Our summers were full of family vacations out west and to Europe. Unfortunately, about 10 years ago, Bob had a couple of strokes, which forced his early retirement and put him in a wheelchair. Then we moved back to Virginia, where we live now. Bob's condition has slowed us down a bit, but hasn't stopped us from traveling to see Peggy in Utah and Paul in Oregon, or kept us from finding new adventures in trips to the Smoky Mountains, the North Carolina coast, and to Florida.

So, you can see that I haven't had much time to dwell on my trip even if I had wanted to. But when Peggy and Brian decided to follow in my tracks, they started asking lots of questions about where I went and what it was like. They came here a few times and together, we looked at my scrapbooks, journal, and photos. It's amazing, what with all the moves Bob and I have made over the years, that I still had as much from the trip as I did.

While Peggy and Brian are on the road I'll be right here at home with all of my old memories and trip information, all spread out on my dining room table. This way, I'll be able to tell them where they should go and what they should try to see.

I start thumbing through my mementos and find an article from *Newsday* written by Audrey Clinton before my trip:

> June Meyer of Baldwin wants to see the U.S. this summer and she's going to do is the hard way—by bicycle. June is quitting her job as teacher with the Lakeside Elementary School in Merrick to make the trip.
>
> "I like teaching but I want to get some traveling experience in now. We'd like to see Las Vegas and the Grand Canyon, but most of all we'd just like to see the things you'd miss by traveling by train."

Here's a photo of Teri and I shaking hands with Millard More, President of the American Youth Hostels. Here's another one of us with the mayor of Simcoe, Ontario. He sure was a nice fellow. Further down the road, the *St. Thomas Journal* took a picture of us getting directions from the Canadian Provincial Police. Oh my, look at this one—we're talking to a reporter in Iowa and wearing bathing suits! Well, I do remember it being hot in Iowa. And look what the *Denver Post* had to say about us as we reached our halfway mark:

> The pretty travelers who have been providing extra highway scenery for automobile travelers are Teri Foster and June Meyer. Unlike most women travelers, baggage is at a minimum. They each have a windbreaker, saddlebag and bed roll strapped to the "luggage rack" of each bike. The saddlebag contains their wardrobe.

And here's the *Bicycle USA* article I wrote after our trip:

> Now our trip seams like a dream—a very vivid dream. Just a year ago I was planning in a flurry of excitement on leaving, and here it is — a wonderful memory. For my whole life I will recall incidents, places, people, and feel the satisfaction of accepting the challenge, of actually doing instead of merely talking about something you would like to do. Yes, my bicycle trip to California was everything I expected and something I can recommend to everyone.

Well, I just hope that Peggy and Brian will be able to say the same thing when they are done with their trip.

Peggy

Brian tells me it's raining out as I lay in bed; the pillows are curled up around my head. He opens the blinds and grayness seeps into our motel room as the mist hangs in layers over the hills outside. "Maybe it will clear up," he says, and I notice that he's massaging his leg. He probably has another muscle cramp, but at least his face isn't contorted like it was yesterday along the highway, his bike lying at his feet. The bed feels especially dry and comfortable, but we've told Phil that we'd meet him around La Anna and I tell myself that I'm just going to have to put the polypropylene on and deal with the rain. "Let's get pancakes," I suggest. Anything to procrastinate.

Brian is quiet as we sit down to an all-you-can-eat pancake special, with greasy bacon and bottomless coffee. He's probably worried about cramping up again and I feel a little guilty about having a wonderful first day. I loved the humidity and the green of New Jersey that pushed itself up and over everything in its way. The hills were a challenge, but they curved and angled past streams and waterfalls so my eyes stayed busy as I ignored my lungs.

Our morning coffee seems to be just the ticket for outlasting the weather. The rain stops and the mist continues, but I figure that this will keep Sweat Boy (my affectionate new nickname for Brian) cool. So we pack our bags and take off toward the Poconos.

Soon the weather clears, and as we pull into a fruit stand by the side of the road, I tell Brian that I want to move back to the East Coast. "I miss the green, the ferns and the smells, the lakes, the clouds ... it's all so alive." Sure, Utah has beautiful mountains, but by the end of the summer everything turns pale brown, bleached by endless days of sun. In our Salt Lake neighborhood, the sound of crickets is replaced by the sound of automatic sprinklers.

I just love fruit stands, especially if they have little old ladies in mismatched clothing behind them. We stop at one such stand in the afternoon and I talk to Marlene, the owner, who was wiping off peaches and apples and plums. "You look hot. You should stand in the freezer," she suggests while leading me towards a walk-in freezer full of fruit soaking in barrels. I motion for Brian to join me, but he is busy looking for Phil, who was supposed to catch up with us somewhere along this route. It's amazing how quickly sweat chills into goose pimples and I almost have to run out of the freezer.

Marlene gives us ice water and fresh fruit with napkins, "because it's juicy and you'll ruin your fancy biking clothes." Brian and I sit on some stumps in the shade of the stand and are entertained by Marlene's grandson, who is shooting his BB gun at rusted cans lined up on a fence next-door, as crickets and cicadas chirp out their songs in the billowing heat.

Later that afternoon Brian have to take a lot more breaks because the day grows sunnier and hotter. As if on cue, his pores open right up and I imagine his shoes filling up with sweat like miniature swimming pools. Hills are now our constant companions; even the flat sections of road seem to be going slightly up. I notice that Brian's face is looking less anguished, so I am encouraged that we can make it another 30 miles. I want to get to the lake region so we can find a cabin on the water and then dive into its coolness and drink beer while watching the sunset. That vision keeps my sweat glands occupied.

We stop along bridges and side rails to take frequent breaks. While Brian stretches out his muscles I pass the time staring at the trees. I suddenly find myself remembering days growing up, sitting in the grass of trees in our yard with my mother, listening to her make up stories and talk about her favorite trees. She said she liked aspens because of the way they reached up tall and skinny toward the sun. I liked oak because of their strength.

Luckily, as Brian sits on the guardrail, his arms between his knees, Phil drives up with "the last rental car in New York City" and a trunkload of Gatorade, bananas, peanut butter sandwiches, chips, pretzels, and PowerBars. Brian's face looks like he just won the lottery as we sit in the air-conditioned comfort of the car and relish every last thing that Phil brought for us.

That night, Phil scouts out the lodging and reserves the last room along Lake Wallenpaupack, just outside of Scranton, while Brian and I finish slogging up what seems to be our 100th hill of the day. With a sunset spreading itself over the tops of dimming trees, we sit in Adirondack chairs with a six-pack, watching Phil do backflips off the dock. Brian writes in our journal and I find myself doing nothing for the first time on our trip.

As the evening wind blows waves toward the shore, I realize that at this moment, I am in a moment of perfect place.

June

It's strange to be thinking back to 1956 like I hadn't a care in the world. I wonder now if I even gave my own mother something to worry about. I really don't think so, to tell you the truth. I know Daddy would have worried and he probably would have convinced me not to go. Daddy was the worrier in our family and my Mom was the entertainer.

After our *Today Show* appearance, Mr. More, the president of AYH, gave us a ride out of the city to Montclair, where we spent the night at Mother's—she was a camp counselor friend of mine. I called her "Mother" because she was a worrier—something I'd never be. Until now, with my own daughter.

Mother threw us a grand farewell party. My dearest friends came, and I knew that after the laughter the moment of parting would come. They had prepared a feast of relishes, baked beans, salads, and a huge chocolate cake. We should have left soon after, but we were having so much fun drinking beer and singing camp songs that we partied until the early afternoon. Our friend, Chuck, asked if we wanted him to drive us to camp, but we were persistent and ready to ride. We took some pictures and after a round of kissing, the tears started leaking out. As we rode out everyone started singing, "So long, farewell, we'll see you again."

I looked over my shoulder at the hands waving at us and could hear them breaking into "When it's Twilight on the Trail." It's my favorite Girl Scout song, and I couldn't stop crying. The tears were rolling down my face and I could barely see. I knew my life would never be the same again and this was both exciting and frightening at the same time.

Our first few days of bicycling were a period of adjustment, and I had difficulty just trying to figure out all the gears. I had only ridden bicycles with one gear before and now, here I was with three of them to choose from! I started to think that I really should have practiced changing gears and pedaling up hills before I hit the Poconos. I'd be riding along when all of sudden—*poof!*—a hill would appear. Invariably, I'd shift the bike into the wrong gear and then barely make it up the hill. I guess that a little training before our ride would have helped me, but nobody trained for things back then like they do now, they just went out and did them. Anyway, I figured that I'd be riding enough that I'd just get in shape by doing the trip. Nowadays, people train so much that there's no adventure in just going and doing. Peggy and Brian trained and practiced so much that I told them they should slow down and enjoy all the publicity beforehand. Of course they didn't listen to me. They just went out and continued to ride up and down those mountains outside of Salt Lake. Too serious for my bones.

As Teri and I rode to Stroudsburg, Pennsylvania, the weather cooperated and the days were beautiful with bright sun and fluffy cumulous clouds. The riding was difficult because of all the rolling hills, but I just put my mind onto the beauty of the countryside and up I went. It was delightful going downhill, passing pine trees, seeing little flowers along the road, hearing the birds and feeling the breeze blow against us.

On the third day of our ride, I remember it was so hot that Teri and I rode in just our bathing suits. A boy walking along the road sold us a couple of sodas for five cents each. Five cents each! Today, it's usually a dollar in those vending machines and that's just too much. That's why I like to go to Taco Bell now, because they give out senior citizen drinks for free. I keep a few of their cups in my car just so that I can always get a free drink.

Usually, when we were thirsty, we would stop at a farmer's house to fill our canteens or ask for cold glasses of iced tea. You have to remember back then, there weren't any of those 7-11s and Circle K convenience stores like they have now. We were out there on our own and had to depend on the hospitality of strangers. If we didn't, then we would've been dead on the road from thirst. We'd see a nicely-painted farmhouse and walk right up to the door and ask. No problems at all. People were happy to help us and often they'd keep us for dinner and maybe even let us camp in their barns or else out in the fields.

As we rode along, people sometimes recognized us from *The Today Show* or from the newspapers. We were in a lot of newspapers, let me tell you! And word would get around and soon we'd be on the local radio station telling our tales. I think I was very professional on the radio. I would tell a joke or two to liven up the interview and then explain why I was doing this trip. "I was bored," "I want to see the Pacific Ocean," "Next time I'll use roller skates!" were some of my more poignant comments.

We spent the third night camping alongside the road and Teri and I even went skinny-dipping in a stream to clean off after a hilly day of travel. There were fishermen around while we were there, so we had to be discreet. I found some large rocks and Teri and I cooled down and washed quite easily behind them. There's nothing better than skinny-dipping at the end of the day.

As we left camp on the fourth day, we headed towards Dingman's Ferry, to a river. We discovered that the bridge that we were supposed to go over had been washed downstream. We were very disappointed, but we surveyed the river and found a place that we could walk across. The rocks were slippery and the going slow, but it was all quite invigorating. On the other side, we headed toward the Delaware River. Fortunately, the bridge across this wide body of water was intact and we were able to cross safely into Stroudsburg.

While in Stroudsburg, we were interviewed by their radio station. After that, a local family, the Wicks, offered to put us up for the night. They were the nicest and friendliest people. Right away they made us a big farm supper of hamburgers, fried potatoes, carrots, and salad. After supper I watched them milk the cows. They even let me put the milking machine on one of them. The cow didn't like my technique and kicked the bucket of milk all over me just when a man from the newspaper came to interview us. I looked a mess, but it was a good story and provided a funny picture for the paper.

After watching a radiant sunset over the hills, the Wicks showed us their slides from a trip they had taken out west. The photos were wonderful and seeing those beautiful places really got me excited about what was ahead in our trip. We all stayed up until midnight sharing stories and camaraderie. I think I even taught them a Girl Scout song or two.

The next day the radio station called and asked to interview us again. Madelaine Malony pre-empted her daily "Thrifty Shopper" segment to talk with us about our trip. After that, Bill, the station manager, took us out for breakfast and gave us each some film. Everyone in town said hello, because they recognized us from the article in the morning newspaper. Some people thought that our trip was terrific, others were skeptical. All wished us luck, though. Even passing cars beeped their horns as we rode by.

The Pocono Mountains proved to be more of a challenge than we had anticipated. One hill went on for about five miles. A passing motorist told us about a good mountain stream ahead along the road and he joined us for a drink of cool, clear water as we filled our canteens. Nowadays, they say you shouldn't drink stream water because it's dangerous and filled with chemicals from people's lawns, or garbage thrown from cars. It's a damn shame because I liked that I could just fill up my canteen and drink. Peggy and Brian probably are buying those fancy bottled waters for two dollars and it's nothing but the same water from the same stream I drank from 40 years before. Only now, someone is making a bundle bottling it and putting labels all over telling you how good it is.

Finally, after climbing for some time, we started going downhill. We passed through quiet woods sprinkled with sunlight falling on a floor of ferns. We sped down the back roads towards La Anna, Pennsylvania. I felt as if I was entering Shangri-La as the wind blew in my hair and the tall trees arching across the road on either side created a marvelous tunnel of green.

The morning of our sixth day started off at the La Anna Youth Hostel with a scrambled egg breakfast with big slabs of bacon, cooked by a Mrs. Wolff. She even packed us some BLTs for the road. As we set out, we rode through a brief thunderstorm. It was more noise than rain, and I just kept thinking that God was shouting his hurrahs for us, urging us up the hills.

Soon it was clear again and we were riding mostly downhill through lovely farm country. Coasting downhill is such a joy. All you have to do is steer and enjoy the visual feast as the wind whistles softly like a sweet symphony.

We pulled into Scranton after riding about 40 miles that day. I purchased some liniment for my sore muscles because my legs felt like they were weighed down with anchors. That evening, staying at a retired schoolteacher's home, we had a quiet dinner and went to bed early for some much-needed rest. It felt nice to be between two sheets again.

I wrote in my journal: "Six days, 130 miles of riding, and already our adventure is off to a glorious start."

June and Teri with their bicycles
and cocktail dresses

3

"A bicycle was more fun than a motorcar. You saw things better and it kept you in good shape."
                    —Ernest Hemingway, *Islands in the Stream*

Brian

As Peggy and I were preparing for our own trip, we often spoke with June about her 1956 ride. During those conversations she would always manage to slip in a comment or two about the difference between our equipment. She would boast about the fact that she crossed the country "without all that newfangled bicycle equipment: No padded pants, no helmets, no slick silky outfits, or special gloves, or those shoes that clip to the pedals. Just bikes and legs, that's all we needed."

An article about June's ride that appeared in the *Montclair Times* described her bicycle as a brand-new "lightweight" touring bicycle. Though it was state-of-the-art at the time, this "lightweight" bicycle was a far cry from the 25-pound, 24-speed bicycles that Peg and I have. It had a heavy steel frame, steel wheels, spokes, fenders, and handlebars. Forty years later, technology had given us lightweight aluminum alloy frames, gears, and plastic fenders. In fact, June's bicycle weighed nearly 50 pounds—twice as much as ours.

Schwinn's 1956 brochure touted the Traveler as, "America's best-selling lightweight: fully equipped with three-speed gears, light and generator set, stainless steel fenders, and leather touring bag. For sport, utility, or touring, it's the top favorite of them all!" The model that June and Teri rode was the 19-inch "girls" version of the bike. "Girls" meant that the top-tube, common on most all bicycles today, was lowered to just a few inches above the bottom tube. Evidently, this design was supposed to accommodate a woman riding with a dress or skirt—or a bathing suit if that woman happened to be June Meyer.

Thanks to our nationally-televised *Today Show* appearance, Schwinn kindly gave Peggy and me each a brand-spanking-new Schwinn 96.1 mountain bike. Schwinn's brochure on this model boasted, "more computer engineering, laboratory testing, and real-world abuse than any other frame on the market. The ride-tuned™ aluminum frame features a sloping, bi-oval top tube and Epicenter™ seat stays. In fact, we feel strongly that the 96.1 rides better than the flagship models offered by most other manufacturers."

Before the ride we installed high-pressure road tires in place of the knobby-treaded mountain tires the bikes came with. These tires work more efficiently on paved roads.

Our bikes each come equipped with a Rock Shox Quadra 21R long-travel suspension fork—in other words, a shock absorber for the front wheel. We adjusted these shocks so that they would remain stiff most of the time. We aren't planning on doing much off-road or singletrack trail riding on the trip, but having them up front gives us some cushion for any potholes or other bouncy obstacles we might encounter across the country.

Schwinn also provided us with several other necessities for the trip. They gave us each two polyester jerseys (made of material designed keep us cooler in the heat because it wicks away moisture and dries quickly), two pairs of Lycra pants with chamois padding in the seat, one pair of long polypropylene pants, polyester wind jackets, padded cycling gloves, insulated winter gloves, front bicycle bags, aerobar handlebar extensions so we can tuck down to break the wind, rear bicycle racks, battery-powered lights, and shoes with cleats that attach to the pedals for more efficiency. This new innovation in shoe design lets us utilize our legs, not only in the normal down stroke, but up, back and all through the pedaling motion. It took Peggy awhile to get accustomed to clipping her feet in and out of those pedals. Her first time out riding with them in Salt Lake included a fall right in front of about 20 cars waiting at a traffic light. However, she soon mastered the fine art of clipping out before coming to a complete stop and now she really likes the shoes. That's a good thing, because I'd hate to have to keep picking her up off the road all the way across the country.

We also brought along rain pants and jackets, polypropylene vests, two polypropylene long-sleeved shirts, a baseball cap, two changes of underwear, swimsuits, a pair of shorts, a pair of long cotton pants, tennis shoes, polo shirt, towel, lightweight sleeping bags, a tent weighing only three pounds, tool kit, two tubes, toiletry kit, two 24-ounce water bottles, rear cordura bicycle bags, rain covers for the bags, sleeping bags, and bungee cords to lash everything on the bikes. And, of course, helmets—something that wasn't even available to bicycle riders in 1956.

June's cycling clothes were made of good ol' cotton, while ours are of Lycra, polypropylene, CoolMax™, and Spandex—space age fabrics one and all. Her sleeping bag was a heavy cotton one. Our sleeping bags are made of lofted, lightweight Thinsulate™ fabric, which stays warm even when wet; cotton is no good when it's wet. Where she had Bermuda shorts, we have Lycra cycling pants with a chamois padding. Her seat was made of hard leather. Ours has synthetic gel for cushioning. She had regular leather saddle shoes and flat pedals. We have cleated cycling shoes that attach to the pedals.

To keep track of our progress, Peggy and I have computerized speedometers, which keep us up-to-date with the latest data about our trip—time, distance, average speed, and maximum speed. I also have a watch that measures our altitude. Peggy calls me Gadget Man—among other nicknames that she likes to tease me with—for all the facts and figures that I spew daily. To keep track of her progress, June simply had a mechanical odometer on her bicycle with which she could monitor distance covered in a day.

Peg and I each have a Camelback™, a device consisting of a plastic bladder built into a backpack. Peggy's holds about 40 ounces of water and mine, about half a gallon. We fill the packs with water, put them on our backs, and we're able to drink all day from a tube that extends from the bladder around front. This gives us the ability to keep both hands on the handlebars, imperative when you're going downhill with a full pack.

My backpack also has room for some of the trip's more vital essentials. In it, I carry my wallet, identification, credit cards, telephone numbers, and a cellular phone. The phone is definitely an improvement on June's equipment. Having it along is a comfort just in case we encounter physical or mechanical difficulties on the open road.

My brother Phil developed our very own web site, where he can post our daily progress and photos of the trip. He tells us that he's looking forward to doing our trip "interactively" instead of physically. He'd like to ride a bike across the country someday too, but says that his bike would have a motor and be able to go 75 miles an hour. We'll be lucky to do 75 miles a day.

Though Peggy and I never actually weighed all of our gear, we figure that our bicycles and equipment together weigh about 65 to 70 pounds. June figured that altogether, the things she took weighed 35 pounds. Therefore, her bicycle and gear must have totaled nearly 85 pounds, a pretty hefty load for 3,000 miles.

When one compares all of our high-tech gadgetry to June's low-tech approach, it's easy to see how she can boast about her endeavor. We considered riding three-speed bicycles across the country; Peggy even joked about dusting off her mother's bicycle and tuning it up for the ride. But in the end we felt it truer to the ride to stick with today's technology for sake of comparison. Anyway, we know there is no topping June, because she just pointed her bike west, rode with no clear destination, slept in fields, parks, and even by the side of the road, and thought nothing remarkable about her undertaking. Peg and I have more of an agenda and plan on enjoying the comforts of inexpensive motels along the way, so why worry about riding the same bicycles?

Ironically, coinciding with our 40-year commemoration of June's ride, Schwinn is celebrating its 100th anniversary. The catalog that came with our new bicycles features the motto, "Schwinn Quality—The Second Century." It also highlights the history of this famous bicycle brand, including a very small note that says, "1993. Schwinn files for bankruptcy. New management takes over." Their 1994 snippet mentions, "Schwinn moves from Chicago to Boulder, Colorado."

Peggy and I see some continuity in riding Schwinns on our trip. To us, they are a microcosm of the difference between the 1950s and the 1990s. Our 96.1 models are an amalgam of American, Japanese, Taiwanese, and Chinese components. The frames are built in America, the front fork/shock, likewise. Almost everything else originated in other countries. But that too is the story of today's global economy. To find a totally American-made bicycle, components and all, is nearly impossible. Outsourcing and specialty factories have long since replaced the assembly line process of building bicycles that June witnessed in 1956. Bicycle companies now simply engineer, specify, and market various models based on their own frame designs, piecing together the components to fit the model. Not that this is bad—our bicycles are sleek, lightweight, and versatile. Technological improvements have given us 24 gearing options and clip-on pedals to make our muscles work more efficiently.

But with all the technology available to us in 1996 compared with June's trip in 1956, a mile is still just a mile. The roads we will ride on are still made of concrete, asphalt, stone, and dirt, identical to the ones that June encountered. Likewise, all the terrain is the same as in 1956. A hill to her will be the same hill to us. The mountains she had to go over will be the same height when we cross over them. And the wide-open plains for her are still the same plains for us. We are traveling east to west, just like June. We're still using two legs each to propel our human- powered machines across the country. Above all, our goals for the trip are the same as for her: Freedom, discovery, and adventure.

June

I never thought about documenting my trip with a bunch of pictures and writing. I just wanted to experience it all without all that stress of lining people up for snapshots and spending time writing about what I saw and did each day when I could be singing or taking a bath after a long day of riding. But a friend at Mother's party gave me a journal and scrapbook and told me, "You better write in this book because if not you'll get old and forget everything and memories will be buried with you in the grave for no one to know." Well, I took her advice and wrote as much as I could each night about our travels. Some days I wrote more than others, but overall, I'm glad that I did because my memory has gone a bit fuzzy in forty years.

Brian and Peggy have enough gear documenting their trip that I figure they could open a movie studio: a video camera, a 35mm automatic camera, fancy journals, tape recorders, a cellular telephone, calling cards, and a web site where people will be able to keep track of their progress every day. I don't know how they'll have any time to ride the bicycles with all the things they have to keep track of.

For my trip all I had was just a little Brownie-type camera that an old boyfriend—Charley the Chest—sold me before the trip. I think he should've given me the camera, but Charley was more in love with his muscular chest than he was with me, so I had to pay him for it.

I told Peggy not to worry about spending so much time writing about her trip. "That's boring," I told her. My only other advice was to take pictures in her mind throughout the trip. Sometimes snapping parts of places that you're passing through are just that — parts of places. I told her that it's better to just be in the place and feel it. Not worry about trying to capture it through a camera's lens.

However, I know that my advice to her will be just that. She's got a mind of her own and would do as she pleased anyway. Just like her mother.

Peggy
We are overjoyed to see a convenience store as soon as we get to Elmira, with its coolers full of every bottled and canned beverage available to the parched public. I stop pedaling and dash into the store, reaching into one of their coolers to get my favorite: grape Gatorade with the squirt top. There's nothing better than squirting that cold liquid down your throat as you sit on the concrete sidewalk and lean against the shaded wall of a 7-Eleven. You really feel like an athlete when you drain the Gatorade, sweat pouring in your eyes as you get one of those "I drank my cold drink too fast" headaches.

While recovering from one such headache, my hands on my temples, I notice a gentleman ambling over to me. He has eyes enfolded in crinkled skin and Rockport walking shoes, double-tied and Velcroed. "Sure is hot enough," he says to me, "but I walk every day since my emergency bypass surgery a few weeks ago in Florida. Sure did give me a scare, but the doctor says as long as I slow down and get more exercise I'll be all right. That's why I walk everyday. Even in this heat." He examines my bike as Brian and Phil come out with chips and pretzels. We talk about reasons for slowing down.

"It's not just the heat that should slow us down," he declares. "Weather shouldn't matter much. It's our heart that reminds us. It stops for us when we're racing too fast and we learn to walk down the sidewalks, past the fields, listening for things we never had time to listen to before."

"You never know when things like this will hit you, so stay in shape. It's great you're doing this now. It'll keep you young. Good luck!" he shouts as we pedal on. He salutes us as we ride away from him, pleased with the fact that we are young and appreciative of the slowness of life now, before the heart orders us to slow down.

I think for a moment how this man could be my mother's friend. They share the same philosophy: slowing down, look around, and listen. Perhaps she has sent him—a guardian angel messenger— to check up on us.

We head back out into the fields through Elmira, the staccato symphonies of cicadas ricocheting on either side of the valley we follow. I start looking at the maps Brian hoards in his zippered bike bag, and he gets a little frustrated with my questions: "Where are we? Are you sure we're there and not here?" He guards his knowledge of roads and landmarks carefully. "I know where we are," he says over and over, but I really don't care. I need to know for some strange reason where I am at this exact moment. Maybe it is the fact that Phil and our support vehicle will be leaving us in two days and then I'll have to find comfort in things drawn and numbered and named. Or maybe I am enjoying the fact that with each landmark we pass, I'll be closer to a pool and a cold beer. I like riding along knowing the Chemung River will stay on my left and that we won't have to hoof it over the ridges of green on either side.

"I think we're lost," I say to Brian as we come to a gate closing off the route we thought was the secret way past the highway to Corning. He's perplexed by the map and turns it left to right while I suggest upside down, just for a humorous moment. I guess we should have noticed the electric plant signs along this road, or perhaps the "Do Not Enter" warnings, but hey, we are daring bikers and should be able to find the shortcuts. We decide to ride back up the hill (why is it whenever you get lost, you have to ride back *up*, not *down*, a hill?) to the main road where I see two bikers idling along—a father and a daughter. Knowing that Brian (and basically any man) will never ask strangers for directions, I take it upon myself to introduce myself to these friendly cyclists, hoping they will tell us the quickest, most efficient way to Corning and a hotel with a pool. They carry ears of corn in little plastic bags that they try to balance while steering, and they look happy to stop for a minute to answer my questions.

We are only ten minutes from town once they point us to the secret road that awaits beyond the overpass directly ahead. I think how wonderful it must be to be carrying those dozen ears of fresh corn home for supper. Too bad they don't invite us over. But they do wish us well on our trip.

The richer the town, the more they try to return the streets and shops to earlier times. It's as if the city officials, in combination with a high cash flow, pour the history back into the town by sprucing up the brass street lamps, cleaning the glass store fronts and ringing in time with corner clocks that gleam and point to the hours, even if their big hands aren't moving. Maybe that's the point.

We find that Corning has chosen to stop time, preserving it when things were comfortable and resplendent, rather than constantly rambling towards the future. Their Main Street is just what the name implies—a throwback to an earlier time when people strolled along and gazed in storefront windows, looking at the latest styles in clothes or at technological innovations. Couples strolling at night, hands in pockets or arms pressed tightly to each other, after a good meal at a local restaurant. We notice that there is even a Woolworths five-and-dime store around the corner, complete with an old-fashioned soda fountain. I remark that this place probably isn't much different from when my mother passed through in 1956.

"Yeah, except no parade for us today," Brian replies.

"No parade?"

"Well, the way June tells it, people rolled out the red carpet for them every place they stopped, so they must have had a parade or something like that for them here."

"You have to remember, Brian, that's the way *she* tells it," I say.

I like Corning, especially because the motel gives us a special "biker's documentary" rate. Phil and Brian laugh at me for asking for a discount, but I'm like my mother, who's motto should be, "You've got to get what you can get when you can get it—especially if it saves you a few dollars."

Growing up with a mother like mine—who has a purse full of coupons, who asks for special rates at Taco Bell and McDonalds, and who still demands senior citizen discounts at gas stations—gives a person a strong nose for a deal. It's as if my mother will be around the corner shaking her finger at me if I don't at least ask for cheaper prices. And now, we're in this swanky motel where bellboys help us with our bikes in the elevators and conventioneers seem perplexed by our modes of transportation and shiny cycling garb. I make a mental note to be sure and tell my mother about the deal I got. I'm sure she'll chuckle and will probably say "that's my girl!"

After checking in, we immediately take a dip in the pool. Then we just sit quietly, sipping cold beers in the shade, before finding an authentic Italian restaurant for dinner. It has checkered table clothes and empty wine bottle candles and cheap draft beer by the glass and loads of pasta piled high. It has been in business for 60 years, and as we lumber out of the place, walking back to our room along the gas-lit cobblestone, I think about how history is something we keep track of to look back on later. I mention to Brian that this is one place that my mother might say is, "just like I remember it."

June
Teri and I started our seventh day with another interview, this one with the *Scranton Times*. The reporter took us to a local cafe and we were astonished by the fact that he seemed to know more about our trip than we did. He told us about our whole itinerary from all the news reports he had read and he seemed to be surer of it than we were.

After that we took off and rode through more hilly terrain that included a long climb on a dirt road. We rested and refreshed ourselves at the top and then enjoyed the ride down through a solitary country road lined with pine trees. Finally we found the road leading to Camp Great Neck, an Episcopalian boys retreat located deep in the woods by a river. Charles Bryant, the camp director, welcomed us and introduced us to many cute camp counselors. I was still, at that point, thinking about Charley the Chest, so I didn't pursue romance with anyone. But I do remember one cute sailing instructor wanting to take me for a sail. I didn't go, but I should have.

We were treated to dinner and it brought me back to good old Camp Madeline Mulford. I taught some of the boys some Girl Scout songs because who needs to learn Episcopalian songs at camp! So boring. Even though I'm married to a minister, I still don't like Episcopalian music. All their songs sound like funeral marches.

Reinvigorated by a good breakfast and a beautiful morning the next day, we set out on what would end up being one of our longest days of riding—64 miles. We had more mountains to climb, including one hill that rose 1,200 feet.

We made it to Towanda, Pennsylvania, just in time to catch the 5pm train to Sayre, Pennsylvania, just below the New York border. We wanted to make it to Elmira that evening, so the train helped us cut out about 15 miles of riding. While lazing around on the plush seats in the train and enjoying the train ride, we christened our bicycles with names. I named mine "Ali," from an Indian song, and Teri named hers "Tumba."

We got off the train and started to ride the bicycles again from Sayre, where we were passed by a car blaring an advertisement for a rodeo in town from a loudspeaker. They made comments about us between their plugs for the rodeo. I felt like I was in a parade all by myself. We played right along, so they doubled back and passed us a second time, much slower than the first. They probably wanted a date, but all I wanted was a steak—and a nice, tall Manhattan.

After 17 more miles of mainly flat riding, we arrived in Elmira, where Teri had gone to college. We stayed with a friend of hers and enjoyed a steak filet dinner, just like I wanted. I was proud of riding 64 miles, the most I had ever done, but made sure to remark in my diary twice about being "really pooped out."

We took the next day off. Teri took me to see her old college campus. On the way there we got mixed up with an American Legion parade heading right toward us. The town was really alive with a Legionnaire convention going on. We were caught up in the pageantry and sang right along with "The Star Spangled Banner" as we rode by.

Another clear day greeted us the morning of July 1. We altered our riding schedule because we were asked to be honored guests at the Corning Glass Company in Corning, New York. Mr. David Pearce drove down to Elmira and picked us up with our bikes at

10:30 in the morning. Lillie Verdeham, the town youth director, met us along with three men who took us around for a tour. The place was fascinating. The museum was full of everything to do with glass, including ancient pieces from the early days of glassmaking and a mirror cast for the telescope at Palomar Observatory. It was the largest piece of glass I ever saw. We all had lunch together and they gave Teri and me each a beautiful Steuben vase, handcrafted out of the finest crystal. After that, they took pictures of us on our bikes with their employees at our side. As Mr. Pearce drove us back to Elmira, I commented about how nice everyone was and thanked him for such a splendid and relaxing day, free of pedaling and sweat. However, I knew that the next day would bring that all back.

Brian and Peggy ready for another day on the road

4

"Two deeply tanned, attractive pedal pushers cycled into Bath yesterday."
—*Steuben County Courier*, Bath, New York, July 6, 1956

"My goal is to have fun," Peggy said. "I just want to enjoy life on the way and not just rush past things."
—*The Leader*, Bath, New York, August 27, 1996

Peggy

We're in Bath, New York, where we have all the local authorities and media gathered around us: the chief of police, Chamber of Commerce folks, a bicycle shop owner, two newspaper reporters, a fireman, a local historian, and a man off the street who "just happened to walk by and noticed something going on."

Of all the places that we had contacted prior to leaving on our trip, Bath responded with the most interest. The Bath Chamber of Commerce and reporters from their newspapers and the radio station all called us in Salt Lake City before the trip. They all wondered how we were preparing, what we were packing, and what our training tips were. Easy questions with standard answers. But now it's all changed.

We're sitting in the offices of the Chamber of Commerce and Brian Ritmer, the reporter from *The Leader*, hits us with more and more probing questions. He is relentless. "How has this changed you? What experiences will you take with you for a lifetime?" I am sitting on a desk, trying to sound intellectual about all I have gained, assessed, become, evolved into, but all I really want to do is go to the bathroom and wash my face. A squeaky ceiling fan blows the humidity around the little room as both reporters take pictures of us.

"Why did you take this trip?" the reporter fires at me.

Finally, a question I can answer. "Because I wanted to get out of the psychiatric hospital ... " Gasps and sighs, followed by silence. " ... that I work in." As with most of my humor, I find myself having to explain my joke.

"Oh, that you *work* in. How amusing!" The reporter says, with apparent relief. It actually would be more interesting to be an escaped psychiatric patient going across the country following in my mother's footsteps. Imagine the headlines.

To be honest, it is nice being treated like a celebrity. But I can empathize with the Madonnas and Whitneys of this world as we sit at the local diner—the Chat a While—the same one where my mother ate when she passed through in '56. Strangers keep coming up to us, asking about our trip and if we are the bikers going across the country. "Isn't your mother proud?" they ask. It's tough answering these questions while trying to dine on my tuna fish sandwich, chips, and pickle, but as the celebrity biker, we have to be cordial. Maybe Brian and I should have prepared written statements or at least readied ourselves with witty answers to their questions. For a moment, I wish that I had my mother here to take over for me. She would relish the moment and I'm sure that she would have them rolling with laughter in no time. I try my best, but I'm tongue-tied and can't wait to just get back to the silence of the road.

After a few more photos in the park and some final goodbyes to our kind hosts in Bath, it's time to bid Phil farewell. After some hugs and thanks for his support on the road and on the Internet, he points his rental car toward New York City, a five-hour drive away. As we balance our loaded bikes against a broken-down fountain, empty of water, it hits me: *Now we've really done it.* We're up in the middle of New York, we don't really know where we're going to stay tonight and *we don't have Phil and his car.* What if we get a flat that stays flat? What happens if my handlebars fall off and I fly down over a cliff into a pasture with bulls and Brian can't find me? What if I decide that this trip is just a little too full of exercise and I want to hop into the air-conditioned comfort of a gasoline-powered machine that can whisk me to a place with soft pillows, a hot shower, and a pleasant waiter who takes my order for French fries and several pints of the best local microbrew? But mostly, what if my legs rebel and won't pedal anymore?

After Phil leaves I gaze at Brian with concern. He looks so self-assured with his maps and that altitude watch and his schedule of where we're going, but I need some self-assurance so I begin asking questions: "Where are we? Point to it on the map. Where will we stay? How many miles? How does the odometer on my bicycle work? What's the altitude here? Are my bags on straight? Will they fall off in traffic?" Brian reacts like any sane man stuck in a modern-day inquisition would—he gets on his bike and starts riding. I have no other choice but to follow him. Pursuing him actually calms me down—I get to watch him riding in those tight, black cycling shorts, his legs spinning rhythmically, hypnotizing away my fears. I rationalize that I can manage today if I only concentrate on this husband of mine, who is concentrating on routes and bypasses and country lanes.

Men and gadgets. I holler "Gadget Man!" at Brian in jest. Why is it that men are so interested in numbers and mileages and where roads actually meet other roads? I'm sure there are women out there who care about the percent grades of hills and the ratio of cars to bikes or even the rotations of pedal to gear in a two-hour period, but I'm just not one of them. Instead, I find myself veering off the road because I see a woman hanging brightly-colored boxer shorts on a clothesline, or I slow down to listen as the wind catches the arc of a hawk's wing sailing effortlessly above me. These are the times that Brian nearly crashes into me because I'm not going 15 miles per hour and he has to swerve around me. I'm sure that it irritates him when I pedal and coast no faster than an 80-year-old driving an Impala in Palm Beach, but Brian does pretty well with me. He sighs my name in mock disapproval, then smiles. Such moments reassure me that I wouldn't want to be anywhere else than with him, riding over mountains and through fields of corn and soybeans.

June

"Has my daughter called yet?" I haven't heard a word in days from Peggy and Brian so I've been calling Jane, my Girl Scout friend in Buffalo, over and over again.

"Is she there yet? Have you heard from her?" Each time I ask Jane her answer is no. I tell her that I think a mother deserves the right to a phone call when her daughter is riding a bike across the country. She assures me that lack of contact is a good thing, because I would have heard if something bad had happened to them.

I remember the horrible road from Corning to Bath and I just know that Peggy and Brian are on that one today. I told Brian to stay off that road but he seemed to think that the new highway would keep the traffic down and that they'd be fine. I saw a head-on collision on that road in 1956. A woman, the mother of nine children, was trying to pass a Cadillac that was ahead of us. I watched as she passed us on the left and then a couple of minutes later— *boom!* A car hit her coming the other way. It killed her, leaving all those kids of hers to grow up without a mother. I suddenly can't get that image out of my head. I'm a mess and it's all because Peggy hasn't called me yet.

Peggy has always been one to push my buttons. As a little girl, she was a demon—just like me, I suppose. And so infuriating sometimes. But to be mad at her is to be mad at me since she's so like her mother. I guess I let things go discipline-wise with her. She'd laugh right in my face when I'd threaten to spank her with the fly swatter. But I never wanted to use my hand on my children so I'd always get a fly swatter from motels we'd vacation in and use it as a threat. Only it never was a threat. In fact, I think Peggy hid most of the fly swatters from me. Maybe I just gave up reprimanding her because she'd make a funny face at me and then I'd laugh and forget what I was angry about. On the other hand, my son Paul was a perfect angel. Didn't talk back or create problems. Maybe he just didn't have time to misbehave because Peggy was always doing enough of it for both of them.

Bob tells me not to worry and to just calm down. I hate it when men tell you to calm down, like it's a switch that you can turn on and off. Besides, someone has to worry, so it might as well be me. I sure wish she'd just give me a call though. I tell Bob that maybe we should try to go to the library and have them show us where they are on the computer. He shakes his head with approval and says, "First thing tomorrow, June."

"All right," I say, "But it's going to be a long night of worry."

"You wouldn't have it any other way, would you?" he says.

"I guess not, but I sure couldn't forgive myself if something happened to her out on the road."

"Well I guess you've got a point," he responds, "But she's got Brian to take care of her. He'll keep her on the right roads."

Peggy

As we head toward Dansville, New York, the atmosphere is slowly changing. We start seeing buffalo heads on garage doors. Blue and red banners follow quickly behind. Bumper stickers are on every car passing by us—a buffalo snorting and angry in red. People are wearing buffaloes on jackets and hats for the Buffalo Bills football team. Luckily our bicycle outfits are the same colors, so we fit right in.

The Chamber of Commerce in Bath told us about a quaint motel on the outskirts of town. "Cheap with a porch" was the description, and when we pull up, it does look affordable and it does have a porch. Surprisingly though, there are no buffalo paintings or flags waving. The woman at the front desk is a charming sort, hair pulled severely into a bun, with frown lines between her eyes. After I inquire about the price, she says, "Forty dollars cash," and out shoots her hand. Now I know that after a long day of biking, I didn't look especially appealing with my hair flat against a sweaty scalp, dirt encrusted under my nose, my eyes red and bloodshot, all combined with the aromatic stench of road. However, I still feel a little put off when she says, "Thank you, sir," upon receipt of my $40.

Brian starts calling me "sir" after that. Later that evening, while sitting on the front porch gulping down Old Milwaukees and consuming a large pepperoni pizza, I make a point to burp and flex my muscles just to keep up with my newfound macho image.

Brian

We decided to get an early start today so we could make it to Buffalo to stay with June's longtime friend, Jane Sweet, nearly 90 miles away. As we finish our breakfast at The Coffee Cup restaurant, the waitress is nearly beside herself with worry about our plan to ride bicycles so far in a day. "Why, it takes me two and half hours to get to Buffalo in my car, I couldn't imagine doing that on a bicycle, what with all those hills. Oh, my."

"I wonder if Mom is even worrying about us," Peggy remarks. "I mean, this waitress is all concerned about us going to Buffalo and Mom just thinks it's great that we're riding across the country. Sometimes I wish she'd worry more about me and stop making me feel like I have to be so independent and strong."

"June is probably busy selling her memoirs," I say, trying to calm Peg down, but she looks distressed.

"Yeah, that's true. I bet she never even left *The Today Show* studios. We should remember to turn it on in the morning. We'll probably see her out in the crowd trying to sell copies of it to everyone there."

As we start riding, Peg is still concerned about her mother so I tell her that we'll call June tonight and she can tell her mother to worry more about her. That eases her expression, and soon her silver bike is cutting a smooth path through the quiet of the early morning.

At 8:30am, we reach the outskirts of Dansville and look through the mist created by the humidity and out at the road before us—or should I say, above us. We see that another "mountain" awaits—a seven-mile stretch of steady climbing, 1,250 feet in all. Peggy continues to ascend like a champ as I chug along and try to drink lots of water.

At about 10am we arrive in Nunda. We've only covered about 15 miles, but I welcome the break so I can regenerate myself with cold drinks, bananas, and cookies from the local market and pharmacy. I also load up on my newfound ally—pretzels.

Besides Peggy, sweat is my other constant companion on the ride. Once my feet hit the pedals, my pores open up like a faucet and I become one soggy mess. I discovered that I'm not only losing a lot of fluid during the day, but I am also losing salt. Evidence is everywhere—dried crusty white lines of salt decorate my black shorts and my helmet straps every time we get off the bikes.

I start to think of my body as one of those two-cycle lawnmower engines that are so hard to keep running. They require just the right mixture of oil in the gas to make them work right. Too much oil and they whine and blow black smoke. Too little and they sputter and stall. Just right and they'll run like a top. So I start buying pretzels and find out that they are the perfect food to replace the salt I am losing. Low on fat and oils, high on carbohydrates and sodium, I buy a bag of them and put it in my front pack. Soon, my routine evolves into pedaling, drinking water, eating a pretzel or two, drinking Gatorade, eating more pretzels, pedaling, etc. I know that as long as I keep the right mixture of fluid and salt, my legs won't cramp and maybe we'll make it to Buffalo without a breakdown.

Peggy

"Where you folks from?" asks a man with a "Welcome to Byrne's Pharmacy" nametag.

"Salt Lake City."

"You've ridden all the way from Salt Lake City to here?"

It always gets a little confusing explaining exactly where we are from and where we are going. I mean, we live in Salt Lake but we're not from Salt Lake; we started from New York but we're going to San Francisco. Our—or rather my—explanations, always seem to make people scratch their heads. And when I mention the tie-in about my mother riding her bike across the country 40 years before, it really throws things into a tizzy.

"But, did you ride your bikes from Salt Lake to New York?"

"Are you Mormons?"

"Where's your mother?"

"Why are you going east to west?"

At least when people ask you questions in small towns, they give you things. We get free postcards, a magnet that advertises the drugstore, and they even pay for my Snickers bars.

"You've got a long way to go today before you get to Buffalo—that's almost an hour-and-a-half trip from here by car."

I shrug my shoulders and thank them for their concern. I'm suddenly glad we got free Snickers bars.

Letchworth State Park is called the "Grand Canyon of the East," but you'd never know it because you ride through cornfields and farms before you enter its gates. As we start out through the park, I think, *Another marketing ploy to get people to pay entrance fees.* "Pretty enough, but I'm not going to see any canyon in this field," I mumble until I notice some people high up on a railroad trellis looking down over me. Being the adventurer I am, I convince Brian to go up on the tracks, ignoring the "Do Not Trespass" signs, to see the view.

We park our bikes along a stone wall and start walking. Soon, the tracks cross an abyss that seems to fall and fall forever, ending in a gorge of rock, water, and air. My knees instantly feel shaky, but we continue on, our faces peering over the rail as a breeze passes below our feet, the mist rising up along the tracks.

Trees, with roots clawing for whatever scrap of earth they can find, seem to be the guardians of the river far below, their leaves waving a warning to those who wander beyond the safety of their trunks. Using the camera's zoom lens, I peer to the bottom. Rocks lay like slabs of broken bones with a clear pulse of water spraying across and over the haze into the churning falls. You can almost see the walls arching themselves upward from the jagged line of water.

We meander around the park and find a quaint inn by some falls that are probably called Bridal Veil or Honeymoon Falls because all we see are young couples strolling hand-in-hand, taking pictures of themselves on benches and rock walls and on the rocking chairs at the inn. At least I have plenty of couples to choose from when asking for our "couple" picture.

"Are you on your honeymoon?" one couple in matching outfits asks me while Brian fiddles around with his speedometer.

"No, we're riding our bikes across the country," I say, smiling.

"That sounds like too much work," the couple replies, strolling away.

"Easy vacationers," I think to myself as I wipe off the Gatorade spilling down my chin.

Brian turns to me and changes the subject. "You know Peg, that was one heck of a climb this morning. And not the first one of the trip either. It sure has been tougher terrain than I expected. I can't imagine June just jumping on a three-speed without any training and surviving these hills."

I tried to picture her doing these roads herself on that balloon-tired bicycle. While visiting Mom and Dad before our trip, I took that old bike out for a spin. It sat in the garage, like a broken lawnmower, just waiting for attention. Rust spun around its spokes, the bell was broken in half, the mirror long gone and the frame stiff, the seat hard and dried from age, its leather cracked from 40 years of wear. My baby seat, a clunky metal contraption that could never meet modern-day safety standards, was still attached to the dented back fender.

I pulled the bike through the mess and jumble of the garage and out to the street. It shined dully, the paint chipping off, its color more rust than the original red of 1956. I got on and tried to pedal, but the gears were jammed. I spun the tires around until the gear caught on and then, with trepidation, I took off. Initially, the bike rode like an old woman—yawning, slow, and with hesitation. There were no toe clips to hold my feet in place, just plain old pedals; I had to stand up to pump the bike into motion. But then, as if waking from sleep, the bike caught her wind and started to gracefully roll along the road as I held onto her handlebars. The only other problem was stopping. The brakes were still the same ones from the '50s, and when I tried them at the stop sign, one brake clicked, long gone, while the other screeched in agony. Maybe the bike was just telling me that it wanted more attention, more chances to run its tires across the asphalt instead of sitting idly in the garage. As I pedaled on, the wind started to whistle through the spokes and the scenery of suburbia passed by. After awhile the bike started to feel solid under my power. It had the grace of time on its side, its heaviness and thick tires something you'd want to keep with you.

I found a good back road away from my parents' house and rode for about an hour. I felt proud riding that bike, and started to feel the history of my mother's trip right there in my hands, and down through my legs. She rode across the country on this sturdy relic, still shining, with thick pedals to take her past places and over mountains. I felt the wind through my hair and envisioned her sailor's cap jauntily on my head. I glided to a stop and turned for home, slowly, the pedals like ferris wheels, lifting and lowering.

June

I remember that the ride to Letchworth Park was a tough one. Rolling hills, curving roads, and the heat combined to make the 60 miles Teri and I covered that day very exhausting. To top it off, my gears started to give me trouble. First, they wouldn't shift up and I got all tired spinning my legs riding in low. Then, without warning, they'd shift into high when I tried to climb a hill. It was very frustrating. But, when we finally made it to Letchworth State Park I was reinvigorated by the expansive view of its high cliffs that opened up before me. With its river, complete with rippling falls, I could see why it was called the "Grand Canyon of the East," because it really was dazzling. It made me anxious to see the real thing when we got out west. Moments like that always seemed to come at just the right time, and were priceless reminders of why I was doing the trip.

Pedaling out of the park we rode west through the twilight and towards a wonderful sunset of golden ribbons which turned to a red, mackerel sky, and then deep purple. That evening we stayed at the Castile AYH and met an elderly gentleman, Mr. Chamberlain. He had long white curly hair and a very noble manner. He was anxious to hear about our adventures and quite willing to share his wisdom. I found his insights very interesting, but since I was tired from the long day I went to bed fairly early.

Recalling that evening in my memoir, I lamented not spending more time listening to Mr. Chamberlain's stories. "Sometimes we meet angels unaware," I wrote. "There was something very special about this time together and it touched a deep chord in my soul. To this day I have always regretted that I did not stay up another hour with him."

I told Peggy before her trip to pay attention to people that she meets along the way—that they might just become the angels she needs if danger comes her way. Instead of the usual rolling of the eyes I get from her, she smiled at me and said, "I'm bringing along Grandma and Gramps [Bob's parents], Tim [Brian's brother] and Vance [her godfather] on this ride with me, Mom. I'll look for them in the trees and in the sky and feel them in the breeze." I tell you, I almost cried with pride when I heard her say that. "Just like your Momma," I said.

Teri and I awoke the next day at 5:45 because we wanted to be sure to get an early start for Buffalo so we could celebrate the Fourth of July with my good friend, Jane Sweet. A clear morning greeted us as we rode 20 miles before stopping at a cafe for pancakes. We had to cover another 60 miles before Jane greeted us in Buffalo. Eighty miles that day! I was so proud of myself—I felt like The Little Engine That Could. I really was getting strong. It's fun to look back at all my pictures from then and see how trim and fit I looked on the ride. And happy.

Jane treated us to a meal fit for champions—ham and all the fixings. After two back-to-back days of extended riding, this meal provided the elixir that our road-weary bodies needed. That, coupled with the camaraderie of my old camp friend made for a great evening. I remember we sat out in her backyard and sang song after song, trading stories of our lives. I could really tell Jane anything, and I told her about how difficult it had all been with my father's death and my mother's remarriage, how lonely I sometimes felt living in Long Island, and how I hadn't really met the right boy yet to settle down with and have a family.

Jane laughed, "You? Settle down? I think you'll always have an adventuresome lifestyle."

Then we discussed the types of boys I might like to meet and it all ended in a large bout of giggling and hugging. After a few cocktails, we drove out to Olcott, an amusement park on the lake, and went on some rides. Our day was complete when we sat on the beach and watched the Independence Day fireworks show mirrored over the glassy waters of Lake Erie.

July 5 was supposed to be a day off for us. However, I recall not being able to sleep in as long as I would have liked because a reporter woke us with a telephone call at 9am. As things would have it, the reporter was quite inquisitive too, so we had an extensive conversation. That evening, the article appeared in the *Buffalo Courier-Express:*

> Two venturesome gals, out to conquer the continent by bike, wheeled into Buffalo yesterday for a breather ... garbed in bathing suits to catch the sun and save on washing ... Neither of these two girls had done much cycling before tackling this trip but June mentioned that "This is the breaking-in trip for us, after all, we're doing this for the experience."

Ha! A breaking-in trip? I can't believe I said that. In fact, I was probably misquoted. I think that reporter just didn't like seeing strong, athletic girls riding freely across the country. This was before Women's Lib and maybe he just felt like we were silly girls. But I tell you, I felt like a well-trained athlete after 14 days and over 400 miles of riding. Not only that, most of those 400 miles were spent riding up and down the steep, challenging grades of the Pocono Mountains.

Later on in our trip it was satisfying to see that news articles described Teri and me as "tanned in the deepest sense of the word and muscled like Olympic Athletes." Now that was the kind of news coverage I liked.

Peggy

Once out of Letchworth, we get back to work on the road. No more meandering or taking pictures, no more honeymooner conversations or stops to view the falls. We have highways and byways and state roads and traffic to go—more miles than we expected. We have one of those little maps that make distance look shorter and it seems that we stay on Route 32 forever. Even with its gel and my padded shorts, my bicycle seat begins to dig in. To top it off, I lose my balm along one of the side roads and my lips start getting cracked in the late afternoon sun. Then, my pedal starts clicking with each revolution and the constant sound makes me even more irritable.

Brian tries having pleasant conversation with me, but the poor guy gets yelled at. I am in the middle of having the mileage blues, and all I want to do is call Jane to see if she can pick us up in her air-conditioned car. But we ride on. Cars pass us, traffic lights stop us, my seat chafes me, my hands get numb, and my sunglasses become smeared in grease and sweat. But I know that if I quit early, Jane will tell my mother about it and Mom will rub it in repeatedly about getting a lift. She'll say, "So you got a ride? I never accepted a ride *that* early 40 years ago, when I was on a three-speed and had no fancy biking pants ... "

These thoughts make me push on through the pain. But then my mind starts to wander again, and I ask myself unending questions. *Why am I in a competition with my mother anyway? Why do we always seem to try to "one-up" each other? How can I ever "one-up" my mother when she did her trip as a single woman riding just a three-speed?* I know I'll never be able to match that accomplishment, so I tell myself to just let it go, enjoy the trip, and not worry about what Mom thinks about me.

All of my life I've been part of my mother and somehow, everything I do has broken off from her experiences. I wonder why I follow her path over and over again—becoming a social worker like her, a flight attendant like she wanted to be, and now a cross-country bicycler. Sometimes I feel like I'm too much a part of her life and not enough of my own.

Suddenly I realize that dusk has settled in and all the cars have their lights on. Just then, Brian shouts "Clarence!" pointing to the sign up ahead. Clarence is the suburb of Buffalo that Jane and her husband live in. I slow down and pull up next to Brian, who is full of light and numbers.

"Eighty-seven miles in 8 hours of riding—and almost 4,000 feet of climbing to boot!" he says with pep. Looking at his prideful grin, I remember why I am on this trip.

As we ride up to Jane's house she springs up from the lawn chair on her porch and runs out to greet us.

"Oh, you made it! You made it! This is all so exciting! You have to tell me everything about the trip," she exclaims with arms flailing, just like my mother. "You're following in your mother's footsteps and she's so proud of you. She's been calling all day—all week, for that matter." Jane smiles. "She's worried about you, you know."

"My mother? Worry?" I laugh but inside I feel like a soft quilt has landed over my heart. I calm down.

Jane feeds us lasagna, hefty with meat sauce, and has loaves of fresh bread for dipping and scraping. We lick our plates clean and she is thrilled when we ask for seconds.

"Did you cook lasagna for Mom when she came here 40 years ago?" I ask, while Jane's husband, David, pours us beer after beer in frosted mugs.

"Oh, no. Meat and Manhattans and chocolate cake. Your mother always liked a big slab of steak."

There's Mom again. Pounding down the Manhattans and slurping up the meat. It totally amazes me because I wonder how she managed to get up the next day and ride with all that steak sitting in her gut and her head dizzy with a hangover. Maybe it was because she was younger than I am and more resilient.

After dinner, we see ourselves on *The Today Show* for the first time. Jane taped it for us. Immediately, I notice that I looked like Groucho Marx, my eyebrows lined with the darkest eyeliner I've ever seen. What did that makeup person do to me? I really can't listen to how the interview went with Bryant because I become mesmerized by my strange eyebrows lifting and lowering like a silent movie star. Bryant seemed to lose his focus on and off throughout the interview, no doubt distracted by my eyebrows too. It just goes to show you that you shouldn't let anyone put heavy pancake makeup on your face prior to a cross-country bike trip. After we laugh at the June-isms like, "It's great to be back, Bryant," Jane begins with the Girl Scout stories about my mother and her.

"June just loved those Girl Scout songs," Jane says with a smile. "And you could barely get her out of that bathing suit at the end of the day. She'd stay in that suit 24 hours a day if she could."

I hated Girl Scouts. I didn't like wearing that stupid dress with the sash that you had to sew badges on. Mom didn't know how to sew and thought that it would be a "good Girl Scout thing for me to do," sew the badges on the sash. I would refuse and tape them on and those other snotty, gung-ho Girl Scouts—who loved crafts and whittling wood and singing—would tease me. Girl Scouts can be a pretty rotten bunch. I remember my mother happily driving me to one Girl Scout meeting, where I proceeded to write "Girl Scouts stink" over and over again on my songsheet. The leader saw what I had written and told my mother. Mom was flabbergasted—it was like I burnt the flag and stomped on it in our living room. Mom didn't force me to go anymore on those Tuesdays and I got back to building mudforts and playing kick-the-can and "ring the doorbell and run" with the boys in my neighborhood. Too bad they never gave badges for running the fastest from neighbor's houses. However, I still had to listen and re-listen to Mom's stories of her Girl Scout days. After a while I got good at nodding my head in interest. Actually, I do get amused when Mom tells her stories, even though I know them all by heart. I just look at the smile on her face and the laughter in her heart and forget that I've heard them all a million times.

Jane's phone rings and before she even answers I know who it will be.

"Oh, you're in Buffalo! You're in Buffalo! Why haven't you called me? I can barely hear you because Bob has the news blaring on his television."

"Mom, tell Dad to turn down the TV!" I yell into the phone.

"Bob! Turn off your set. I can't hear Peggy!" Mom yells back into the phone at my dad on the other end.

Mom and Dad watch two televisions simultaneously—Dad in the kitchen at the table, Mom in the living room with the remote control. They watch the same shows, only in two different rooms, both with the volume up, as if to say to each other, "My show is louder." I've asked Mom why she and Dad do this, and she always says, "We like it better this way." I think it's because they fought so many times for the remote and now, instead of war in the house, there's Maury Povitch.

The volume is down and before I can say a thing, Mom corners me. "So you don't care about your mother? You just let her worry for four days?"

I try to respond. "Well, we have been ... "

"Oh, it doesn't matter. I'm just glad to hear your voice. Did you get lost yet?" It's just like Mom, asking that kind of question. But before I can answer or explain she'll tell me that it doesn't matter. But I do the same thing to her, not that I acknowledge that too often. Mom continues, "When I was on my trip, we got lost a little bit trying to get up to Jane's house, but then we didn't have detailed maps like you two have."

"Mom, we only need maps so we can follow your route because it was so wacky and went all over the place—not in any kind of a straight line, you know."

"Oh, who needs straight lines to anywhere, anyway? I certainly didn't. When I was a Girl Scout leader, I'd always tell my scouts that crooked lines lead to adventures."

Jane jumps on the other phone. "June, you'd always tell those girls strange things whenever you got lost on one of your adventures. Remember the canoe trip on the Delaware River in 1955, when you almost got washed away in a flood and you told those girls that if they sang loud enough that good luck would come their way?"

"But good luck did come our way—we got rescued, didn't we? Dark clouds are always surrounded by silver linings."

Mom has always been one to find the positive in any negative. "How many times have I heard that saying?" I interject.

"Oh, maybe once or twice," Mom laughs, even though I've heard that phrase hundreds of times. "How have the roads been?"

"Not too bad. The hills are everywhere around New York State, though."

"Oh, I remember the Poconos. They nearly wore us out. But we didn't have 24-speed bikes like yours. We just chugged up on our three-speeds and jumped in lakes. Have I told you how proud I am of you?"

"Only about 20 times in New York."

I remember how Mom looked in New York City before our trip, like a sunbeam was caught inside her skin, glowing from her every pore. She'd walk up to strangers and tell them that Brian and I were riding our bikes across the country following her route from 1956. If they listened, she'd tell them more.

"Jane, have you serenaded these two yet with any songs?"

Oh, no. I knew it was coming. The Girl Scout sing-a-long. "Remember when we arrived at your house 40 years ago and you had a party for us and we sang all the songs we knew, like "Twilight on the Trail" and "More Rapids" and "Day is Done"?

"Peggy, which song would you like to hear first?"

I listen to "Twilight on the Trail" and one other Girl Scout song before I can't stand it anymore. I tell Mom that I have to go to sleep, but before I can hang up she discusses how much fun she had in Canada and how people gave them keys to the city and bought them dinner and how a Canadian Girl Scout camp gave them presents and sang them the Canadian National Anthem. "Jane, I think we should sing the Canadian National Anthem for them, don't you?"

"Mom, it's just me, Brian's already off the phone. He went to e-mail Phil for our web site."

"What's that web site anyway, why can't you just send postcards and call me? You can even call collect."

"Goodnight, Mom. We'll call you in Ohio." As I hang up and walk away, I hear Jane talking to her on the other line, trying to explain e-mail and web sites and computer log-ons to her. Then, as I'm getting ready for bed, I can hear them singing song after song, giggling in between.

Greetings from the Mayor and Clerk of Dunnville, Ontario

5

"A pair of pretty pedal pushers—and not the kind you buy over the counter in the ladies wear store—visited Dunnville briefly this week."

    —Dunnville, Ontario, newspaper article, July 7, 1956

Brian

On the morning of our sixth day, Jane and I talk while she makes us a big "biker's breakfast." Peggy isn't up yet and I decide to let her sleep in until the reporter gets here.

Jane just can't get over her excitement for us. "It's great you're doing this together—not many couples would even think of such a thing. Go for it. Do it while you're young," she says to me, smiling.

"People along the way have warned us that we may not be a couple when we're done," I joke.

"Oh, you two will be a couple for a lifetime, I bet."

Peggy trudges in and responds, "Yeah, a couple who will have aches and pains from this trip—for a lifetime."

Jane is a big cyclist too, and has done weeklong tours in Vermont and Maine. She's even the founding member of a local women's bicycle group called "Outspokin'." This particular day just happened to also be the day that they met for their weekly ride—a 20-mile jaunt around the countryside of Clarence. So, after an interview with the reporter from the *Clarence Bee* and watching our *Today Show* video again, we set out to meet the Outspokin' women for lunch.

The crowd is overwhelming. Women decked out in matching pink Outspokin' tee shirts and cycling outfits line the main road in front of Berrafatos Char-Pit. They scream and shout our names and take pictures of us in our Schwinn outfits. They bombard us with the usual questions about our trip while we wait for our grilled hot dogs; the women pat me on the back and hug Peggy.

"Oh, your mother must be so proud, Peggy!"

"How long have you been married? Where are your children?"

"Don't you get tired? Maybe you should rent a car sometime to take a little break."

"It's good you brought along a handsome man to protect you, Peggy!"

"Who organized this trip for you? A travel agency?"

It is rather humbling to be admired by such a friendly group of women, all cyclists themselves. I lose count of how many times I say thank you. It's strange, I've been one to admire other bikers doing cross-country from afar, sitting back and imagining myself doing their trip and wishing it onto myself. But here I am now, the one doing the trip, the one on the bike, and I feel like I'm in a movie. It just doesn't seem real sometimes. I'm usually on the periphery of things, being the organizer, the behind-the-scenes kind of guy. I'm not looking for credit or accolades; I just want to see a thing through. Like this trip. To see Peggy and I, as a couple, accomplish it. I know that this is her mother's trip revisited, but in the end, it will be ours too.

Jane shuttles us through the city and to the Peace Bridge in her van, complete with its "I'd rather be bicycling" license plate frame. She bids us well as we wave goodbye and begin to push our bicycles across the bridge's walkway because there isn't much room for us on the road. We pause briefly to admire the view, expansive and blue on this crystal clear day. We look out at the lake and watch its waters converge into the Niagara River below, on its way east to Niagara Falls, Lake Ontario, the Saint Lawrence Seaway, and eventually, the Atlantic Ocean.

The Canadian side beckons us with clusters of red and white

maple leaf flags waving in the breeze. The Canadian flag has always been one of my favorites—simple, yet bold—and the country a pleasant place to visit.

As Peggy and I cross into Canada, the questions and curiosity of the guards is less than when June entered the country in 1956. They simply ask us to state our citizenship and the purpose of our visit. No searches or detailed inquiries. I guess that bicycle tourists are a common sight these days, or maybe it was just the fact that we are a married couple traveling together, not two young and pretty single women like June and Teri. Or maybe it's just that Peggy, traveling with a male companion, tended to discourage would-be suitors and gawkers. Nevertheless, with a simple wave of the guard's hand, we are in Canada.

We round the corner from the Port-of-Entry and head towards a park that lines the Canadian shore of the lake. This strip of green parkway, complete with a nice bicycle trail, is in stark contrast to the docks, highways, and skyscrapers that line the Buffalo side. We pull over and enjoy the silence, taking a break in the shade of the trees and enjoying the blue horizon that stretches before us. We also need a bit of time to unwind from the hustle-bustle of the last couple of days. We both remark that it is nice to have everyone so interested in our trip, but to ride all day and then have to be pleasant company afterward is a difficult task. Though we enjoyed the attention and eagerness of people wanting to talk with us during the first six days of our trip, we are ready for a little time out of the limelight. Canada offers just the release we need as we anonymously cycle west along the coast towards Long Beach Provincial Park, 40 miles away.

That evening we set up camp in the park and head out for a dip in the still, cool waters of the lake. We ride our bicycles to dinner that evening and nobody gives it a second thought when we park the bikes inside the hallway while we eat. Anonymous we are—heck, we couldn't buy attention now.

June

After a day of welcome rest in Buffalo, Teri and I were ready for the road again. But first, we had to stop by the Schwinn dealership to pick up our bicycles. We had dropped them off the day before so that a mechanic could fix our gear problems and make other adjustments. The repair bill came to $22, quite a sum for two women who were hoping to cross the country for less than $500. Fortunately, the mechanic was really nice and he said, "Schwinn has agreed to pay for all of the repairs." He asked how the riding was. When I said that pedaling up the mountains was a bit hard, he asked me to sit on my bicycle to see how it was fitting me. "Well there's your problem, your seat is too low." When I said that the seatpost was as high as it could go he just took it off and put a longer one on. "That ought to take care of it," he smiled, and off we rode towards the Canadian border.

We crossed into Canada via the Peace Bridge as a dense fog settled in, obscuring our view of the Niagara River below and Lake Erie on our left. We stopped at the customs booth when we got to the other side. The customs officials didn't spend much time looking at our things, though. They just asked lots of questions. I think that they were just stalling for time because they were curious about our trip. They said that it wasn't every day that they encountered two young women cyclists doing what we were doing. Again, we felt quite the celebrities.

We rode on to Dunnville, Ontario, about 45 miles away. The mayor, Mr. McQuarterly, rode his bicycle out to great us and give us the red carpet treatment. He and the town clerk made some telephone calls to the paper, the radio station, and the local Girl Scout camp, Camp Owasa. The clerk noticed that there were no licenses on the bicycles, so he issued us complimentary ones. Then they treated us to dinner, keeping us company until one of the Owasa camp counselors came and picked us up.

Queen Elizabeth herself couldn't have had a finer welcome to the Girl Scout Guide camp in Canada. The campers were so excited to meet foreigners that they sang "The Star Spangled Banner" to honor us. After that, the whole camp mobbed us like we were a couple of movie stars, asking for autographs and taking pictures. Then Patty, the camp director, drove us back into town where the mayor and a photographer were waiting. All of this attention was a bit overwhelming, but certainly got my first trip to foreign soil off to a good start. If only the weather was as nice to us as the people were.

Riding out of Dunnville the next day we immediately encountered a harsh headwind, making for a hard day of pedaling. We decided to stay in Simcoe instead of Delhi because we were so tired. We called the mayor, a Mr. Carter, and he drove out to meet us. A dashing gentleman, he took us out to dinner and set us up in a hotel, all paid for by the Board of Trade. Did we enjoy taking a shower and sleeping in big beds!

It was nice being able to take a break from talking to people about the trip. Maybe I was just being temperamental, but I was feeling a bit homesick. I was missing the wedding of my friend, Dot Minelli. Dot was a good friend of mine who, a few years earlier, stayed with me and my mother for a couple of months. She'd had a difficult life and was on her own as a young woman. Now, she had met the man of her dreams. Friends and family had their own lives and were living them, and here I was, riding along, passing through, and trying to figure out what I was supposed to be doing. I guess I wanted the things I had left behind to stay at a standstill while I was on this adventure, and when they didn't, I felt like I was missing out on something. I felt like a nomad. A pilgrim.

To raise my spirits, I decided to plan my own wedding. It would be by the ocean and I could imagine myself in a sailboat on the bay with all my friends sailing close while the minister had us state our vows. Or else, it could be Camp Madeline Mulford with everyone in Girl Scout uniforms serenading us while we had a big bonfire. Or even at Mother's Lutheran Church with a German band playing polkas and my husband spinning me around. The only problem I had back then was that I really couldn't picture who that husband would be or what he would look like. I tried putting my old boyfriend's faces into that daydream but none of them seemed like the right fit. I thought, *Maybe I'll meet him during this trip.* He might be a cowboy out west or even a sailor. If nothing else, thinking about the possibilities kept me pedaling through those difficult winds in Canada.

The next morning was Sunday, so Teri and I got up early and rode to Delhi to find a church to attend. The first one we came to was the Hungarian Presbyterian. A woman, Mrs. Medved, said, "No English here," directing us to United Church where there was an English service. I remember really wanting to go into that Hungarian church and see a different way of believing in God. Who needs to pray to God in English anyway? I didn't. But we left and went to the English service and it wasn't anything special. Mrs. Medved must have realized that I was disappointed, so upon leaving, she invited us to lunch. At least, I think she did, because we couldn't really understand her and she couldn't understand us, but she said something about food so we just went. We sat at a table with her Hungarian family. They stared at us and we all tried to talk, but no one understood a thing. That was okay—we smiled and that was all that was needed. I felt honored to be invited to this stranger's house and I gave her a hug upon leaving.

Sometimes I think that when you meet with strangers, it's like leaving fairy dust in your wake. Happiness carries itself inside of you even after you leave that stranger's company, and I think that's what God and Jesus and Mary want of us anyway. To just be with people and share simple times with them.

Soon after leaving Delhi we encountered road construction that was so bad that we had to hitch a ride. Fortunately, an usher from the church was passing by and he gave us a ride past the mess.

Back on the bicycles again, we headed towards St. Thomas. Our destination for the day was Rondue Provincial Park, about 75 miles from Simcoe. We had to push ourselves because I didn't want to miss the Girl Scout rally in Detroit the next day. Girl Scouts from all over the nation were going to be joining up for fun and food and songs and I just had to be there. I wanted to ride right into the rally on my bicycle and sing "God Bless America" at the top of my lungs and wave the flag that was taped to my handlebars. I was feeling very patriotic, happy for the world and ready to show it off.

Unfortunately, we hit a rainstorm just as we entered the outskirts of St. Thomas, so we took cover in the police station. Of course, the police officers called the press and the radio, and we all had a lot of fun. Then the strangest thing happened: A call came into the station. Two ladies from the hostel in Detroit were calling all over Canada looking for us. Apparently, the local AYH representatives had expected us to arrive in Detroit that day. Having heard nothing from us, they had been calling all over our route so they could drive out to pick us up in time to attend the Girl Scout Roundup. As soon as they found us, they gave us instructions to stay put because they were sending a couple of girls in a car to pick us up.

It was midnight by the time we made it to Detroit. Though we were tired from our long day of travel and misadventure, we still couldn't believe our good luck. We'd make it to the roundup rally after all. I didn't get to sing my song or wave my flag that evening, but you can bet I belted out many songs the next day.

The camp had a terrific setup with tents and displays all over housing 6,000 people. I rode my bicycle from camp to camp and serenaded everyone with the biggest smile on my face. Everyone knew who we were and what we were doing and they even made an announcement for those who didn't have any idea about our adventure in progress. I think we even got a picture taken of us for the National Girl Scout newspaper. After supper all the units paraded into the arena and I found the group of my friend, Carol Jayner, and just started to walk beside her. When she saw me she was so surprised she started to cry. Then we all went and sat in the arena. Before us was an awe-inspiring sight: 6,000 Girl Scouts on the hillside at sunset, colorful flags and banners all around, everyone sitting in groups from their home states. We all started to sing and it was like a heavenly choir, especially when the other side serenaded us to "Peace." The evening ended with everyone marching into the center from the hillside, linking hands. A terrific feeling of patriotism and sisterhood prevailed, and I couldn't have been any happier.

Thinking back on that day, I wish that Peggy could have experienced the emotions that I had. But she never liked Girl Scouts the way I did. Maybe it was because I pushed her too hard. Or maybe it was just the times. Being a Girl Scout in my day was a great honor. Peggy had other things to do when she was that age, like playing softball and cheerleading. That's okay, I guess—over the years she taught me a lot of good cheers that I've been able to add to my repertoire of Girl Scout songs. Sometimes, we even sing them together. Now *that's* a special treat.

Brian

We get an early start on our second day in Canada because our destination is Port Bruce, 100 miles west. The day is clear and a slight tailwind helps us make good time. By noon, we have covered nearly 60 of those miles, so we pull into Port Dover for lunch. Peggy says that this small, lakeside community, full of bait, tee shirt, and souvenir shops, reminds her of the New England shore towns she knows from summers growing up in Maine. She says that if she didn't know any better, she'd easily mistake this place for Kennebunkport, Camden, or Cape Elizabeth, complete with tourists looking for a good parking place and kids running on the beach.

Then we make the first real nutritional mistake of the trip. Peggy has been boasting that with all the riding and exercising we're doing, we can eat anything we want. With that in mind, she downs a large strawberry milkshake before we leave.

It's tough starting up after the break; we quite enjoy the shade, the beach, and watching the tourists mingle about. That, coupled with the fact that the heat of the midday sun is bearing down on us, makes the afternoon ride all the more difficult.

About the time we hit the 75-mile mark, Peggy starts to feel a bit woozy from the heat and the strawberry milkshake. I should have known better than to let her drink that thing, because it's doing nothing but curdling in her stomach.

The scenery turns quite surreal; suddenly we are in tobacco country. Small green and red tobacco-drying barns line the country roads. It must be harvest time, because everywhere we look workers are in the fields picking tobacco leaves and loading them on the backs of tractor-trailers. Heat, tobacco fields ... what next? I thought this was supposed to be Canada! I almost check my map to make sure we haven't taken a wrong turn and somehow ended up in Virginia or North Carolina. Peggy's cryptic journal entries capture the character of today's riding, which also happens to be her first-ever 100-mile "century" day:

> 100 miles. Oh Lord! Tobacco fields. Sun on the road through my sunglasses. My butt hurts. I do the neck exercises. Look at yellow flowers. Change position of hands. Eat veggie sub and strawberry shake at Port Dover and watch relaxed people on the beach

with their families. Fill water bottles a lot. Feel delirious and irritated, then numb, then get second wind. Brian realizes that maybe we're doing too many miles in the heat. Stop in Port Burwell and walk into a lighthouse to use the bathrooms. Decide to ride 10 more miles to Port Bruce where there's only one restaurant, Bert's Burgers. While we're getting greasy food I ask the cashier if there are any cabins for rent. "Oh, you mean cottages," and she hands me a card to call a lady to see about renting when that lady just happens to be eating dinner there. She shows us a cute cottage on the beach for only $30—American. Brian hands her the money before she can say "no," we had a place for the night. A Deal! I go swimming in great waves, floating around and diving under, feeling refreshed. Tomorrow is another 100 miles. I can do it. Then it's a two-day rest.

Planning our trip, I spent endless hours poring over maps and working on our itinerary. I basically researched the route that June had taken in 1956, coupled that with my cycling experience—which included a number of previous pack tours—and started to work on what I thought was a reasonable schedule. Our plan was to cover the 250-mile Canadian portion of our trip in three days, then catch a ferry across the lake and spend a couple of days in Port Clinton with my mother and her husband. However, getting a later start than we wanted out of Buffalo had set us back a bit. Therefore, in order to make it to the ferry in time for our two days of rest and relaxation, we have to do back-to-back 100-mile days. I'm up for it, having bounced back from my early woes with the heat and the hills, but I worry about Peggy. She's in great shape—better than I am—but her body just isn't built to handle more than about six hours a day on the bicycle. As trim as she is, she doesn't store as much reserve as I do. The next day is going to be tough.

As we settle down that evening, a full moon crests over the lake and fills our bedroom with stark, white light. I'm anxious about the road ahead and having doubts about my ambitious itinerary. On the other hand, Peggy is already sound asleep. Looking at her relaxed expression, I realize that it won't be the end of the world if we don't make the 100 miles to the ferry the next day. We'll just have to settle for one less day in Port Clinton. No big deal. What's important is our purpose and our journey. "We're doing this for the experience, Brian," Peggy keeps reassuring me. Looking at her, I know that she is right. Being with her on this journey is all that matters to me anyway.

Peggy

I just love our little cabin with it's naugahyde orange couch, lime green terrycloth-covered armchairs, and the homemade needlepoint sayings in the bathroom: *Please be neat and wipe the seat.* I feel like I'm at my grandmother's house—it even smells like mothballs, making me want to stay awhile longer. As Brian sleeps, I pull the rocking chair with the crocheted seatcushion out to the front verandah to watch the sunrise coming up over the lake in pinks and purples. I'm not ready to leave, but I know we have to go. Unexpectedly, I find myself empathizing with the trucker's lifestyle, driving from city to city, never having time to stay put and soak in any of the smells or sights. So, for today, I figure I'll just start thinking of myself as a trucker on two wheels instead of eighteen.

Drinking coffee and looking out at the crystal waters of the lake, I'm almost tempted to jump in the water one more time. I just couldn't get enough of it yesterday after that 100 miles—jumping in and out of the waves and floating, looking up at the darkening sky. But it feels good sitting and rocking and burping up the fish and chips from yesterday's dinner.

Brian finally pulls my coffee cup away and hands me my biking clothes, and we hit the road. I'm still feeling the aftermath of yesterday's trials and tribulations, but the morning air and the throngs of retired Canadians out on morning walks perks me up.

Then again, it could be the three cups of coffee in quick succession that did it.

The roads are empty of traffic and Brian and I ride side-by-side as we pass more tobacco fields, the men shirtless in the morning breeze, looking almost peaceful lifting and stacking the plants onto the scales. One man waves a stalk of tobacco at us, his face an uproar of a smile. The day is set for me—I can ride another 100 miles, no problem.

At mile 40, we hit the dirt fields, farmed earlier and blowing hot in the sun. And like a fryalator finally warmed up for cooking, my stomach becomes a broiling mass of bubbling lard that escapes up and down my throat. Those damn fish and chips! What was I thinking? But last night, starving and sweaty, fish and chips just sounded so good, so filling, so satisfying. Not anymore. I tell Brian to pull over at the next shady spot. It just so happens to be in a graveyard, which is appropriate, given the way I feel. I throw up on some poor soul's grave while Brian eats an apple and looks on with worried eyes.

After my stomach finishes the first of its many spin cycles, we join the traffic that seems to have emerged from thin air, from all directions, at high speeds. Cars, 10 in a row, whiz past us as we labor on, my face green, my vision concentrated on Brian's butt. *If I can only focus on watching Brian's butt in front of me, I'll be okay, I'll keep going*, I tell myself, and that little visualization works for another five miles. We have to stop again and luckily, there is a store with a bathroom. I sit in the dark bathroom and wonder what the hell we're doing. You can get a little pessimistic when you're sick in a bathroom in Canada with 60 more miles to ride on bikes. Brian is busy calling his work, doing his manager thing, so I just lay down on a picnic table, ignoring the screaming children playing catch near me. *If they hit me with their ball, I'll throw up on them*, I decide, and that very thought makes me feel better.

"We'll see how far we can make it today," Brian says. I know he is disappointed, because if we don't make the time up today, we'll miss the ferry and lose a day of rest in Port Clinton. I want those two days of rest, too, but I just don't know how we can do it.

Back on the road, I decide to soak my headband in cool water. An elderly gentleman, Glen Stephens, pulls over in his blue Chevrolet and gets out of the car to talk to us. "Where are you from?" he asks, and we get into a discussion about Utah and how he likes Westerns and how he and his wife don't do much traveling anymore because she has Alzheimer's Disease. "Do all this while you're young. My wife and I can't go anywhere now," he says longingly, leaning against the hood of his car.

"Peggy's not feeling like she can go much farther today," Brian explains. "She's sick from fish and chips."

"Well, there's a nice hotel around here to spend the night," he offers. We explain that we are going to Leamington and have to make a ferry in the morning.

"That's 50 miles from here—an hour in the car." Glen feels badly about not being able to help, but he needs to take care of his wife. He offers to call some of his relatives to give us ride, but we decline.

Even though we don't take him up on the assistance, it's really nice to have a complete stranger want to do whatever he can for us. We have his number in case we need to call, and that is enough to help me ride a few more miles. However, 15 miles later, at Blenheim, my body just shuts down. There will be no more biking today; all I want to do is lay in bed, eyes closed, and throw up for the rest of the day. We see a visitor's center in the distance where we might ask about lodging. Unfortunately it's closed. I sit on the wooden deck of the center while Brian looks at maps, figuring out the mileage and pondering our options. Cars pass in a steady stream, east and west.

A couple walks over to us and asks about our trip. I just don't have any energy to talk to them—especially when the gentleman tells us to eat in the diner next door. "Best fish and chips around!"

he exclaims. Brian relays the tale of my own fish and chips episode, and how we won't make it in time to catch the ferry tomorrow, as the couple climbs into their van and wishes us luck. *Please give us a ride, please give us a ride,* I plead telepathically, and as biking miracles never cease, they back up and offer to drive us to Leamington. "We have grandchildren there we can visit and we'd love to do it. By the way, my name is Mary Cleveland and this is my husband, Glen." We load our bikes into the van and ride the 40 miles to Leamington in air-conditioned comfort. Relief and disbelief gradually displace my nausea.

At Leamington, we find out the ferries now depart from Kingsville, another 10 miles down the road. "Oh, you can let us off here. You've done enough already," we say. There are hotels around here and chowder houses and a beach.

"No, no, no—we can't just leave you here with 10 miles to go in the morning and Peggy sick. We'll drive you to Kingsville." There is no telling Mary "no"—she's a lot like my mother: determined and generous.

At Kingsville, we purchase a ticket for the ferry for the next day and the Clevelands take it upon themselves to find a hotel for us. "I can only feel good if we have you safe and sound in a nice place for the night," Mary explains. Unfortunately, there are only two hotels in town; one is out of business and the other is above a bar, a by-the-hour, -week, or -month kind of place, with men smashing bottles of beer on the floor at three in the afternoon. "Absolutely not," Mary says. "I know a place that is open and very nice and free."

Before we can say anything, Mary and Glen deposit us—dirt, sweat, and bikes—onto the front yard of her son, Jim, and his wife, Sue. "They'll love having you spend the night. Let me go talk to them." Now I can really see the connections between my mother and Mary. Mom would happily drop strangers off at our house in Salt Lake if she had the chance. I remember coming home from school to the house that was connected to the church where my father was minister and there would be some sort of guest staying in an extra bedroom or camped out back. It would usually be someone just passing through, or a person down on his luck. I have a sudden case of déjà vu, only now *I'm* the surprise guest.

Brian and I sit in the Cleveland's van, my burping and nausea starting up again, until Jim and Sue walk out with Mary, forced smiles on their faces. I can almost read their looks—*What has my mother done now? It's Friday night, and we have some homeless, sick bikers on our front lawn.*

" ... and so I told Jim that we picked you two up by the side of the road ... " Mary is smiling, full of the adventure, while Jim just looks at us with our dusty faces and our clothes stained in sweat. "I just knew you'd love to have such an exciting couple with you, Jim." After we take all our packs and bikes out, Mary and Glen drive away in the van. We stand there, smiling shyly at Jim, Sue, and our situation. There is a long pause until Sue breaks the silence by asking, "Would chicken be okay with you two for dinner? If it's not, we can make something else." She leads us into their spacious living room, telling us to put our gear in their daughter Jillian's room for the night, complete with a double bed recently made up with fresh sheets and pillowcases. "We've got plenty made if you're hungry."

I feel like a vagrant sitting down at the table in my sticky bike clothes between Jim, Sue, Jillian, and Jack, their 11-year-old son. We all hold hands and pray to a heavenly father while Jim adds a plug for our safety back on the road tomorrow, or maybe he's just putting in a gentle reminder to God that we need to leave tomorrow. The conversation picks up as Sue and Jim fill our plates over and over again with potatoes, chicken, rolls, and salad. "Have more, we have plenty," they insist while we gorge on their food. I feel like Tiny Tim at Christmas dinner, my eyes wide and my stomach filling, the nausea subsiding with each mouthful.

We talk about our trip and they talk about their family and life just across the Canadian border. They seem more all-American than us, talking about shopping in Detroit and who their favorite college football teams are. They bring out watermelon and strawberries with ice cream for dessert. I think about how amazing it is that Brian and I leapt so quickly from desperation to heaven.

"How about a swim or a hot tub?" Sue asks after dinner and, like two kids in a dream, we throw on our swimsuits and relax in the warm, bubbling waters while she brings out hot tea and cookies.

"Can you believe this?" I ask Brian. "Just when it could not have gotten much worse, luck brings us to the comfort of food and hot tubs and free lodging only eight miles from the ferry." Brian lowers his head into the heated bubbles, not answering, just shaking his head in disbelief. I almost pinch myself, but don't want to risk changing our good fortune. You don't question fate; you just let it happen and thank your lucky stars.

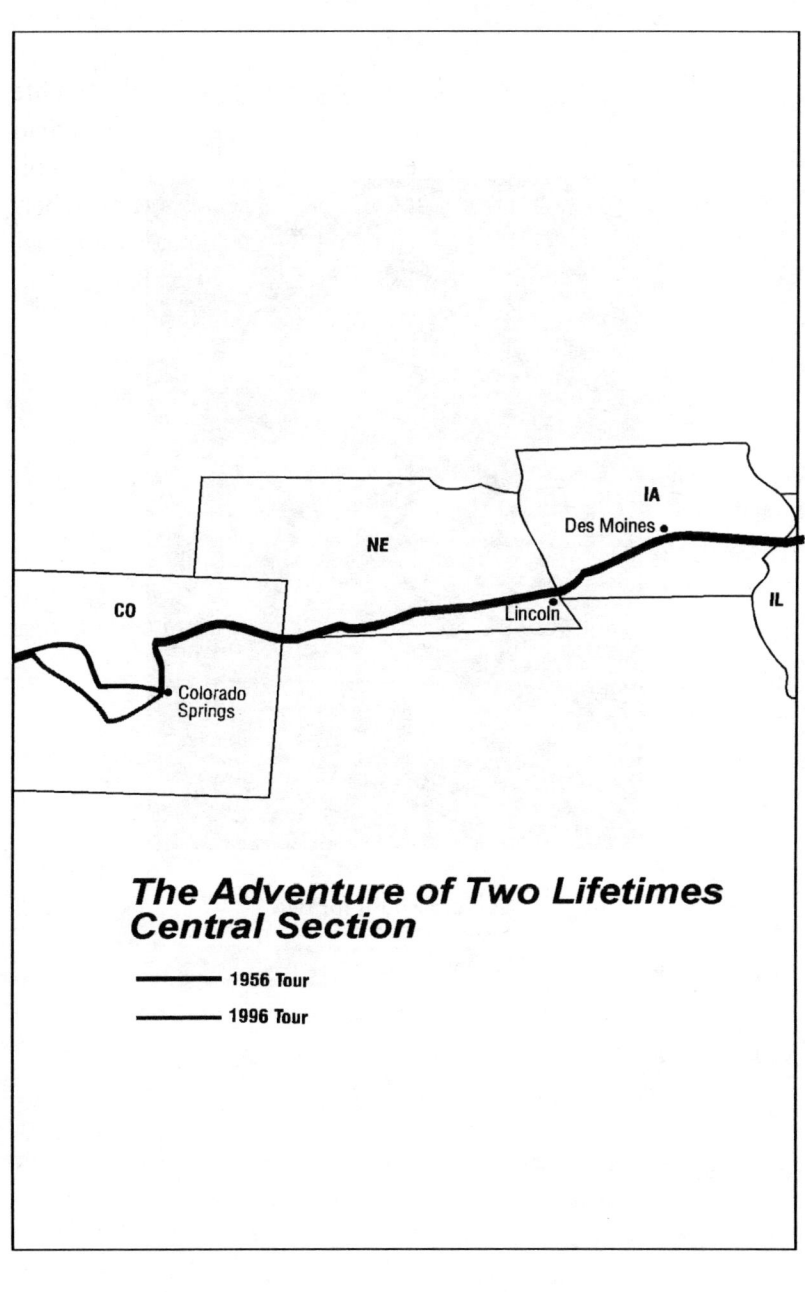

The Adventure of Two Lifetimes
Central Section

— 1956 Tour
— 1996 Tour

A bicycle built for two

6

"Two touring New York women cyclists got tangled up in parading Shriners when they reached Detroit Tuesday."
—*Detroit Free Press*, July 11, 1956

June

Those days that Peggy and Brian were riding across Canada were almost too much for me. Finally, after the third day, I loaded Bob and his wheelchair into the car and drove us down to the library. I walked us right in there and told them that my little baby was riding her bicycle across the country and I just had to see where she was on the computer. The fellow in charge of information seemed a bit confused, because he just cocked his head a little and pointed to the corner and said, "They can help you over there." I wheeled Bob over to the corner where there were all these people plopped down in front of flashing screens. Images and words were all over the place and everyone was mesmerized.

I walked up and asked a cute young lady if she could help us. "Sure," she said. Her name was Jackie and she told me she was getting her degree in computer technology at the community college so she could teach kids how to use computers.

"Kids!" I said. "How about helping a couple of senior citizens who don't know the first thing about these gizmos?"

"Okay, that's what I'm here for," she said, "What do you want to know?"

I started to explain that my daughter and her husband were riding across the country and his brother was helping to track them on the computer.

"So they have a web site?" she asked.

"Yeah, I guess that's what you call it," I said as I pulled out the card that Peggy had given me in New York with the address typed on it. I handed it to her as she told us to come around behind her desk. I wheeled Bob up on her left and then pulled up a chair for myself on her right. Before I knew it she was typing away. Suddenly, up came a picture of Teri and I riding our three-speed bicycles in front of Rockefeller Center.

"Oh, look at that," I exclaimed, "How did they get that?"

"Oh, it's nothing Mrs. Newland," she said.

"June—call me June. What else do they have about my trip on there?"

"Let's see ... Looks like they have photographs, a daily journal, quotes from the road, statistics, and mail," she said. "Why don't we try the daily journal and maybe that will tell us where they are."

She typed quickly and clicked this little thing she called a mouse and the screen changed. "Travel Notes" appeared on the top and we read "Day One—the combination of heat, humidity, and climbing toasted the riders. At 20 miles Brian hit the wall. Peggy looked unfazed."

"That's my girl," I said to Jackie as she started typing again.

"Let's look at where they are today," The screen changed again, showing their schedule.

"Day Seven—Long Beach, Ontario, to Port Bruce ... 102 miles."

"One hundred and two miles!" I marveled. "I hope she's eating right."

Bob and I must have sat there for over an hour as Jackie clicked and typed. All kinds of information came up about their trip, their bicycles, my trip, and everything in between. It was fascinating. Bob especially liked the part where Peggy wrote, "Dad went to

Episcopal Divinity School while Mom was pregnant with me. In 1990 he had a second stroke and retired from the church. He loves anything that has to do with Celtic history and cries every time he hears bagpipes."

"That's true, isn't it Bob?" I said as I looked over at him. His face was aglow with pride.

"Let's read your biography, June," Jackie said. Up came that same photo of Teri and I on our three-speeds. Next to it I read, "She has always been an outdoor kind of girl. From Girl Scout to river runner, anything out in nature is where you'll find my mother."

"Oh, that Peggy," I said, "She sure does know her mother well."

We read on: "In 1954, her dad died in an industrial accident and after her mother re-married she remembers singing 'Everybody's Got a Home But Me.' Mom didn't like her new stepfather. She remembers wanting to move out of the house but didn't have a good reason. Then, her bike trip came along and changed her life..."

"You can say that again," I said.

"Looks like it changed for the better," Jackie added. Then she clicked on the mail. She explained that other people with computers like this could send Peggy and Brian messages. We read a few of them. Then we came across one written by Laura Sweet, Jane's daughter. She wrote Peggy and said, "I had the pleasure of spending time with your parents when they came to our house a few summers ago. I'll never forget the entrance June made at Mom's pool party. She appeared in full Girl Scout uniform! She even managed to steal the show from the synchronized swimming performance my mother had lined up. I remember laughing and singing all night."

"Oh, isn't that nice," I said to Jackie. Then I asked her if she had ever been a Girl Scout.

"Yes, for awhile," she said, "but I liked sports and piano lessons much better so I quit in the fifth grade."

"Just like my daughter," I said. "Must be your generation."

We spent some more time looking at the photos and then thanked Jackie for her time. She gave us the library's telephone number and said that we could call her Mondays, Wednesdays, or Fridays and she would look on the computer and give us an update about Peggy and Brian. Back home I put three pins in my map to mark their days riding across Canada. I looked west and realized that they still had a long way to go.

Brian

The next day dawns bright and clear as Sue asks, "How did you two sleep? I hope it was okay."

Okay? On a scale of 1 to 10—10! Or maybe some other superlative would do: "A-plus" ... "four stars" ... "magnifico." I suppose I could've picked any number of clichés to describe how great our sleep was. Deep ... Restful ... Just what the doctor ordered ... all of the above. Our good fortune continues into breakfast as Sue lays out muffins, fresh fruit, coffee, and juices. Though we are still full from the night before, we can't help but to gorge ourselves again on the McCullum's hospitality. It was so fine that the thought of calling my mother and telling her to take the ferry to Canada crosses my mind. But no, that would be a bit much. There is certainly something to be said about overstaying a welcome. But we can't overstate our thanks, which is immeasurable. So we exchange hugs and addresses after packing up. As we mount our bicycles we promise to send a postcard from the Rockies, since Sue had mentioned how much they loved seeing them on a family vacation a few years ago. As we ride down to the end of their cul-de-sac driveway I check to make sure our tires are really on the ground, floating as we have been the last 18 hours between dream and reality. We both suspect that powers beyond our legs are at work in keeping our scheduled departure on the ferry intact. One of June's journal entries springs to mind: "Sometimes we meet angels unaware."

We make the eight-mile ride down to the docks in Kingsville in plenty of time to catch our breath and take a few photos. The crystalline blue water of Lake Erie combines with a cloudless sky to form a geographic anomaly, a dividing line visible in the southern horizon. Just beyond that imaginary boundary, my mother and her husband, Dutch, wait for us in Sandusky, Ohio, USA.

Peggy boards the boat first as I take some photos of her being swallowed whole by the *Jiimaan*, its hinged nose open like a shark's mouth to accept passengers, cargo, and automobiles for the 2-hour, 50-mile journey across the lake. We park and lock our bicycles in the area designated for them and walk up four flights of stairs to the upper deck. People are everywhere, all ready for their own getaways; a three-day weekend on Pelee Island; a trip to the U.S. for some shopping; or maybe they just plan to enjoy a beautiful day on the water. One thing is certain—they aren't taking this trip just for transportation. Everyday ferry riders—like the ones who commute on ferries from Bainbridge Island to Seattle in Washington, or across the Hudson River from New Jersey to New York—don't pose for photos, look at maps, or gesture enthusiastically like these people. There is genuine good cheer on this boat today, matched by the spectacular weather.

As we pull out of the docks and the boat aims its stern towards Ohio, I remark to Peggy that today is unlike most of the days I knew growing up in Ohio. Ohio's weather is not the most friendly to body and soul. Sometimes, days, weeks, even months can seemingly go by when the sun doesn't shine. Winters can be brutally cold and dark. Summers can be equally brutal with heat, humidity, and thunderstorms. However, when the clouds would break and a pleasant, sunny day would appear, it was relished. This day is no exception, as the lake is abuzz with activity. From our perch on the benches of the open-aired deck we can watch all sorts of people enjoying themselves on the water—sailboats flying their multi-colored jibs at full-sail; jet-skiers jetting about and around the motor-boats pulling water skiers; and armadas of boats gathered in groups around the hot fishing spots, everyone working to catch their limit of bass and walleye.

Peggy and I just sit there on the deck and enjoy the breeze and sun. We don't say much for the two hours until I start to reminisce about family trips in the summer, staying at a cabin along this lake, and our annual excursion to Cedar Point to ride the newest roller coasters. I'm getting that friendly, homey feeling and it's great to share it with Peggy.

Soon, the docks come into view and sure enough, Mom and Dutch are waiting. We exchange waves and point cameras at each other. The boat pulls into port and we step back onto American soil. After a quick check of our identification and bicycles by the American authorities we're off to a celebratory lunch.

From Sandusky we need to get over to Port Clinton, where we are planning to spend our two days by the beach. To get there we have to cross the Sandusky Bay via a four-mile-long bridge that spans the shortest distance from shore to shore. To get around the bay is about a 50-mile ride. I have driven across this bridge a number of times before, but I'm not sure whether bicycles are allowed or not. I keep my doubts to myself as we ride through downtown Sandusky and west towards the bay. When we get to the bridge, sure enough, "No bicycles" is clearly posted next to the on-ramp of the highway. We look at the map. Peggy questions our alternatives.

"Well, to go around the bay is about 50 miles," I admit.

"No way, Brian. We're supposed to be here to take a break," she insists.

"No problem," I say, "We'll just flag down a pickup truck."

Two vans pass us first. Peggy wants me to try to stop them. "No, we need a truck. It's only four miles across and it would be too much of a hassle to get the bikes in and out of a van for such a short distance." No sooner have the words crossed my lips than a red pickup with two fishermen rounds the corner. They laugh at our predicament and gladly toss the bikes into the bed of their truck as Peggy and I climb in back. Five minutes later we are deposited on the other side. Unloading the bikes, we explain our trip. They almost don't believe us.

"Really? Nah ... really? All the way to San Francisco?" they ask, dubiously.

"Really. No joke."

They laugh some more, shake our hands and drive off. We figure they'll have more than fish stories to tell their friends and family when they get home. Laughing ourselves, we re-mount our bikes and ride the final five miles to the motel my mother reserved for us on the lake.

Within minutes of arriving, Peggy and I unwind with a dip in the fresh waters of the lake. Mom joins right in while Dutch laughs and relaxes on the deck. Later, we stake our spots on the beach, pull up some chairs, and wait for the sunset. The sky turns from orange/red, to red, to red/purple, to purple, and finally, to a hazy darkness. Silence fills the air, and warmth is in our hearts.

Following two days and nights lounging, swimming, eating and watching Lake Erie sunsets up at Port Clinton, Peggy and I head for my hometown, Findlay. I haven't lived in Findlay for almost 10 years, but I still call it home. Always will. Twenty-five years of using it as my permanent address—grade school, junior high, high school and breaks from college—has solidified its impact and hold on my life. And why not? Findlay is the kind of place you think of when you think of a hometown. Tree-lined streets with sidewalks, a classic downtown with streetlights, courthouse, and shops, football games on Friday nights, churches on every other corner. Main Street runs north and south through the center of town, providing the plumb line for other streets that run east and west of it. Main Cross, the major east-west route, inter-sects Main Street right at the heart of the downtown and at its corner lies the Hancock County courthouse. The roads lead to the edges of town, where they reach out into expansive horizontal run-ways between fields of corn, soy, and wheat.

Growing up in the midst of these fields and flatlands I didn't have mountains around me to climb, a lake or ocean to swim or boat in, or even much in the way of woods to hike through. How-ever, these roads blessed me with endless miles of straight, flat, paved, country roads. They were lightly traveled and great for riding a bicycle on, so that's exactly what I did. For nearly 25 years my bicycle was my ticket to escape and these roads were my suste-nance. Riding alone, I often daydreamed about riding my bicycle across the country.

When I moved to Seymour, Indiana, in 1987 to take a job and eventually attend graduate school in Bloomington, I was excited about the prospect of being able to ride my bicycle on the rolling hills of southern Indiana. I wasn't disappointed. Six years of riding those beautifully winding, tree-lined roads gave me reason to bi-cycle more than ever, one year totaling nearly 3,000 miles.

By the time I was 30, the realization of doing a cross-country bicycling trip had still eluded me. Then, by an act of blind good fortune, I met Peggy at her brother Paul's place in Chicago. It was the first weekend of October 1992, and I was up there visiting a mutual friend, Glen Hodgkins. We were there to have a "boys week-end" and share photographs and memories of a canoe trip to the Boundary Waters we had taken earlier that summer in Minnesota. By sheer coincidence, Peggy decided to fly to Chicago to visit her brother too. I had no idea who she was when I walked into Paul's apartment. I thought that maybe she was Paul's old girlfriend because Glen said that she might be there. Finally, we were introduced to each other and I learned her true identity. The rest of the weekend was a blur of laughter and good cheer. However, I do recall one of our first conversations, and that it revolved around our mutual desire to ride bicycles across the country: hers to do what her mother had done in 1956, mine because it was a life-long dream.

So here we are, four years later, tooling along on the roads of my youth. Later on, Mom and Dutch will be throwing a big barbecue party for us at their house. My cousins and an aunt and uncle from Tiffin are going to be there to celebrate our journey along with some local friends. As I look forward to that, I realize how wonderful it is to be able to route us through my hometown, fulfilling a life-long goal on the very same roads that I daydreamed about such a trip—and to be doing it all with someone as special as Peggy. It's the tenth day of the trip, and we are finally hitting stride.

June

I was relieved when Peggy told me that they wouldn't be riding into Detroit and were going to take the ferry down to Ohio instead so they could visit Brian's mother, Rhoda. I know that she's as worried about her little boy as I am about my girl. She'll make sure that they get a few good meals, too. That'll be nice.

I wasn't the greatest cook for Peggy growing up, because I've never followed a recipe in my life. A dash here, a dab there, my meals were always a creation. I must have done all right though. To have such a beautiful daughter and handsome son takes good nutrition. Good genes too. That must be why Peggy is such a good cyclist—it's in the genes.

I remember looking forward to a little rest and relaxation while we were in Detroit. Up until then, we had ridden 14 of our first 17 days and had encountered wind, weather, and a few brief hardships, including the trouble with my gearing. Our plans were to stay in the Detroit area for three days and four nights before we started pedaling west toward Chicago.

After our day at the Girl Scout camp we got a ride back into Detroit and spent the night at the YWCA. The next morning two newspapers and the local television station, WXYZ, interviewed us. I remember this day being as hectic as any we had on the road. We awoke early and were rushed to their TV interview before we even had time to shower. For the first time on the trip I had to wear dirty socks, and when the TV camera pointed at us it focused on my hairy legs and dirty socks. We could see ourselves in the monitor and boy, were we a sight! After more interviews and photos with the newspaper reporters, we had lunch with Sherry Metyger, the local liaison with the AYH, and she drove us out to Greenfield Village, home of the Henry Ford Museum. There, she set us up with accommodations for the night. Of course, our first priority was to finally take showers and clean up.

During our visit, Teri and I found out that Ford not only preserved the history of the automobile but also some noted bicycle innovations, like the first two-seater. We were asked to ride this contraption so they could take a picture of us. The bicycle was unlike any tandem bicycle I had ever seen before. Instead of one rider sitting behind the other, the bike was constructed with two side-by-side seats, pedals, and handlebars, all attached to one front and one back wheel. It took us forever to figure out how to ride the thing, but when we did it was hysterical. We looked more like a couple of Weebles wobbling than cross-country cyclists. I told the folks taking pictures of us that we'd better stick with our three-speeds for the rest of the trip because we wouldn't be able to stop laughing long enough to get anywhere on that thing.

We left the village on July 12, the 21st day of our trip. We ended up riding 40 miles over nice country roads, which unfortunately turned to dirt just as rain started falling. It lasted long enough to make the going a little rough and muddy. We ended up just south of Ypsilante and stayed at the Saline Valley Farm and Hostel. Corn and soybeans were ripening in the fields as we approached the farm, a lovely pastoral setting, with a classic white arched barn and pine trees surrounding the house as windbreaks. The three-story farmhouse had been added onto over the years, telling the history of a typical Midwestern farm family who didn't uproot themselves when quarters got cramped. Instead, as the family grew, the house grew right along with them, accommodating new babies, children, teenagers, and parents all under the same roof, new and old together. Much to my delight, the farm had a nice lake where we were able to take a swim. The days that I was able to take a swim on my trip were always the best ones. We set up camp next to some Girl Scouts out on a three-day bicycle tour of their own. My journal recalled that evening:

> We finally cooked out for the first time on a lovely point on the lake with pine trees, a fireplace, and a bench—a setting sun in the background. It was delightful. For supper we had two helpings of salad, steak, potatoes, onions, asparagus, corn, rolls, milk, cake, and iced tea. Were we full after that! I had coffee and a cigarette afterwards as I sat on a bench by the lake in the twilight. Later, we circled around the Girl Scouts' campfire and sang songs. Here's one we learned:
>
> > *A canoe may be drifting at sunset*
> > *and the sky all purple and gold*
> > *and there's a campfire down by the water*
> > *with a song that will never grow old*
> > *Now these things may be found anywhere*
> > *and not mean a thing at all*
> > *for the love and the friendship that dwells here*
> > *makes this the best camp of all.*

We left the farm the next morning in a thick fog and headed towards Jackson, a 40-mile ride. There, we unwound a bit, spending time with three of Teri's cousins. We walked uptown to see the Cascades, fountains with colored lights and music. We also enjoyed separate rooms at the YWCA, where I finally had some time to kick back with a novel and slept very restfully on a most comfortable bed.

We decided to try and cover some extra ground the next day so we rode on to Kalamazoo instead of Battle Creek. We had to make up a day to get to Chicago anyway, so we did two days travel in one, covering 63 miles. The day was clear and warm, so we rode in our bathing suits. As always, this attracted the attention of pass-ersby, including some college boys from Albion who stopped to share some beer and conversation with us by the side of the road.

We also confronted a lot of traffic that day. At one point, my wheel got stuck where the pavement met the berm, which was soft sand. I almost tipped over and barely missed being hit by an on-coming car. The edges of roads can often be full of obstacles like this; we noticed that a lot on our trip. Roads were designed so that cars could zoom from place to place. Bicyclists had to fend for themselves and be extra alert for drivers coming close to the edge. Fortunately, Teri and I made it to Kalamazoo in good time and enjoyed a pleasant evening of dinner and walking about town.

July 15, 1956, was a sad day for me. As I awoke and readied myself for the day's riding I thought about my father, Perry. This was the second anniversary of his death. My journal entry from that day reads, "Two years have passed and I think of Daddy every day. His spirit is so much a part of my life." I remember too that I felt his presence with me as I pedaled. I gained strength knowing that he was watching over me. In a way, he was with me every mile of the trip.

We rode 47 miles through more heavy traffic and stopped in Benton Harbor for the evening. The next day we headed south towards Michigan City, Indiana. It was very hot riding and we were covered with sweat when we met the mayor of Michigan City. He was very friendly and helped set us up in a plush motel for the night. I enjoyed the ac-commodations so much that I remember taking a shower, going out to dinner and then taking another shower afterward. Boy, did I enjoy being clean after that day of sweat and grime.

Peggy

Mayonnaise in the Midwest is like lobster in Maine or the omnipresent Jell-O in Utah—it's included in almost every meal you eat. At Brian's mom's house it's so comforting to eat mayonnaise salad with pasta and carrots, mayonnaise raisins and apples, mayonnaise and roast beef, and my favorite—mayonnaise dip with onion soup. The party that Rhoda and Dutch throw for us in their backyard is filled with relatives and friends. Cameras, video cameras, overloaded paper plates, running children knocking Dixie cups of Kool-Aid and cans of soda over on the lawn surround Brian and I as we recount our adventure and show everyone our bicycles. It's a three-ring circus and we're the clowns on bicycles, making people laugh.

"Brian was so sweaty in New York, you could've used him to water this lawn!" Laughter.

"Peggy asked for a documentary rate in upstate New York!" Laughter.

"The Outspokin' women's club sang us a song along the highway to Buffalo!" Laughter.

Laughter goes a long way with relatives and people who have known you for years, even if the jokes aren't that funny. We sleep well that night in Findlay knowing that all these people are supportive of our endeavor.

Rhoda is up early to give us a great breakfast before we start riding again. Then, she tells us that she has something else to give us that is in the other room. A minute later she comes back with a little card in her hand.

"I was in church the other day and picked this up on my way out," she explains, handing me the card, which pictures a nun holding a crucifix in her hands. "Each month, they highlight a different saint with these cards. This is the one they had out the Sunday before you left on your trip."

The card describes the life of Saint Rita: "She is known as the 'Saint of the Impossible' because of her amazing answers to prayer, as well as the remarkable events in her own life." Rhoda mentions the irony of her picking up the card just prior to our trip. "I knew it must have meant something, so I've been praying to her every day for your safety."

I take the card and tuck it into my front bicycle pack next to the guardian angel pin that Jane Sweet gave us in Buffalo. Our church, All Saints Episcopal, had also given us an angel in Salt Lake City prior to our trip. The same Sunday that Rhoda had picked up this card, our minister, Bradley Wirth, was blessing our bicycles. After reading an interview with my mother and me that was in the Saturday edition of *The Salt Lake Tribune,* he called and told us to bring our bicycles to church the next day. Brian and I felt odd wheeling bicycles up to the altar that Sunday, but it was a good feeling too. It gave us a certain sense of comfort heading into the unknown. Just like they were for my mother in 1956, these blessings and prayers are becoming welcome trip companions.

Rhoda cries in the driveway, waving, while Dutch waves and we are off again, heading toward Indiana. It feels strange riding bicycles down these streets that I've only seen from the window of a car on other visits, but Brian feels especially good about today's ride because we are on all his old biking routes; he doesn't even look at his maps or calculate mileages. He confidently leads me through the cornfields, taking haphazard lefts and rights past rusty tractors dead in the sun, flaking red barns, muddy "criks," and patches of oaks that seem out of place among the vegetables growing on either side of us.

Near Defiance, a giant Campbell's Tomato Soup can appears in our line of vision, painted on an old storage bin outside of the grounds of the Campbell's soup factory. We get off our bikes and take pictures of this 25-foot monument to soup, the red of the Campbell's label in direct contrast to the green fields.

Haze rests on our shoulders as we hike down the water gully to the icon that made Andy Warhol famous. Telephone poles line the road like modern day totems, blocking my "artist's eye" as I try to catch the playfulness of the bins. But I take picture after picture through the wires and wood anyway, the haze shrouding the Campbell's brand in mystery.

I'm melting in the soup of Midwest humidity and any thought of warm tomatoes just sends more sweat down the back of my Schwinn shirt into my already soggy shorts. I think my shoes are filling with sweat and I know Brian's are already filled and dripping. As we pedal away, another car stops to take a picture as well. Their windows are rolled up because they have air conditioning and I instantly detest them for it.

As we approach the city limits, we see what looks to be several oversized backpacks on wheels. Another biker—a comrade on wheels! A compatriot on the road of adventure! This guy has packs all over the place, filled to the brim, bulging out and bungeed over. Books he has read across the country fill his left front pack. An American flag taped high and proud on a makeshift flagpole is behind his seat, alongside a smaller Canadian flag. Woolly sweaters and Teva sandals are velcroed over his back tire. He looks and talks like a '90s version of John Muir or Daniel Boone—on wheels.

"Where are you heading?" Brian asks. He likes to know where people are going.

"Where have you been?" I ask. I like to reflect on where people have been.

"Going from Portland to Portland, via Tennessee. Out exploring and watching, taking my time," he responds.

His name is Chris Anderson. He has red hair curling behind his ears and the makings of a mustache that may have been growing since he left Portland, Oregon. He looks to be about 20 years old and says he has been on the road for three months, zigzagging his way across the country in no particular hurry. He shows us one of his front panniers, loaded with books.

"I know they slow me down," he said, "but I'm in no real hurry. Better to go slow with a good book than to be stuck without one at the end of the day. How 'bout you?"

Brian explains our route while I attempt to explain my mother—which is not a very simple thing to do. I really wish we hadn't eaten all of Rhoda's cookies within the first hour of our trip from Findlay; this kid looks like he could use one. He could be a whip; he's thin, with quick movements of hand and head.

"Has the road been kind to you?" he smiles, offering us a stick of gum.

"Oh, yes, we've had all sorts of adventures so far." I notice that I sound like my mother and—surprisingly—I'm not worried by it.

"No accidents or close calls with traffic," Brian explains. How different Brian and I see the road in our descriptions. He describes realities—the smoothness of the pavement, the percentage of cars passing us, the heat that picks up instantly from noon on, and where all the intersections go before they intersect again. I'm a metaphor kind of person, not seeing what's in front of me, but what's underneath it all; I see the road as a pulse leading us to an unknown heart somewhere. I think I drive Brian crazy most days trying to describe what the roads mean to me.

We take photos, wish each other well and pedal away, our west to his east, but our three souls are heading the same direction.

I love spinning along the flat roads of Ohio. You don't have to do much shifting here, so I ignore the gears and let my mind wander to things like the clothes blowing in the wind on the clothesline directly in front of us and the farmer churning down the cornstalks on the left. Our bike lanes are almost wider than the road. Brian explains that this is so the tractors can drive on the far side and cars can pass them, but I imagine the bike lane is made just for us. Brian picked a good route because we haven't seen a car in over an hour. That is, until we hit Indiana on Highway 8.

Like a dividing line between heaven and hell, the "Welcome to Indiana" sign is the only warning as the wide shoulders turn to cracked asphalt falling in chunks into muddy gullies right next to the road. Cars, angry and full of exhaust, come close to knocking us off the road, and our day of peace has changed to something more sinister. We turn a corner and pass houses piled one on the other, broken beer bottles lining the rusted fences that say, "Get OUT!" and "No Trespassing" while dogs leap at us through their pens, the hair on the backs of their necks mimicking our own. All I want to do is get the hell out of here, but it's the only road Brian sees on the map. I suddenly wish we had that other biker's American flag scotch taped onto our backs to ward off the Rebel flags we see raised on each house's flagpole. I hate Rebel flags—they remind me of stupid men in trucks with guns bolted to back windows and those naked women mud flaps waving obnoxiously at me.

As luck should have it (or prayers to the road goddess), we soon arrive in Auburn, Indiana, where a nice gasoline station manager points us in the direction of a Bob Evans restaurant attached to a clean motel. He must see on my nervously twitching face the need for Bob Evans' biscuits and honey.

Brian and I have become very programmed to ritualized behaviors, especially at the end of the day. As we arrive at each motel, Brian says "Hold on, hold on!" That's my cue to hold onto the bikes outside of the motel room so that Brian can move and adjust the room for our bikes. He moves tables and chairs into corners, pushes a bed against a wall, while I sit outside of the room, laughing at him. Brian likes things to be ordered while I just push things on in—Brian knows this and it scares him. As soon as our Hold It Ritual is done, it's time for the Clean It Ritual. Off come the clingy, stinky biking clothes, which we pile into the bathtub while we take our showers. The water in the tub occasionally turns brown from all the dirt, which is rather disgusting to see. We pour Woolite on the still murky spandex; then, like grape smashers in Italy, we jump up and down and in circles on the clothing, pulling the dirt and juices out of the fabric and into the water. The only difference is that Brian and I don't drink the bathwater afterwards in celebration.

Our third ritual, the Organize It Ritual, is Brian's favorite. Before we can go out to eat, we organize our packs and get out a fresh spandex outfit for the next day—"So we can get going in the morning," Brian says. I usually ignore him and find my dining outfit (for more immediate concerns) and urge him toward the last and most important ritual: The Eating Ritual. We can eat whatever we want—as long as it isn't fish and chips—and this is the best part of the day, especially with a Bob Evans so close.

There is nothing better than walking into a Bob Evans and hearing that lovely canned music and knowing that your menu will have colorful pictures of all the food you can eat. You don't have to talk in a Bob Evans; you simply point at the menu and nod in agreement with the perky waitress. Good thing, because Brian and I have Post Traumatic Road Disorder. We are unable to talk, the visions of trucks careening past us, Rebel flags, and flipped "birds" from pickup truck windows still too close to discuss. The biscuits are nirvana, the honey dripping down my chin, chased by the all-you-can-drink Sweetened Iced Tea. Brian and I both pick the same picture for dinner—Chicken Noodle Casserole, a Bob Evans specialty. We don't complain that the actual food looks different from the bright, overstuffed plates on the menu. It still tastes great, especially with a second helping of biscuits.

Brian

The Northern Indiana roads that take us through flat, glaciated farmlands are far different from the Hoosier hills I had ridden so much during my six years living in the southern portion of this state. In fact, not so long ago, this part of the country was altogether different. Ian Frazier describes it in his book *Family:*

> Emigrants rode through unbroken forests for days on end. Some said that you had to have the experience to understand how solitary and unrelieved it was. They called the tree-covered expanses wastes and the occasional sunlit openings oases. A view extending two hundred yards was rare enough to draw comment. When travelers came out into an opening where they could see sky and clouds and distance, they rejoiced.

One hundred and fifty years later, that scene has done an about-face. Nowadays, to find a 200-yard expanse of trees is a noteworthy event. Trees—some with trunks as large as 60 feet around—have all but vanished. Settlers tamed these northern Indiana lands by lumbering or burning the trees to free up the soil for farming. Then they constructed roads, enabling more people to follow and settle. They drained and tilled the soils, displacing the local fauna with corn, beans, tomatoes, wheat, and barley. Forty-, 80-, and 160-acre farms sprouted up everywhere. About every 5 or 10 miles a town would soon establish itself to provide the services that supported the farmers and their families.

I mention all of this to Peggy as we ride through these parts on our second day in Indiana. However, she isn't as interested in my history lesson as I am because she dislikes the roads themselves, which are skinny, heavily traveled, and don't provide much of a shoulder for our bicycles and packs. To complicate matters, the map I have isn't detailed enough to get us off of the busy main routes.

About 10 miles out of Auburn, riding west on Highway 8, we

get forced off the road by a pre-fabricated double-wide house. We pull over and almost get blown into a ditch as the truck whizzes by, house in tow. I joke, "I never figured we'd be run off the road by a house!" She chuckles a bit, but I can tell she isn't too comfortable. Some things you can laugh about later. For now, we need to find some alternative route.

When we get to Cromwell I ask around for a more detailed map that can get us onto some side roads. I find "Hoosier Hank's" map of the lake counties, which is mainly intended to list all of the hotspots for fishing in this "Chain-of-Lakes" region of Indiana. But it's detailed enough to allow us to find some lesser-traveled roads and avoid collisions with more houses. We also catch some beautiful scenery along the way as we pass between Lakes Wawasee, Dewart, and Tippecanoe, prompting me to sing the song "Tippecanoe and Tyler Too."

I mention to Peggy that her mother probably would have wanted to stop for a cool dip or a canoe ride if she had passed through this region in 1956. We are looking forward to a dip too, but that will come later at our hotel in Plymouth. We also look forward to a visit from Francis and Betsy Disori, who plan to drive down from their home in Elkhart to have dinner with us this evening.

I know Betsy from my college days in Bowling Green. She was the lead singer in a band I was in, Boats on Sand. We played local clubs and parties during my freshman and sophomore years. Later on, when I moved to Indiana, I did a few bicycle tours with Betsy. Her husband, Francis, is an avid cyclist himself, having done two cross-country tours from New Jersey to California. I remember visiting their house and looking at the United States map he had up on the wall, complete with pins marking the routes he had taken on those rides. Next to the map were photos of him on the open road. He's the only person I know—other than June—who has ridden a bicycle across the country.

That evening we drill Francis with questions about his east-to-west treks, especially the one he took in 1988. Ironically, on that trip he rode across much of Iowa and Nebraska on U.S. Highways 6 and 34, the same roads we were planning to ride ourselves. We ask him what we might expect.

"Iowa's hilly, don't be fooled by your concept of riding the roads from any trip you've taken on the interstate. The interstates cut through the hills and fill in the valleys. The roads you'll be on are like rollercoasters. It sure is pretty though," Francis explains across a table of mashed potatoes, gravy, and chicken. Betsy is busy following their restless daughter Zoey, who shows little interest in her father's bicycle adventures, around the restaurant.

"Nebraska is hilly too, but the roads are nicer," Francis continues. "I got run off the road twice in Iowa. I think it was two buddies from a small town that I had passed through, since they were both young and driving old pickup trucks. They also passed me within minutes of each other. That was it, though. Traveling alone can be that way. Some people saw me out riding by myself and just decided to give me a hassle. I didn't mind; it was worth it. I even rode 200 miles one day, from Hastings, Nebraska, all the way to Colorado—a double century. I'd do it all again in a heartbeat."

The Disoris drop us off at the Days Inn, our home for the night, and wish us well. We tell them we'll send a postcard from Nebraska, maybe even from Hastings. That evening I dream about the rolling hills and wind we have ahead of us. But first, we have to get out of Indiana.

Riding out of Plymouth the next day I route us on some roads I remember from riding in the Blueberry Festival Century a few years earlier. I know that these roads will be good to take because people who know which roads are friendly to bicycles organize century rides. They are generally either paved side roads that don't have much traffic, or roads with good shoulders that allow enough room for safe riding. When you sign up to ride one of these centuries, they give you a map and a general idea of the type of terrain you will be covering. They also mark the roads with painted arrows that point the way. Intersections will have left, right, or straight arrows, depending on which way the ride is headed.

We take Route 17 out of Plymouth and soon find the first of these friendly arrows. It gives me a strange feeling riding this road again, as the Blueberry Festival ride I had done along this same road a few years before had about 3,000 other participants. On such rides, you're never alone because there are always riders ahead of and behind you. Today it's just Peggy, a few passing automobiles, and myself. They all give us the "Indiana Wave" though, a subtle lift of the hand off the steering wheel and a smiling nod. Nothing too conspicuous, but a neighborly greeting nonetheless. Peggy chuckles at this quaint Midwestern mannerism and practices waving a bit herself by lifting her hand ever so slightly off the left handlebar and nodding. I chuckle too. "Stick with a smile and a full wave, Peggy. They know you're not from around here, so just be yourself." She laughs and speeds on ahead of me.

The day heats up considerably after our early 8am start. Together with the heat comes more traffic. Passing through Lowell at about 1:30pm we stop to load up on cold drinks. I have two Gatorades and a Mountain Dew to pep me up. By the time we reach the Illinois border at about 3pm, my watch/altimeter/thermometer reads 100 degrees.

Peggy

"Do you think this is Oprah's house?" It's hot and we're on a dirt road at the very definition of "in the middle of nowhere." In a field of dust sits a rather large mansion, surrounded by a wrought iron fence and a yard filled with nude statues, extending their plastered arms to the 100-degree day. We stop under a tree and notice a gardener pruning those awful bushes that rich people shape into animals. I just can't see Oprah having topiaries, but she does live in Indiana somewhere. Just outside of Illinois, I've heard.

I have to ask the gardener. He has a bored expression on his face and he would probably love to have a conversation with two dirt-stained, sweaty bikers. "Is this Oprah's house?" I have to shout because he's behind the bush. Brian shakes his head at me because I've broken one of his rules, asking directions or questions.

"Naw, she lives further north from here. This house is in bankruptcy and I just keep it up. I think some Arabians are lookin' to buy it so it has to look good." His name is Sam, as stated on his workshirt, and we talk about the whims of the wealthy. "You should see the inside—2 pools, 6-car garage, 10 bathrooms, a grand hall for dancing—all out here in this field."

We discuss the merit of having so many bathrooms and Sam gives us some fresh water for the water bottles and tells us where we are exactly.

"Just go down this dirt road for a few miles and it'll turn into pavement just about 15 miles from Manteno. Follow it straight into town, but be careful of the freeway. How'd you get on this road anyway?"

"Peggy wanted to go on some country roads, and here we are," Brian says as he pulls his map out again and points at a faint line on the map.

"Is this where we are?" He asks, adding, "I thought so," after the man shakes his head in agreement.

Men always think they know where they are when it's sometimes better to be lost than found. I have to say, though, I was getting a little nervous on the endless dirt road before we hit not-Oprah's house. *Where the hell are we?* I thought. *We're lost and we don't know where we are. I can't ask Brian any questions because I got us into this mess with my need to bicycle down country lanes instead of major straight-*

aways, and if I ask, he'll rub it in and I'll never hear the end of it.

Sam sprays us with the hose. Ah, the pure pleasure of it all. We put our baseball caps on under our helmets and head out into the dirt fields, the sun directly in our eyes and waves of heat distorting the view ahead.

The farms lay like islands in a brown sea of worn-out fields, hazily green and red in this heat, at evenly spaced intervals. Twisted trees protect barns and houses from the howling winds of winter. In the late summer, oaks and sycamores shade sleeping Dobermans and pit bulls, waiting and watching with one eye open for the changes in weather. I feel like I can look over the whole expanse of Illinois into Iowa, the flatness allowing me to see the distant roads slicing straight through land, intersecting and reappearing again near the horizon. I'm mesmerized, and Brian thinks I'm experiencing sunstroke because his conversations with me run one-sided as my mind wanders over and past the fields.

We come to a sign, boards nailed to boards, depicting mileages with arrows to towns and cities from New York City to San Francisco. Denver is over 1,000 miles away, and the New York arrow points in the opposite direction. Manteno is only three miles, and we can even see the water tower in the distance announcing our hallowed resting grounds. We are close to Chicago, and I can suddenly taste the delicious flavor of a Chicago-style deep-dish pizza and the crispness of an Old Style beer to go with it.

Four years ago, when I worked as a flight attendant, I would fly east to see my brother, Paul, for long weekends in Chicago. We'd walk out from his apartment with all his 20-something roommates to the bar across the street, the Schubert Inn, and we'd drink glass after glass of Old Style and play darts and pool, bracing ourselves for the windy, icy walk to the bars of downtown. Blues followed us from loudspeakers in each hole-in-the-wall bar, with their smoky singers sitting on chairs with slide guitars and deep-dish pizzas.

Our cheeks were red from the combination of beer and wind—it couldn't get any better. It's only logical that I'm craving pizza and a beer as we cross into Illinois.

We find a new motel right off the freeway and—joy of joys—it has a pool, hot tubs, and washers and dryers. No Woolite-bathtub-wine-laundry-dance on our sweaty clothes today. Instead, after dropping our clothes into the hotel's Maytag, we have time to go convenience store shopping. There, behind the frosted doors of a glassed-in cooler, are quarts of Old Style.

Back in the motel, we pour the "beverage of choice" into our Styrofoam motel cups and sit decadently in the bubbles of hot tub heaven, taking an occasional dip in the empty pool which seems to have been left private just for us. Then, with our clothes in the dryer, spinning away without any of our effort, we dial for pizza and spend the night in our room watching TV and eating on the bed. We've ridden 95 miles through the heat, but now, safe and sound in our room, we take photographs and videotape ourselves looking healthy and refreshed. If you didn't know any better, you'd think we were on a Carnival Cruiseline holiday.

7

"The 1950s: Young veterans, back from foreign wars, settled their families into Cape Cods and ranch homes in identical suburbs sprouting across the nation, they bought Philco television sets, Frigidaire and Kelvinator refrigerators, and the latest model Buick or Chevrolet. Americans no longer purchased goods solely for function, using them until they wore out. They sought style, status, and sparkle. Not just new, but *brand new* ... Mom in her cashmere twin-set, plugging in the Mixmaster; Dad in his Ray Bans, plucking the maraschino from his Manhattan. And the kids? Of course, outside in the fresh air, plying the streets on their Schwinns."

—Judith Crown and Glenn Coleman,
No Hands—The Rise and Fall of the Schwinn Bicycle Company

June

During our stay in the Chicago area, Teri and I appeared on the Bob and Ray television show. They had us on for seven whole minutes and it seemed like an eternity. We were impressed with the color monitors, as color TV was just coming out in those days. However, I found out that it presented a whole new problem for my appearance. Before the show they assigned me to a makeup artist who must have been in training, because my face looked like nothing more than a bunch of gray gook. Ray assured me that most of the people who would be watching the show only had black and white TVs anyway, so that was a relief.

I used the opportunity on camera to put in a good word for United Airlines. You see, my ultimate goal was not only to ride across the continental United States, but to try and fly to Hawaii and ride there, too. I figured that since United's headquarters were in

Chicago, surely some executive would be watching the Bob and Ray show and would jump at the opportunity to get some publicity by flying us over to the islands after we got to California. So when asked at the end of the interview what we were going to do with ourselves after our trip, I hinted, "Oh, we plan to go on to Hawaii if we can find an airline to sponsor us. I understand that United Airlines has a lot of flights there. Maybe they will give us a good deal." Ray chuckled as they went to commercial and nudged me after the show that I should go into marketing. Then I told him that I was from Brooklyn and knew how to bargain. He reminded me that my part of the bargain would have to be to make it to California, so with that in mind we left the studio.

The next day Teri and I were given a tour of the Schwinn factory and headquarters. Russ Gunderson, an executive with Schwinn, picked us up at noon on July 20, 1956, and drove us to the Schwinn complex, located on the northwest side of Chicago. I recall that they showed us the assembly line where they made all of the bikes, including Travelers like the ones we were riding. It wasn't all that fascinating—though I must say that I've never been much interested in factories—but they did give us the red carpet treatment. Before we left they took a few photographs and gave us a lot of golden bicycle pins that we could hand out to people along the rest of our trip.

Peggy

It's always a joy to try to eat breakfast in a cloud of smoke. It seems like everyone in our little Super 8 continental breakfast room has a coffee in one hand and a lit cigarette in the other. It's just too much for us, biting into muffins and tasting nicotine. We decide to take breakfast back to our room and watch *The Today Show*. Bryant is out on the street receiving crocheted hangers from a retirement community from Pennsylvania and it brings me back to our own chance to talk to him. Perhaps I should've given him one of the crocheted hangers that my grandmother made for me 20 years ago. as a gift. Nanny, a true adventurer like my mother, would show up at our house with grocery bags full of her stuff—crocheted hangers, sea shells, plastic placemats from some restaurant she ate at. All "treasures" for us.

The day is sticky again but the cornfields engulf us in green as we follow the Illinois River. Pushing out of the flats of corn, we rise on roller coaster hills through patches of oaks and cows chewing at fences, their eyes following us. Suddenly, butterflies appear on all sides. Monarchs fly in waves of flitting color over our shoulders and down past our wheels like guardian angels leading us further west. Some lay dead on the ground, smashed by the roaring trucks that blaze along from time to time carrying pigs and cows to market. But most remain, carried by the breeze of our pedaling. A couple even land on Tim's scarf that I have tied around the handlebars for good thoughts.

Tim, who died from AIDS the previous year, was Brian's oldest brother and my dear friend. A photographer with an eye for wisps of light hidden in grains of shadow, his death has created an enduring void in all of us. I wanted to bring something of his along on this trip. Even though I know he is with us, following us like the haphazard butterflies, having his scarf on my handlebars gives comfort every time I look down at it.

Light hits leaves in translucent patterns as we pass a pile of abandoned barns, scattered like ghosts in the fields. Leaning on my handlebars, I take picture after picture of the frayed, weathered barn wood that's exposed nakedly to the peeling sun, and I think of Tim. I know that his eye frames the photos I am taking; I only push the button.

With the river continually on our right, we see town after town across the water, their steeples raised high like patriotic flags. I count seven steeples within one small downtown. Faith, these towns seem to say, lies in the center of us.

We are excited to stay in one of these small towns—LaSalle is our destination, the mileage clocked out by Brian as a six-hour day. The map shows two bridges across, one inaccessible to bikes because it's an interstate highway. The only option is to take the smaller bridge that crosses the river into the heart of the city.

The only problem is that our little bridge is under construction. Riding towards it, sign after sign warns, "Detour," "No auto traffic," "No access." Brian becomes frustrated, knowing that the next bridge across is 30 miles away and that we can't ride across the highway bridge without hitchhiking. We stop at the edge of the rather short bridge and I survey the construction workers, their shoulders hunched over jackhammers, and I decide that this crew needs a break. What better way to take a break then to allow two tired bikers to cross the bridge? I was June's daughter, after all, and with that genetic link comes a knack for making people do what I want. "Brian, you stay quiet and I'll get us across. Just smile and don't say a word." Brian looks skeptical, but construction workers on a hot day are a piece of cake.

"Hi, we're riding across the country and I'm *so* tired. We've been on these bikes for over six hours now and I'm telling you—I need a cold beer and a warm shower," I say, appealing to what these construction workers want, too. "Can you let us cross, please?" Brian does a good job of staying quiet while I smile broadly.

Luckily, the manager is in the group of men I approach. I know I have him when he shakes his head, saying, "*You're* going across the country on a bike?"

"Yes, can you believe it? We're really tired today and the other bridge is 30 miles away from here ... "

"Sure, go on. Just don't tell anyone."

We wheel our bikes across the broken-down bridge as construction workers stand up against the railing, jackhammers quiet at their feet, the cool water running slowly beneath us all.

Once over the bridge, LaSalle unfolds like a history book forgotten in a school basement. The downtown seems to have crumbled in the wake of time gone past and the cute bed and breakfasts and diners we had envisioned are lost somewhere outside of town. "So much potential," I remark to Brian, as we see the "Going Out of Business" banners and fluorescent-painted windows advertising 50% off televisions and ovens. Coming out of LaSalle we ride past failing houses peeling into unkempt lawns, and only when we get closer to the highway do we see the new paint, the thriving businesses, and the reason.

The highway is a vampire to old Midwestern river towns, sucking the vibrancy out of the old town centers and nourishing the strips of chain stores and restaurants near the interstate. People in cars don't want to see the quaintness of towns, the history or buildings. They want the fast-in and fast-out, get-back-on-the-road kind of service.

We end up finding a new motel in Peru, right along the highway, next to a mall. A variety of faceless restaurants serving generic food are on all sides of us. We decide to walk to a Denny's for dinner.

"You can't walk over to Denny's from here," says the front desk girl, horrified. "It's across the highway and there's no sidewalks from here."

We decide to brave it anyway. Cars wheeling off the highways on high-speed ramps careen past us, some with horns blaring, the drivers shaking their heads. We're walking on their territory. Broken bottles, soiled baby diapers, and wrappers from gum, potato chips, and various other snack foods lay on the side of road. We jump across a drainage ditch to reach Denny's, climbing over a barbed wire fence to reach the parking lot in full view of shoppers and families who are pulling over for a quick bite during their summer vacations. Unfazed, we go in and enjoy our dinner before braving another walk along that road back to our motel.

*   *   *   *   *

"Where are you now?" Mom asks on the phone. She wants to know because she's putting pins into a map she got from National Geographic. The pins represent us as we ride our way west.

"I can't find LaSalle on the map!" she blurts.

"Did you put Dad's glasses on?" Mom doesn't have her own pair of reading glasses. She steals them from Dad, explaining, "Who wants to pay twice for something we can share?" They really don't fit her so they fall off her nose and sit cockeyed on her face; she looks like a crazed professor with one eye enlarged by the magnifying lens and the other eye half-covered by the frame.

"Yes, I did and he's mad at me. He can't read the paper right now, but these pins are more important. Now where is LaSalle? You said in Illinois?"

"It's right off I-80. Just follow the highway and then you'll see Peru and LaSalle."

"Why are you staying next to the highway? I didn't stay next to the highway. I stayed in a nice little downtown motel and we walked around to a restaurant and got dinner for free. We always did that—we were treated like celebrities you know."

"Mom, the only motels we could find in LaSalle were the 'by the hour' kind with motorcycles out front and with tattooed clerks who looked like they sold illegal weapons. We had to go toward the highway to find anything decent. A policeman even told us to go to the highway for clean, new hotels and to stay away from downtown."

"Well, isn't that sad," she says.

"Yeah, it is sad," I respond, adding "Brian and I really wanted to find a bed and breakfast and walk around town, but we ended up in a Super 8 and had to walk across the highway to get to a Denny's. I guess we could've been anywhere."

"Weren't there any parks to camp in by the river?" she wonders.

"We just couldn't find a nice spot to stop." I feel embarrassed suddenly that we haven't camped more, pitching our tents in city parks or behind bushes next to streams and rivers like Mom did.

"I'm glad you're being safe. It's nice that Brian's with you." she says, but I feel like a wimp. On her trip Mom was a single 24-year-old who camped in the woods with 25-year-old Teri. Here I am with my husband staying in a Super 8 off the highway.

"Yeah, life has changed over 40 years, hasn't it?" Now I sound like an old lady.

"Did you have a nice dinner? What did you have?" Mom loves to hear about food and how we're eating. She worries about me not eating enough and becoming so skinny that I won't be able to have children after we're done with the trip. On our last conversation two days ago, Mom had asked me when Brian and I were going to try to have children and I sarcastically answered that we'd try after we got back from our bicycle trip across Europe and Russia.

"Chicken and pasta … " I go on to describe our long list of foods as Mom asks additional questions about how the pasta was cooked, if the vegetables were overdone, if we got whipped cream on our pie.

At the end of our conversation Mom says that she wants to sing me a goodnight song. She starts singing "Baby's Boats, a silver moon, sailing on the sea…" and when the ending comes, we sing it together: "out across the sea … only don't forget to sail, back again, to me … "

June
"Well, at least they're all right," I say to Bob as I hang up the phone. "And I'm sure glad she has that Brian with her."

Bob wheels himself over to the map as I put a few more pins in to mark their progress. When I can't find Illinois he reaches down and shows me where it is, right below Lake Michigan.

"It's amazing you ever made it across the country, June," he says with a laugh.

"We had the sun, the stars, and the moon to guide us," I reply.

"As long as we kept them over our right shoulder I knew we would be all right."

"*Right* shoulder! Don't you mean your *left*? You were going east to west, weren't you?"

"Details, details."

After our stay in the Chicago area Teri and I headed west again on July 21. However, we got a late start out of Park Forest and immediately ran into a thunderstorm which soaked us to the bone. But the sun came out about a half hour later and soon we were dried out. We stopped to ask directions from two elderly women and ended up sharing coffee and cake with them. My journal entry recalls, "They really made quite a fuss over us as they thought our whole trip was quite exciting. They even called the press. When we left we gave them each a Schwinn pin."

As we neared Morris, Illinois, we noticed two shady characters following us. We quickened our pace and were soon in town where we wisely stopped at the police station. Our purpose was twofold: one, we wanted to get rid of the men following us; and two, we needed a place to stay for the evening and figured that they could help us out. They set us up with lodging at the Gebhard Woods.

The caretaker of the woods gave us a lovely spot for the night. It was a log shelter with a fireplace and picnic table located under big trees next to a lake. The other campers soon invited us over for coffee and conversation. Soon, we had the whole camp surrounding us. A father and son even offered to let us stay in their cabin for the evening when we told them about the shady characters that were following us earlier. We declined, feeling safe enough with all of these people close by.

Later on, we went back to the shelter and started a fire. Everything looked lovely as the trees framed the moon on the lake. But as we bedded down I began to have regrets about not taking the men up on their offer of a bed for the night. It wasn't because of the shady men, either—it was the hard ground we had to sleep on. As pretty as our campsite was, I failed to recognize all the cobbled rocks that surrounded our spot. Needless to say, I spent lots of time tossing and turning. The one benefit of a restless night was that I was up early to enjoy a wonderful sunrise. It was lovely getting up with the new sun, dew on everything, the campground silent except for the singing of birds. Two cardinals perched themselves on a tree and sang their song just for me. I tried to join in, but when I did they flew away.

After we packed up, the caretaker took our pictures. We traveled 25 miles before we found a place for breakfast at 11am in Ottawa. It was a hard day, with a strong wind against us and traffic all around. In Princeton, the police made some calls for us but the Salvation Army wanted us penniless and a Catholic priest didn't know of a place we could stay. So we ate supper and started riding the last 15 miles to Sheffield in the fading light.

The only place open in Sheffield was a bar, so we went in and got ginger ale and asked directions to the minister's home; when we got there he was out. By now it was dark, so we stopped at a large house and asked if we could camp in their backyard. Instead, they made arrangements for us at the house of an old couple who took in roomers. The light on my bike wasn't working, but somehow we found the place. After a bath—absolutely necessary following two days of dirt and grime—we sat with them and had coffee and cake. We watched TV and looked at pictures of their children and grandchildren. It reminded me of how Daddy used to show everyone that came to our house the pictures of us. They were a cute couple who thought that science was progressing too fast. I agreed and told them that is why traveling by bicycle was so nice. "It gives us lots of time to meet people and see the sights," I said.

When I went to bed I wrote that we had covered 75 miles that day. The trials and tribulations of finding lodging for the night and then trying to be gracious guests made a long day even longer. Fortunately, I knew that the next day we would be crossing into a new time zone and would gain an extra hour of sleep. Traveling east to west did have its advantages.

We got an early start the next day but were detained by a lot of townspeople interested in our trip. Once on the road we made good time even though there was a pretty strong crosswind blowing.

We stopped in Atkinson for some lemonade. The people at the store took the opportunity to tell us all about their centennial celebrations and of the virtues of small town living. Refreshed and ready for the road again we headed towards the Moline Airport. There, we stopped for lunch and got to talking with some of the pilots. Before we knew it, one of the pilots offered us a place to stay for the evening in Rock Island and whisked us away for a tour of the area. The tour's highlight was a flight over the Mississippi River in his Piper Cub. Needless to say, I thought that all of this was quite exciting. And all by chance.

For a trip that started with few expectations, an open agenda, and a limited budget, Teri and I certainly had a knack for ending up in the right place at the right time. We figured that the angels were doing a good job watching over us so far. I knew that Daddy must have had something to do with that.

Peggy

After enjoying our pizza and beer party, Brian and I turn in early so we can get an early start the next day. In the morning, we ride away from the hum of the highway and strip malls through the quieter fields and rolling farmlands on our way toward Iowa, watching as boys in football uniforms kick footballs in elementary school practices while fathers look on from the sidelines, steaming cups of coffee in their hands. It's strange to think of school starting up and footballs being kicked in such hot weather, but fall is just around the corner.

The humidity comes out of hiding and before long, Brian becomes a human IV tube, hooking himself up to any liquid that gets near him. He drinks one 16-ounce orange juice, one 64-ounce Gatorade, one 16-ounce Snapple, and one 12-ounce Coke—all before noon—and he is still thirsty, so we stop in Princeton to re-supply.

Nothing feels better than entering an overly air-conditioned supermarket when you're past the point of simply being hot. As we walk in the air hits us in cool, moist waves. We gravitate toward frozen foods and juices. Senior citizens and mothers with babies push carts around the nearly empty store, and we must look strange with our helmets in hand, stringy hair sticking to our necks, and eyes red from the sweat pouring into them. We really don't care; our needs are more important to us than appearances.

"Are you the couple from *The Today Show*?" Our checker recognizes Brian first; his hair isn't as matted to his head as mine.

We discuss our trip and where we are going and how hot it is and when we are finishing. Bagboys and the manager come over to shake our hands and we feel like celebrities.

"I thought you were blonder on television," the checker says, and I try to explain what sweat can do to hair. She doesn't want to listen. "You look the same," she says to Brian.

We ride on Highway 6 most of the day. Cars rarely pass us; the road is ours. But the interstate soon catches up with us again as our road parallels the four lanes of 18-wheelers and moving vans. We watch the traffic back up on the interstate after a car accident, pleased that our bikes are moving faster than the stalled cars.

About every five miles or so we pass through a small Midwestern ghost town with cracked streets and flowers growing out of the sidewalks, a few people sitting out on their faded porches, staring out at the sky. Sometimes we take a break, sitting in the shadows cast by rusting grain storage bins and empty savings and loan buildings. I wave at a man in a wheelchair, his newspaper on his lap, as he watches us pass. I get the feeling that this is a place where clocks are rarely watched or wound. Time goes slow, and that's all right.

When we finally get back into the vein of traffic, we are 20 miles out of Davenport, Iowa. Cars and trucks roar past heading toward the tri-city area and we hang on the shoulder, our eyes in the rearview mirror. After a day of quiet solitude on empty roads, this rushing traffic in the heat of the day sets our nerves on edge. Brian and I trade off leading and following as cars come dangerously close. Luckily, a turn-off to the interstate pulls some away from us and we take a well-shouldered road to the Centennial Bridge.

Unfortunately, the Centennial Bridge is closed due to construction, and this time there are no construction workers to flirt with. A rickety Armory Bridge is a mile upriver. But we don't care—we have reached the 1,000-mile mark on our trip! With the sound of revving engines and army personnel in tanks and jeeps filing past us, we set our camera on self-time and smile into its lens as our speedometers clock in the mileage. Our peeling, sunburned faces beam at our accomplishment.

Davenport is a very busy city—especially on a Saturday night. We roam like Mary and Joseph with our bikes from hotel to hotel, hearing "No room in the inn" time and time again until we hit the Radisson.

"Try the Documentary Rate, Brian," I suggest; it had worked so well in Corning.

No go with a cheap rate for an expensive hotel, but they have a room and we treat ourselves. We wheel our bikes into the glass elevator and listen to a jazz quartet serenade us as we ride in style to the 14th floor. Our beds have feather pillows, the bathroom is fully stocked with gourmet shampoos and creams and shaving kits, and the hotel even gives out free toothbrushes if we need them. We take advantage of it all.

Dressed to the nines in our Teva sandals, wrinkled Grameci pants, and tee shirts, we walk through the elegant lobby and ask the concierge about brewpubs. Happily, there is a new one right next door and we eat pub fries and drink pilsners with our large orders of pasta. Another photo is called for so I "pull a June" and ask the waitress to take a candid shot of Brian and I with our beers raised high.

The night only gets better. While walking along the wharf by the Mississippi River we notice groups of people heading toward an outdoor pavilion, blankets, picnic baskets, and small children in tow. "What's going on?" I ask a couple strolling near us.

"Pops concert, last of the season, with fireworks," explains the man. He frowns. "But you need a ticket."

We soon find a piece of the fence torn down and follow other rebels streaming into the concert as the sun fades to cooler twilight. Card tables laden with grapes, cheese, wine, and cakes sparkle in the candlelight of people out for a full evening of music. Children scream and chase one another while couples walk hand-in-hand toward the symphony, which is belting out the theme to *Star Wars* and Disney classics. Brian and I merge right in with these farmers and businesspeople and families from Iowa and Illinois.

"Isn't it nice that they're doing this all for us?" Brian jokes as the cannons go off during the William Tell Overture. I just look at him and nod as he smiles and pulls me closer. Arm-in-arm, we sigh in unison and awe as the fireworks light up the night sky and the reflecting pool of the Mississippi.

8

> "The next day was a grind. We made eighty-six miles, but we had to win every inch of it from a strong head wind, and it rained almost every day. But we didn't mind. We'd been living on a bicycle for nearly four months now, and each succeeding day, whether easy or tough, had increased our love for this kind of living."
>
> —Elisabeth and Jim Young, *Bicycle Built for Two*

Brian

In 1989 I described my fondness for bicycling in a paper I wrote for an Environmental Ethics class I was taking at Indiana University:

> I ride my bicycle whenever I can and try to do a few extended tours each year. Hemingway wrote, "A bicycle is more fun than a motorcar. You see things better and it keeps you in shape." Good enough for me. Ten miles in a car usually means ten minutes of watching the road and adjusting the volume on my tape deck. Ten miles on a bicycle is an experience not only with the road up ahead, but with the elements: Conquering wind, friction, and gravity, not with just the body, but also the mind. Overcoming those barriers because the stimulus of the ever-changing fragrance and scenery can be absorbed and appreciated better at 15 miles an hour than at 65.

Riding in the early morning is best. All the crazy, rowdy, "three-out-of-six-pack" demons are off the roads. Birds are singing and the air is as crisp as it will likely be for the rest of the day. Misty. Like opening the refrigerator on a hot day. Long shadows lead the way as the sun comes up behind us. If we happen to be riding south or southwest, its rays filter through the trees, flashes cutting in and out, creating a strobe-lit wonderland. It's like an old movie, where the frames are slow and movements are jerky. Riding like this gives you more time to see and feel things and react to sudden changes in your surroundings. Looking down, you see the discarded bits of life—soda cans, beer cans, paper bags, a sock ... A sock? Now, that conjures images. Laundry? Thoughtlessness? Murder? Your mind wanders, but your legs keep spinning.

All of this is harder to do in a car. And if you haven't experienced it, or haven't ridden a bicycle for years, I don't know that it can be explained. Sure, almost everyone has ridden a bicycle, probably growing up. From age 6 to 16, bicycling means freedom and independence. Crawling, walking, running, biking—these are the steps along the way to that inevitable day when turning a key and pushing a gas pedal finishes the evolution. Most people never go back; their life has immediately jumped from 10 to 15 miles per hour to 50, 60, 75. The old bike gets hung in the rafters or tossed in the corner of the garage behind the lawnmower. The rubber on its tires gets brittle and the cables start to rust and freeze up. Oh, there might be the occasional hope of restoration, a warm spring day attempt at a ride, but the reflexes aren't as quick as before, and the bike doesn't feel as nimble. And there's too much traffic, more than you remember as a kid. Eventually, it's time for a move or a garage sale. In an instant, the bike is gone.

A lot of people have made remarkable treks across the country—and around the world, for that matter. While researching for our trip, I stumbled across humbling accounts of amazing achievements. Inevitably, a lot of people look at these adventures from the athletic perspective: How fast? How far? How high? How long? Others, the comparison perspective: Who has gone farther? Did you stay directly on her route? How many days? How many miles a day? Like June, Peggy and I are riding for the adventure alone, knowing that our trip won't break any records or set any new standards. Such an attempt would put us in some tough company.

The *Guinness Book of World Records* notes that the greatest mileage amassed in a cycle tour was more than 402,000 miles, by Walter Stolle. His tour encompassed 154 countries and lasted 17 years, from 1959 to 1976. They credit Thomas Godwin, of Great Britain, with the most miles ridden in a year. Godwin cycled every day in 1939, totaling 75,065 miles—an average of 205.6 miles a day. The women's record for crossing America was set in 1992 by Seana Hoga, who won the Race Across America (RAAM) by riding from coast to coast in 9 days, 8 hours and 54 minutes. That same year, Tal Burt of Israel circumnavigated the world (13,523 miles) by riding from Paris to Paris in 77.5 days. The husband and wife team of Ronald and Sandra Slaughter hold the U.S. record for tandem bicycling, traveling 18,077 miles around the world from December 30, 1989, to July 28,1991.

A March 27, 1996, article in *the Sacramento Bee* recounted a 15,000-mile trek by Sarah Patek and Fernando Barrios. The couple rode from Fairbanks, Alaska, to Ushuaia, Argentina, starting on June 22, 1994, and finishing on December 1, 1995. In between, they traversed Alaska, the Yukon Territories, British Columbia, Montana, Wyoming, Colorado, Arizona, Nevada, California, Mexico, Costa Rica, Guatemala, Honduras, Nicaragua, Columbia, Paraguay, Uruguay, Chile, and Argentina. But were they the first couple to do this? Of course not. The article mentions Greg and Jane Siple: "In 1975, the Siples became the first male/female couple to pedal the Western Hemisphere from north to south, taking 2¾ years to complete their journey. Jane was the first woman to accomplish the feat in either direction." The article added that Greg Siple's unofficial record of trans-hemisphere riding had probably been matched by about 70 other people.

Others have ridden around the world, and written about it too.

David Duncan's book *Pedaling the Ends of the Earth* recalls his ride around the world from December 1981 to December 1982. In *Miles from Nowhere*, Barbara Savage recounts her around-the-world bicycle adventure from 1978 to 1980. *Women's Sports* magazine said that her adventure "makes us sigh with pleasure ... there truly is a world of opportunity if only we are brave enough to go after it." Fred Birchmore circumnavigated the globe by himself just prior to World War II. He re-published his biography in 1996—at the age of 85—proudly stating that he was "still riding a bicycle."

While we are on the road, crossing America by bicycle, a fellow Bowling Green State University graduate, Bruce Ohlson, is leading a group of cyclists around the world. When asked by the local press why he wanted to do such a trip, his response was simply, "Just because."

I tried to do some research to figure out how many people ride across the country every year. There is no official account or resource like *The Guinness Book of World Records* that tracks these things, so any guess is simply an estimate. But I tried to give it at least an educated guess, so I called a few of the touring companies listed in the "Travel and Tour Directory" of *Bicycling* magazine to see what they thought.

Tim Kneeland and Associates (TK&A) has been leading cross-country bicycle trips for 10 years. Their brochure claims, "Since 1987, more than 1,100 individuals have made their dream of crossing America a reality with us." When I called I spoke with Karen-Ann, a friendly woman with a down-under Australian accent. She said that their rides are so booked up that they have added a southern route from Anaheim, California, to Orlando, Florida, as an alternative to their normal northern route which goes from Seattle, Washington, to Asbury Park, New Jersey. Their rides are fully supported with vans to carry your gear and "take care of the details—you simply ride your bike." Riders pay a set fee or work with TK&A to raise money for charity.

Big Wheel Bike Tours is a Pennsylvania touring company, which has just started offering a coast-to-coast option. I called and spoke with Evan Trubee, who proceeded to tell me that he has ridden across the country twice himself. He said that their Portland to Portland (Oregon to Maine) route was "filling up quick" and that they expected anywhere from 30 to 40 riders who will ride about 70 to 80 miles a day.

The Pacific-Atlantic-Cycling Tour (or PAC Tour) leads "Bicycle expeditions across America for the exceptional cyclists." Started in 1985 by cross-country record holders Susan Nortorangelo and Lon Haldeman, PAC Tour offers four cross-country routes. Susan and Lon are both former Race Across America winners and their tours are not for the faint of heart. They average anywhere from 125 to 140 miles a day and get you across the country in a little over three weeks. Fully supported, riders on a PAC Tour are people who, according to their brochure, "have been cycling seriously for at least three years with over 5,000 miles of cycling per year. They are looking for an adventure where good cycling is the priority while seeing America." Riders are rewarded at the end of the day by staying at "the best motel in town." Their information packet also includes training tips for a PAC Tour: "Ride 200 miles in less than 14 hours at least twice before the tour—this is a minimum standard; ride back-to-back long hard days; and be comfortable training 200-350 miles per week for 10 weeks before the tour." To top it all off, I looked at the itinerary for their "Elite Tour," a 2,881 mile ride from Yuma, Arizona, to Charleston, South Carolina. Riders are scheduled to complete the ride in 15 days, average 192 miles a day, and climb a total of 74,000 feet (5,000 feet a day) over the course of the trip. So much for our training and itinerary. These riders would even scoff at our 100-mile Canada day!

Adventure Cycling is perhaps the best known of the cross-country bicycle tour organizers. They lead unsupported trips across

America every year. Trip leaders and participants all carry their own gear and ride for 70 to 90 days across their popular northern route, which goes from the Pacific coast in Washington to the Atlantic in Maine. "We lead 4 to 5 tours a year that average about 10 to 15 riders each," said Kevin, when I called their 800 number. "We like to go at a pace that allows everyone time to enjoy the sights and all the great National Parks we go through," he added. Adventure Cycling also sells maps of their preferred routes. Kevin said that they sell about 1,500 cross-country maps every year. I asked if that was a good indication of how many people really ride from coast-to-coast each year. "That's tough to say, because how many buy the maps for two, maybe three people ... and what about those who just do a portion, or those who just put the maps in a drawer and never start?" Venturing a guess, he said, "Add up all the supported trips and then figure all the people who do it themselves, I guess it's got to be at least 2,000." Finally, I asked him if he knew who the first people were to ride across the country.

"Sure, Thomas Stevens did it on a highwheel bike," he said with assurance. "He left Oakland on April 22, 1884."

"What about women?" I said.

"Hmm, I never thought about that."

In journalist David Lamb's book, *Over the Hills,* a chronicle of his solo ride across America in 1994, he describes one such woman. "In 1886, a young American named Margaret Valentine LeLong bicycled alone from Chicago to San Francisco in two months, carrying only an extra skirt and underwear, toilet articles, and a pistol." However, John Weiss, a bicycle historian and cyclist who has researched and collected more than 450 bicycle touring narratives, has looked into Ms. LeLong's story and says he hasn't been able to come up with any corroborating evidence that she actually did this ride. "I looked and hoped to find something in the San Francisco paper's archives from her arrival there, but had no success. And I was unable to find a good index or microfilm of any Chicago papers. Perhaps she started from Chicago and never completed the ride. Or it may be just a piece of fiction."

In his accompanying letter, Mr. Weiss wrote, "There is another woman's story from that time which is more believable. Annie Londonderry also left from Chicago in 1894 to cycle around the world. She went from Chicago to Boston. There were published articles about her that time in *The Wheeler* and *The American Wheelman*. Her around-the-world ride was mostly by boat, but she made it. She returned to the United States from Japan and rode from California to Chicago, riding the last 150 miles with her arm in a sling because she broke it in Iowa."

I came across another interesting story one day in a used bookstore. *How Many Hills to Hillsboro?* is a book written by journalist Fred Bauer, who, together with his wife and three children, took a cross-country bicycling trip in 1962 from Virginia to New Mexico. He and his wife hadn't ridden a bicycle for years, and his kids were 15, 13, and 2; the youngest was carried the whole way on a bicycle seat. They had a great trip:

> There were no phones to answer, no deadlines to meet, no meetings to attend, no trains to catch and no loyalty tests between work and family. All there was was bicycle riding—simple, uncomplicated, uncerebral.
>
> Harmony. All of our efforts were bent in one direction, a novelty for any family with children over ten. To have a successful day, we had only a few basic requisites—properly functioning bikes, healthy bodies, plenty of energy-producing food and a place to sleep. (We even survived in the main without TV). In regard to food and sleep, I can say without equivocation that food had never tasted better and sleep was never more welcomed.
>
> Such a simplistic daily discipline brought with it a satisfaction, a peace, a tranquility, unexperienced since boyhood. Sud-

denly, our senses were pricked awake and we became mobile aesthetes, all of us, appreciative of a fanning maple's shade, a mockingbird's ecstatic song, the taste of dead-ripe blueberries picked from a roadside bush, the afterglow of a sunset.

Bicycling magazine frequently rates the most popular bicycle tours and events. A recent article, "36 Great Rides," lists "classic centuries, sick steeps, cross-state adventures, city tours, and mountain bike fests." In it, their editors describe the Great Five Boro Bike Tour in New York City that has over 28,000 participants riding a 42-mile tour through all 5 boroughs; Fat Tire Bike Week, a mountain bike tour held annually in Crested Butte, Colorado, where "all rides start at 9,000 feet and go up"; The Leadville Trail 100, an epic mountain bike race ("It's a century ride that you have to finish in 12 hours"); Cycle Oregon—a 454-mile, 7-day tour starting in the desert and ending at the ocean; the STP Ride from Seattle to Portland—some people do it in a day, while most take two; The Hotter'n Hell 100-mile ride in the August heat of Texas; and finally, The Ride Across America, a 3,300 mile, 6½-week-long coast-to-coast ride that benefits the American Lung Association.

Bicycle journeys aren't the only epic adventures that people undertake. Peter Jenkins wrote about his 1½-year hike from Alfred, New York, to New Orleans, Louisiana, in *A Walk Across America*. In Louisiana, he met his soon-to-be wife, Barbara, and together they wrote *The Walk West* about their 2½-year, 4,800-mile walk from New Orleans to the Pacific Ocean in Oregon.

Peruse any *Outside* magazine that has been published in the past 15 years and you'll read about mountain climbers, rock climbers, ice climbers, extreme skiers, distance runners, solo sailing races around the world, Antarctic expeditions, kayakers, triathletes, bungee jumpers, cliff divers, river runners, wind surfers, surf boarders, snow boarders, the Eco Challenge, and the X-Games. The list goes on and on, each more extreme, each requiring more distance, more time, more quickness. Between these articles you'll find glitzy adds promising adventure of their own, as if a Royal Robbins outfit or a new pair of Hitec boots or latest model North Face backpack are all that you need to get out there and "do it."

For those who are unable or unwilling to head out into the unknown, the automobile companies have provided them vicarious links to escape via all-terrain vehicles. Everyday, on the highways of America, you can see people heading for adventure in a Nissan Pathfinder, Mercury Mountaineer, Ford Explorer, Subaru Outback, Chevy Tracker, or Range Rover Discovery.

Even *National Geographic* has gotten into the act. Their article, "A Wild Ride: Biking Across the Alaska Range," recounts the journey of Roman Dial, Carl Tobin, and Paul Adkins, who traversed the rugged Alaska Range by mountain bike. "On their 7-week, 775-mile expedition, the trio rode on glaciers, game trails, and gravel bars. They also rafted rivers and climbed icy mountains—anything to complete their daring, high country journey."

But Peggy and I know that an adventure is a relative thing. Heck, adventure is out the door every day for most everyone: jockeying for position on highways, juggling schedules to fit in all of the day's needs, going to college to try to get a good job, hunting for jobs, working hard to keep a job in a competitive environment, raising kids, saving for retirement.

To some people, our attempt to ride a bicycle 65 miles a day is too much to fathom. But to us, the people who are overwhelmed by our ride look like the kind of people who would drive around a parking lot for ten minutes just to get two or three spots closer to a store, or who take the elevator when there are only two or three flights of stairs. We also figure that most of these people haven't been on a bicycle ride for years. After all, bicycles are considered "toys" by many people—not legitimate transportation.

Peggy and I discussed this issue before our trip. We talked about *adventure* and what it means to us; We knew we weren't going break any records or do anything more extreme to our bodies than to get them in good shape. But, despite the fact that these days many other people attempt what we are attempting, many do not.

While I was researching, Peggy noticed a trend—records and numbers surrounded my findings. "What about the simple reason of riding just for riding? Why not choose to travel down the road with time as companion rather than time as a competitor?" she asked. "It seems that in today's world we push past time, knock it around, throw it on the floor and laugh at it. The minutes clicking past us don't seem to matter. It's quickness we want—*now!*" I agreed while Peggy concluded, "Perhaps in our flashes of mini-seconds and mega-moments what we lose out on is time's wisdom." We tried to take that philosophy into account during our pre-trip planning, because we didn't want to zip past everything only to return with a list of days checked off and mileage achieved. Sure, we wanted adventure, but for us adventure was somewhere between a fully-supported and planned PAC Tour, a 3½-week cross-country ride, and pushing the gas pedal of a Nissan Pathfinder on a 75-mile-per-hour windshield cruise. Jon Krakauer, himself a renowned adventurer/author, put it best when he said during a Salt Lake booksigning event that, "To do adventures, you just need imagination and desire, you don't have to set records."

One day before our trip, while out for a training ride up along the bench of the Salt Lake Valley, we stopped to gaze at the city about 500 feet below. The road we were on is a popular tourist destination for people wanting to look at the city, the Great Salt Lake, and the snow-capped Wasatch Mountains that rise 7,000 feet above it. As I reached down to take a drink of water I heard a bus rounding the corner. It slowed down and stopped right next to us. I could see people pointing and taking photographs of the majestic views through the tinted glass, all while they sat in the comfort of their cushioned seats and air-conditioned cabin. I faintly heard a tour guide describing the sites. No one got out. A minute later the bus started up again and drove off, leaving us in the wake of its black cloud. I looked at the sign above the back window: *Adventure Tours*.

Teri and June enjoy an evening as special guests of
the Hotel Fort Des Moines

9

"Life is already too short to waste on speed. I have a friend who is always in a hurry; he never gets anywhere. Walking, [or bicycling], makes the world much bigger and therefore more interesting. You have time to observe the details. The utopian technologists foresee a future for us in which distance is annihilated and anyone can transport himself anywhere, instantly. Big deal, Buckminster. To be everywhere at once is to be nowhere forever, if you ask me."

—Edward Abbey, *The Journey Home*

Brian

After a night celebrating the 1,000-mile mark of our trip, we ride out of Davenport via the Duck Creek bicycle path that connects a few city parks while following a stream for about six miles. We take our time since we can ride side-by-side and the weather is hitting us with a misty rain. Despite the rain, the trail is abuzz with walkers, joggers, and bicyclers out for some fresh air on a Sunday morning.

We don't mind getting a little wet. I point out to Peggy that this is the first bit of rain we have experienced since the thunderstorm that broke at the end of our first day on the road in New Jersey. Sure, the weather has been hot and muggy, but to go 16 straight days without rain in the dog days of summer is a rarity. We rationalize that we have no reason to complain, so we don't. We just put on our neon rainjackets, cover our packs, and ride on. Our day's itinerary is pretty easy anyway—we are riding to Iowa City, a little over 60 miles away.

Soon, the bicycle path ends and we turn onto Highway 391. The road is somewhat narrow and lacks a good shoulder. This doesn't bode well, and I start thinking about what both June and Francis said about the roads they experienced while riding across Iowa. I remember them both saying how pretty the state was, but that they don't give you much of a shoulder to ride on. I remind Peggy of this point. She shrugs her shoulders and accepts it. I decide to get behind her to watch for the traffic in my mirror. We ride silently into a slight wind, making good time under the gray skies of our first day out on the Great Plains. The silence is broken only by the passing cars and trucks, preceded by my occasional bark of, "Get over!" meaning there isn't enough room for everyone on the highway and we have to pull over onto the gravel shoulder. You see, there *is* a shoulder on most of Iowa's roads—a wide one, in fact. The only problem is that it is gravel. Gravel is no fun to ride a bicycle on. Our speedometers tell the whole story: Riding on the smooth blacktop of the highway we can go about 15 to 17 miles an hour, on the gravel it's more like 10 to 12, a difference that over the course of a full day of riding could mean a couple of hours on the bicycles. I start spinning numbers in my head about as fast as my legs are spinning the pedals, calculating times, distances, and days; I'm thinking too far ahead again. Peggy zaps me out of it in her usual way, commenting on the green fields, the cool rain, and the lovely smells in the air. *All right*, I think to myself, *a reality check*. The riding suddenly gets easier.

About three hours into our day we see two things on the horizon: the buildings and trees of Liberty Center, and a very large, very black thundercloud. We speed up, but that only shortens the inevitable. A downpour hits us as we cross the town limits. We pull into the first convenience store we see, but don't stay in there too long because they have the air conditioning cranked up. It can't be more than 50 degrees in there. It must be a plot to keep wet bicyclists from loitering inside during a rainstorm. We grab a couple of drinks and some chips and head back outside, choosing to sit out the rain under the awning of a garage next door. About 15 minutes later, the rain lets up a bit. Putting on the rest of our raingear, we decide to hit the road again, squishy shoes and all. By the time we make it to the edge of Iowa City, an hour later, the clouds have cleared and we are good and dry.

Tonight we are staying at the Iowa House, a hotel located in the Student Union building on the campus of the University of Iowa. Peggy and I like it because it reminds both of us of our days living in college dormitories and our trip to Europe in 1993. During that trip we spent a couple of days in Innsbruck, Austria. Our accommodations were similar—a local college offered inexpensive rooms in one of their dormitories for budget travelers like us. It cost something like $20 a night. It was clean and cozy; all we needed, just like our room at the Iowa House. However, Innsbruck's dormitory had one feature that Iowa's doesn't—a vending machine that sells beer. Ah, the friendly liquor laws of Europe. Before we can have a cold one, Peggy and I have to get cleaned up and walk uptown.

Much to our delight, we happen upon a Mexican restaurant, our first of the bicycle trip. Back in Salt Lake City, Mexican food has become a normal part of our training regime. It's been nearly three weeks since we last tasted a bean burrito or had some chips and salsa. Needless to say, we feast on quesadillas, nachos, burritos, and fajitas until we go belly up. It's good that we have to walk back afterwards, because we need a bit of air to regain our bearings.

During our walk we pass the Englert Theater. I'm sure that it must be the same one that June talked about in her journal. Peggy stands under the marquee as I take a few photos, just like her mother did in '56. Peggy laughs at my perseverance with the camera as I shoot lots of photos and video of her under the blinking lights of the theater's canopy. No matter how funny it seems, we both start to feel as if June's trip and ours are somehow coming together here in Iowa. If not for the fact that the movie on the marquee is *Inde-*

pendence Day, the 1996 summer blockbuster—the setting could easily be mistaken for a scene from 40 years earlier.

June

Tuesday, July 24, 1956. Teri and I had breakfast at the Moline airport and then crossed the Mississippi on a very narrow bridge. Riding into Davenport close to noon, we recognized that the day wasn't going to be very cooperative with our desire to ride from Davenport to Iowa City. We stopped to ask about the weather ahead. "Hot!" was the only response we could summon from passersby. The thermometer read 90 degrees. We knew that as the day progressed it would only go up, so we flagged down a fellow in a bakery truck going from New York to Nebraska. He picked us up and we sat on the floor facing an open door and rode all the way into Iowa City. It was only about 4pm when we got there, so we decided to take in an early show—*The Best Years of Our Lives*.

When we were buying the movie tickets, our bicycles and gear caught the attention of the theater's manager. His interest in our trip proved to be a mixed blessing because he kept calling the press and pulled us out of the show a few times for photos under the title of the movie, because the name tied in so well with our trip. It was a bit annoying, but when I stopped to think about it I just had to laugh. After the movie we stopped at the newspaper office and then had a bite to eat before riding off to find the home of the Olsens, friends of Teri's father that lived outside of Iowa City.

As we rode west I noticed the sky was an odd hazy color with gray and white puffy clouds on the right and black sky on the left. Soon, it was raining on us. We asked directions to the friend's home and other people immediately invited us to stay the night, but we found the right house. Since they were out, the neighbors let us in and we just sat on the porch, bleary-eyed, waiting to give the folks a big surprise.

They came home and were they surprised! We chatted for awhile but I couldn't keep my eyes open.

Lying down to bed my mind drifted as I thought about how many turns the day had taken. It was an odd feeling to be riding around a strange town at dusk with rain coming down and not knowing where we were going to sleep and then having everything fall into place for us. Fortunately, each day seemed to have a way of working out just fine for us. That theater manager was right after all—so far, with luck, good timing, and the kindness of strangers, 1956 was definitely turning out to be one of the best years of our lives.

The next morning we awoke to a nice breakfast set out by the Olsens. Then, we headed towards Grinnell. The day was beautifully clear and quiet, a good day to ride and reflect. My journal notes how I felt on the road during these quiet times:

> Early in the morning my thoughts turned to God with joy and thankfulness for another day. I appreciated the beauty of my natural surroundings, which most often lead into a spontaneous, original song. This was followed with "God Bless America" or "America The Beautiful." "The Happy Wanderer" was popular at the time and I really enjoyed singing, "I wave my hand to all I meet and they wave back to me"—especially when a farmer really did wave back to me.
>
> Sometimes I would concentrate on a friend or family member and remember times together. Although most people think of me as an extrovert, I have always cherished the quiet moments of deep meditation and reflection. Since I was a child, I have never felt alone.

We rode 68 miles that day and made it to Grinnell at about 6pm. There, we called Mr. Smith, a local undertaker who had gone to school with Teri's father. He didn't remember her father, but he and his wife took us in for the night. It wasn't just another typical stop for the evening, though. After we showered and changed into clean clothes, a reporter came by to have dinner with us. Soon after, all kinds of people started showing up—widows, families, children. Apparently, the Smiths had decided to treat us—their cycling guests—to a little open house. And what a crowd there was—people were everywhere. We talked to an elderly lady who had traveled all over the world on a freighter. Later on, more people came and we all went on a tour of the town and stopped for frozen custard. It was all quite enjoyable, though we got to bed very late.

We arose early the next day to try and beat the heat. We rode west to Newton, where we had planned on cooling off with a dip in the city pool, but it was closed until one o'clock, so we rode on as the heat got worse. Soon, we were hit with heat, hills, and a strong headwind. As the temperature peaked at 104 degrees, I took a salt tablet to ward off dehydration. It really didn't do me much good, nor did dumping a canteen of water on my head. Further down the road a farmer treated us to some fresh iced tea. Finally, after riding about 30 miles, we decided to try and get a lift to avoid getting heat exhaustion. Much to our relief, a man driving a big open truck let us hop in back and drove us all the way to Des Moines.

The Chamber of Commerce had made arrangements for us to stay at the Hotel Fort Des Moines for the evening. I recall that when we arrived we were smelly and bathed in sweat. Walking through the lobby everyone looked at us curiously, but the manager noticed who we were and he took us up to our air-conditioned room. There, a basket of fruit and a welcome card awaited us. It was most cordial. My diary recounts the rest of that evening:

> After a shower three photographers were waiting in the lobby and everyone gathered around and asked questions. Another convention was going on in the hotel and there were lots of people everywhere. They treated us to a grand filet mignon dinner in their very ultra Steak Ranch House. It was wonderful to

relax in the room when we got another phone call for us to come down to the WHO-TV studio. Later on, we sat in the lobby and watched ourselves on television and more people came up to us and asked questions about our trip. Then we went to one of the Key Clubs that the bellboys invited us to. You walk in the door and a bell rings. Someone comes to admit you if you are a member. We sure felt like celebrities. What a splendid day.

Peggy

Months before we set out from New York, Brian and I discussed what to expect on our trip. He spent hours looking over maps, visualizing terrain, distances and routes, while I just thought about people and places. My expectations were based more on the years of listening to my mother's stories than on maps and routes. Therefore, one of the places that we are most excited to revisit on our ride is Des Moines and the Hotel Fort Des Moines. We anticipate a grand welcoming party of our own, just like my mother. Now, with only two days to go, our expectations are growing. But first, we have to stop in Grinnell for the night. Even though we haven't reserved a place to stay or arranged for accommodations, we don't worry. We know that, as with Mom, things will work out for us.

We wake to the sculling team rowing in arrowed arcs across the misty river next to our Iowa House dorm room. A megaphone-toting coach shouts "Stroke! Stroke! Stroke!" which echoes off the water up toward our open window. Watching them reminds me of my college days at the University of Maine in Orono—only then, we used canoes to float down the rivers in haphazard lines directed toward keg parties along the shore. We never expected to get anywhere with our canoes. We just floated in the spring sun, our paddles limply pushing water. I guess I wouldn't have made a good sculler.

I've been determined to have a leisurely morning ever since walking past the muffin and coffee stores on our way back from a stomach-loading night of Mexican food. With my double, extra-large latte in hand, Brian and I read newspapers and watch the parade of students walking to and from class. Some look so serious, books piled high in their arms, while others breeze past on rollerblades, not a book in sight. I loved college—the late night parties, no curfews, no living next to a church. At college, Dad didn't wait up for me or walk out to the car to catch me kissing whomever my boyfriend was at the time. Mom wasn't there to ask me question after question about where I went, who was there, what I did, and why I had so many headaches. No one cared that I was a minister's daughter in college; I could stay out late and schedule late afternoon classes if I wanted. If only it could've lasted a lifetime.

Around noon, we finally pack up to go. Brian goes to the bookstore while I check out. I suddenly feel like a celebrity as student after student stops to talk to me.

"Where will you finish?"

"Where did you start?"

"Is your Mom with you, too?"

"I wish I could go with you."

The manager of the Iowa House gives us a nice discount on our room while Courtney, the student working with her, continues with more questions.

"Where are you going today?"

When I said that we were heading toward Grinnell because my mother stayed there and had a party in a funeral home, Courtney grins broadly with recognition.

"Oh, you must mean Smith's Funeral Home. I'm from Grinnell and you know what—you can stay with my mother. She'd love to have you. She has bikers stay at our house during the RAGBRAI."

Before I can say no, don't worry about it, we'll find a motel, she's on the phone with her mother and we have a place to stay.

When Brian returns, students surround him, too, while I hand him the address of Courtney's Mom's house.

"Who's Courtney?" Brian asks, shaking his head, dumbfounded.

Courtney had told her mother, Patti, to expect us at her house around 5pm. It was now 5, and we had 15 miles to go, so we stopped to make a phone call. "We're going to be a little later than expected."

"I've got food in the oven warming for whenever you get here."

Earlier, we had made a detour to the Amana Colonies, a touristy place of old-fashioned cookies, silversmiths, knickknack shops, and people driving quickly past us in motorhomes while snapping pictures. It was a 10-mile mistake on our part to go that way. Okay to do in a car, but on bikes we had to cruise down hill after hill, then push back up those same hills on the way back. At least we had the chance to buy some homemade oatmeal cookies for energy.

The sun smacks us directly in the face for the rest of the day as endless hills necessitate constant changing to and from our "granny" gears. All I can think about is taking a shower and getting food when we arrive at Patti Witt's house.

"Here's the shower. Give me your laundry and I'll meet you in the kitchen for dinner whenever you're ready." Patti, a smiling woman, with a house edged on two sides by corn, knows what to do with sweating, tired bikers—clean them up and feed them. Apparently, a couple of years ago, the *Register's* Annual Great Bicycle Ride Across Iowa—known to cyclists nationwide as RAGBRAI—made an evening stop in Grinnell. 7,500 cyclists camped out on people's lawns, on the high school football field, and anywhere space was available. It was a festive evening that Patti remembers with fondness. She and her family hosted about 40 cyclists: "We had about 10 tents in the front yard and about 15 in the back. It was great fun, especially the group of about a dozen Catholic priests and nuns who camped out back. We went through a whole keg of beer that night and stayed up until about two in the morning singing songs and telling stories. I guess you can say we have a real fondness for cyclists—what a wholesome bunch."

That night really made my summer. Now I've got you guys to thank for reminding me of that."

We fill our plates to overflowing with chicken and rolls and fresh veggies and potatoes with real butter. While Brian and I bury our faces in our plates, dipping and licking and chewing, Patti basically calls the town, explaining who we are and what we are doing. I'm scheduled for a radio show the next morning and the newspaper plans to do an article on us. But first she gives us a VIP tour of the town, with our last stop being the Dairy Barn, where she treats us to hot fudge sundaes.

She drives us around the Grinnell College campus and extols the virtues of having such a great school in her little town. "It really gives us some of the more cultural things; we really like that," she explains as we drive by the new administrative buildings. After that, we head downtown and she shows us the bank that she manages. When we make it to the Dairy Barn, Patti busies herself introducing us to everyone there, since "The whole town comes down here after supper." A couple recognizes us from *The Today Show* and other Grinnellians gather around, sundaes in hand, to listen to our stories of why, when, where, and who.

Afterwards, Patti and I sit in the back yard, the dark sky sparkled with stars. We discuss making choices that last a lifetime. "I chose small towns and children and I've never regretted it. Regrets are for people who aren't strong enough to choose and take all that comes with it," Patti says as the crickets chirp in the otherwise silent corn.

I bring up a point my mother has said about the choice she took in doing her trip in 1956. How her life suddenly took on a different flavor as she risked the unknown while searching for herself. And especially how it changed the rest of her life...and mine.

It is amazing how the random thoughts that circle in my mind during the trip become more and more coherent the further we go. Like the importance of being tired and satisfied in the same breath.

Missing home as a place, and finding a home inside myself while riding on a bike. Sometimes in this world we accept the choices given us rather than running after the things we want for ourselves: jobs, mortgages, 401Ks, and 9-to-5 lifestyles, rather than conversations, watching horizons for changing colors, and silence.

We sleep with the windows open, the farms silent in the night. We make an early start, this time with the sun barely over the eastern hills. Our front packs are filled with enough of Patti's muffins and cookies and fruit to get us all that way to Des Moines. Patti stands outside with a steaming coffee cup in hand and wishes us goodbye and good luck. As we leave her driveway, she calls after us, "You guys made my summer!" *What a compliment*, I think as I shout back with a smile, "And we were the ones who got the free room and board out of the deal!"

So, off we head towards Des Moines, our Land of Oz, the place where the red carpet was rolled out for Mom and Teri—free rooms, free food, flowers, the royal treatment. We are looking forward to the same welcome.

"Hi, this is Peggy Newland Goetz. My mother rode her bike across the country in 1956 and the Hotel Fort Des Moines put her up for the night 40 years ago. My husband and I are arriving in Des Moines this evening and I was wondering what your management could do for us?" *I'm such a wheeler-dealer sometimes*, I think to myself as I call the hotel from a convenience store, where we are stocking up on juices and Gatorades. We trudged up the "killer" hills Patti had warned us about and now, 20 miles from Des Moines, the roads are finally leveling out.

"*Who* are you?" I have to explain our story again to the secretary of the manager, who doesn't seem too impressed. I really don't expect her to be impressed, just to give us something resembling what my mother got. "We'll see what we can do when you get here."

To get there seemed fairly easy because within miles, we can see the metropolis of Des Moines, shining in the distance. The problem with seeing the town is that it's like a carrot being dangled in front of a donkey—we think we are getting closer and closer, only to have to turn right or left to avoid the direct routes the highways have to the city. Haphazardly, we take country road after country road, finally hitting the jackpot (we think) when we find an industrial straightaway to the city. Then, someone in an old car throws a half-full beer at Brian. Fortunately, it misses and goes between his legs. Dogs strain against their metal chains as greasy trucks hauling what looks to be nothing more than garbage rattle past us. On one side of the street a mill belches smoke while we pass houses on the other side, old cars on blocks decorating their yards. Brian tells me to ride as fast as I can, which I'm already doing. We finally ride over a series of railroad tracks past warehouses decorated with fluorescent graffiti and we see the capitol—a gold Mecca on the hill—a couple of blocks away. Businessmen and women walk in groups of two and three to cars, their briefcases shut snugly while they talk on cellular phones. Children explode off a school bus as they go on a tour, their teachers looking like they have headaches. We ride by, feeling safer in all this business and bustle. The capitol shines in the sun as picnickers sit on benches under trees spilling autumn leaves. We're ready to be pampered.

Brian holds the bikes while I go into the Hotel Fort Des Moines, a rather prison-like brick building with a flapping awning. The lobby is as silent as an empty church and clerks stand behind the reception desk, soldiers guarding their post. Sweat is streaming down my face and I notice that my fingernails look like I've cleaned out car engines all day. "Hi, I'm Peggy Newland Goetz. I'm the biker following in my mother's footsteps."

The clerks look at me, their eyebrows up, their lips pursed. "And...?"

"And the manager was going to do something for us since this is a 40-year commemoration."

The clerks still look confused, but I put them out of their misery by asking for a key. They want my credit card so I ask to speak to the manager.

"He's busy all day in meetings. Governor Pete Wilson, from California, is in town and he's staying here." The clerks point the way up the stairs to the manager's office and I notice all the signs for Pete Wilson, decorated with balloons and streamers. Where are the balloons and streamers for us? Ones that say, "Welcome Brian and Peggy! Forty years later on bikes! Celebrities! Athletes! Welcome!"

Businessmen stare at me in my spandex and a concierge snaps, "Do you have an appointment?" then sends me away with a flick of his wrist. "Go ahead and check in, the secretary will call you in your room," he says.

I give my credit card to the three clerks and they make a print. Brian asks about our discount and I sadly shake my head as he follows me to the smallish elevator. We stuff our bikes into it and head to the 11th floor. As we shower, the secretary calls us and offers a half-price room for $75. So much for the red carpet. In fact, the carpet in this room is frayed, we have a view of an alley, and the hotel doesn't have a pool. At least Brian interests the newspaper in talking with us. Our interview is short—nothing like the three reporters who covered my mother in 1956—and soon we are on our own to find a restaurant for dinner. But first, we have to check in with Mom.

"I bet you're having the time of your life there, aren't you? They really rolled out the red carpet for us when we stopped there!" Mom is so excited. She's been talking about how wonderful Des Moines will be for us, how we can finally get a real steak dinner.

"Well, not exactly," I respond.

"What do you mean? I was treated like a queen there in 1956. They should do the same for you."

"We got a half price room for $75." Mom will love that one. She never spends over $50 on a room or else she'll complain to the management and they'll give her a senior discount *plus* the AAA discount.

"Don't they know who you are?"

"No. Governor Pete Wilson is here so they're busy with him."

"Who's he?"

"He's the Governor of California."

"Oh, big deal. He never rode his bike across the country, did he?" Mom talks about how politicians shouldn't get all the deals around the country, how those politicians don't care about senior citizens and how they all have bad hair and cheat on their wives.

I change the subject. "We're going out for a nice Italian meal in the city."

"What? They're not going to give you a free dinner like they did for us?"

This conversation is going nowhere. I really should've made up an elaborate lie about how we got a king-size bed and feather pillows, that the Jacuzzi in the corner came with a free liquor bar, how all the bellboys and clerks and managers lined up, saluting us and throwing confetti, and how they gave us lobster and steak dinners accompanied by champagne while the paparazzi of Iowa snapped photo upon photo.

Again, I change the subject. "I wonder if we're staying in the same room as you and Teri. How did you get your bikes up to your room?"

Mom described the cute college boys who were working as bellhops that summer and how they helped her with everything and then took her out on the town.

"You really should talk with the manager you know. I bet he just doesn't know the whole story. Boy, if I was there, I'd set him straight," Mom rants, as I finally cut her off. "We've gotta go, Mom. We're pretty hungry. Give Dad a kiss for me."

Leaving the hotel, we can smell the musty aroma of meat grilling in their restaurant downstairs. In our street clothes, we're able to slip past the hordes of reporters waiting to interview the governor. I nudge Brian, chuckling. "If they only knew who we are."

Our cozy Italian dinner is quite nice and our waitress is really sweet, too. She's even excited about our bicycle trip and asks lots of questions. I guess she doesn't know that Governor Wilson is in town.

"The Bridges of Madison County"

10

"Days under the hot sun on the open highway had blended their complexions—they were suntanned to the shade of veteran life-guards."

—*Winterset Madisonian,* July 31, 1956

"Forty years later, Winterset's neighborly charm still exists. While the couple was biking into town, local resident Dick Cooper saw them. After talking with the Utah couple, Cooper learned about their journey and offered the Goetzes a car to use while in Winterset to tour the Bridges and see the county."

—*Winterset Madisonian,* September 18, 1996

June

We woke up early after our evening out and were treated to breakfast with three of the Hotel Fort Des Moines' managers. Soon after, we were held over so that more photographs could be taken of us with the hotel staff. Finally, after all of the fuss, we were ready to hit the road again. But as we were leaving the hotel, I discovered that I had a flat tire. This was the start of what would prove to be an endless stream of predicaments for me, both physically and mechanically. My journal entry from that day tells the rest of the story:

> The police came and took away my bicycle to fix the flat. Then they gave us a police escort out of town. One mile out, while riding up a hill, I had another blowout. Four men and a little boy stopped and fixed it. Then it blew again. They were going to drive us back to Des Moines to get a new tube, but instead they drove us west to Winterset. It was so hot that I was feeling nauseous and dizzy. One of the men said that it was 104 degrees out!

I got the tire fixed again in Winterset and rode a mile when it blew right in front of a gas station/general store. The store owner, Mr. Lamport, looked at my bicycle and thought I needed a new tire instead of another new tube. He closed his store to fix the tire and also fashioned a new part in his shop to repair my gears, which were still giving me trouble. While all of this was going on, Mrs. Lamport invited us into her home to cool off and have some iced tea. I think that her husband and son must have sweated more than two hours fixing my bicycle.

People are certainly wonderful and friendly here in Iowa. It would have been so easy for Mr. Lamport to say that he couldn't fix my bicycle, but he didn't give up until he had done all that he could possibly do. It teaches me a wonderful lesson and I hope that I can profit by it and apply it myself.

When he had finished with my bicycle it was still very hot and we were beat, so we took a ride in a cement truck for awhile. After he dropped us off we rode our bicycles up and down the rolling hills for about eight miles. It was getting late so we started hitching for a ride at about 6:30. We got a ride in a station wagon and instead of stopping at Greenfield, we went right on to Red Oak because we were real tired and I was still having gear trouble. As we rode I had the fortune of sitting up front and enjoyed the lovely countryside and a radiant sunset we were riding into.

We stayed at a friend of Teri's family who lived in Red Oak. Boy was it good to get the day's dirt cleaned off of me. After showering we had sandwiches and went to sleep on their open back porch. We had to move in the middle of the night when a terrifically loud thunderstorm passed over.

Three flat tires, gear trouble, 104-degree heat, hills, three rides, more gear trouble, and a thunderstorm—what a day! No wonder, 40 years later, I recall this day like no other. It had all the ingredients of a fascinating short story—maybe even a mini-series.

Recently, I watched Clint Eastwood's movie, *The Bridges of Madison County*, and I caught a glimpse of what appeared to be Mr. Lamport's country store and once again remembered that sweltering day in Iowa. I smiled, and then tears began to fall. Not tears of sadness, but of the kindness and unselfishness of strangers.

I can only hope and pray that my little girl has similar experiences when she passes through Winterset.

Peggy

Madison County—the name brings up images of bridges and kitchens with Meryl and Clint cutting up veggies while eyeing each other hungrily, photoplays of secret passions, and waiting for—wishing for—lovers on country lanes. I must confess that I did get caught up in the romance of *The Bridges of Madison County*. I wanted to see Francesca's house and, of course, "the bridge." Winterset looked like such a cute little town in the movie, and though it's not on our itinerary, I have designs on stopping there for the night.

We start riding from Des Moines under cloudy skies. As soon as we see the signs to "Francesca's House" and "Howell's Tree Farm," the clouds darken and thunder starts rumbling in the distance—right over the promised land of Winterset. We have to keep going.

We ride up a long gravel road—the one that Clint Eastwood, playing a *National Geographic* photographer on assignment to shoot photographs and write a story about Madison County's six covered bridges, gets lost along in his dumpy truck—to the gate of Francesca's House. We stand at the chained fence, welcomed by signs reading "Do Not Enter," "24-Hour Security," "No Trespassing," and "Only Open 10-4." No one is around except for a bus tour across the hill at Howell's Tree Farm, another movie tourist attraction. Lightning smashes suddenly into a distant hill and the bus tour people scurry back into their buses. My bike is metal and we're out in the rain with triple pronged lightning—I'm about to die. Lightning snaps a distant hill, giving the morning sky an orange/red cast, and I want to be in a house with my eyes closed, the curtains pulled shut, and blankets high up to my chin.

With passion, Brian throws my bike to the ground and lifts me into his sinewy, sweat-stained arms, carrying me past the "No Trespassing" signs, his breath in my ear. The lightning crashes on either side of us as we reach the porch, and as luck goes for lovers, Francesca's house is open just for us. We rush into the kitchen, our rain-soaked bodies chilled by the rain, and dance in small, slow circles to the strains of radio music ...

In reality, I have a tantrum outside in the rain. "We're going to die! The lightning will hit our bikes! What are we going to do?" Brian doesn't carry me anywhere; he just tells me to put on my fluorescent rain jacket because we have to get away from this hill and "this damn Francesca's House."

Rain begins to splatter. Precipitation seems to come up from the road as we pull on our bright rain jackets that are so out of place in the cornfields and fading autumn grasses. At least we'll stick out so that, hopefully, the trucks barreling past us won't run us over. Clouds leak green charcoal dust, growling like shadows in a nightmare. We ride the only way we can—west.

Lightning surrounds us. Its haphazard prongs seek out trees, barns, the ground—whatever is most convenient. We're probably next. I'm not breathing too well with anxiety squeezing my insides, so my legs take over, pushing me up hills. Trucks grind past us on a detour from the highway. "Over!" Brian shouts as I stray into the middle of road as rainwater forms a river in the bike lane. The pea-soup green clouds follow us; they won't go away, and I know what I have to do—hitchhike.

I stick my thumb out, the wind blowing my rain pants into linebacker legs, as cars, trucks, and vans blow by, their wipers frantically waving as they pass. Brian stands next to me, not saying a word, because he knows I'll scream at him. Lightning turns his face lime green.

"Where you two off to in this weather?" An elderly woman yells from her porch.

I decide to be theatrical. "This storm is going to kill us!"

"Oh, it'll be over soon enough. Why don't you sit in my porch and wait it out?" I flash a smile at Brian as we roll our bikes up the driveway to her dry porch. "Do you want a Coke?"

We sit in taped-up lawn chairs, staring at the sky with her stray cats. We introduce ourselves and she tells us her name is Mrs. Hess. This storm "isn't nothing" to her and she knows that it will pass quickly because birds are still in the trees and her cats are sitting calmly on the porch.

"We had a storm here a couple of weeks ago, tore through the fields and scooped up bushes and twigs. Lightning was the only brightness in the sky at 9am." We tell her why we are doing this trip and where we are going and she sits in her chair, laughing and smiling. "Why, you're celebrities! Why haven't I heard about you?" Her husband, Bernie, pulls up in his old pickup, which could double for the one Clint drove in the movie—all rusted and worn, but running. He walks up with a TV dinner under his arm while Mrs. Hess whispers to me, "Old Bernie, he's on his last leg. Just do what you can while you got what you have in your bones." Bernie stands under the porch with us for awhile, his Swanson turkey dinner thawing in the humidity, as his wife takes picture after picture with us. "They're celebrities," she says to Bernie.

Brian pulls out a clipping from my mother's scrapbook and shows it to them. It's a copy of the article from the Winterset paper in 1956 about two bike tourists stopping in town. Bernie squints and looks at the article and then comments that he doesn't think that June and Teri would have passed by their house back then. "Oh, we lived here all right, but they didn't pave the road until the '70s. Don't think they'd ridden here unless they liked mud. Now that they've paved it, this road is full of traffic all the time. Big trucks going 75 miles an hour. I call the sheriff about it all the time. Doesn't do a thing to stop 'em."

We ask him what it was like having the movie in town for filming. "Don't know, didn't pay much attention to it myself. Never seen the movie either. Buncha stories if you ask me."

Mrs. Hess gives us refills before we pedal out under a break in the still swirling sky. We take pictures of them waving from their front porch, their hands raised, pushing us off toward better weather with large smiles.

The rain holds off for about 10 minutes. Another storm catches us on our way to Winterset. Black clouds burst open in the fields around us. Panic tries to settle in again, but before it does, I push it out by pedaling as fast as I can. Brian follows close behind as we race between two blowing fields, our heads down, feet spinning. As soon as we are two miles out of Winterset, the storm hits us, whipping from behind with gusts of wind that shove us full force into town. We are drenched but we've made it. We sit in Hardee's with the lunchtime crowd, shivering in the air conditioning as the storm roars past. No one seems concerned except us.

In the town of Winterset, I try to recognize places from the movie. Piles of freshly permed senior citizen women in Rockports are doing the same as they pour out of tour buses. They seem to have brochures that tell them where to find the romance. Brian looks at his maps again while I go into the Chamber of Commerce.

"Bathrooms are on your left, ladies." A tour guide points us toward the back of the Chamber, but I quickly scuttle out of line to look at all the blown-up photographs from the movie. There's Clint shooting a picture of Francesca on the Roseman bridge; Meryl having a picnic with Clint; the kitchen scene; Clint's truck. I notice that they don't have the one of Clint and Meryl taking a bath together.

There are maps everywhere, showing the locations of all the bridges: the Roseman, the Howell, the ones from the movie. There are also slick calendars, tee shirts, books, and tour guides, all available for a price—and to think, I expected this town to be just the same as the movie.

A Chamber lady asks where I am riding today and I explain our trip, just happening to have our booklet with June's pictures, newspaper articles, and diary. "Oh, how glorious! Are you staying here? Will you talk to the paper? Can I have a copy of some of these articles?" Senior citizen women hover around to listen to our story, looking through June's articles and patting me on the back. "It's a modern-day romance story!" The Chamber woman gives me a list of motels that might give a "traveler's discount," and I am ready to tell Brian that we're staying here.

Brian has been doing some work of his own. A couple from Winterset is questioning him about our trip and invites us to lunch in a Chinese restaurant next door. Chinese in Winterset? I wonder where the café where the "fallen lady" is snubbed by the townsfolk might be? The couple, Richard and Jeanne Cooper, convince Brian that we have to stay to see all the bridges.

"You can take my car. It's the only way to get to everything in one day and you can't do it on a bike—they're too far apart and down dirt roads," Mr. Cooper explains. He starts talking on his cellular phone, calling the paper, the radio, and his business. Soon, we're set up in a motel, showered, and warm, and have the Cooper's Cadillac Coupe DeVille at our disposal.

We take a nap to recover from all the storm chases and when we wake up the sky looks innocent, humidity gone. We jump into the Cadillac and tool around the town as school children run out of their classes and bus tours leave for the day. The newspaper interviews us at a local coffee shop—"You don't want to go to the touristy one. Too much noise and their coffee isn't all that great anyway," he says. During the interview, we eat the best German Fudge Cake I've had since the ones that my Grandma Fick used to buy from New York delis.

Afterward, we walk around Town Square, no panic. It's as if the storms pushed us here so we can have fun and get off the bicycles.

Get off our schedules. Take a break. So Brian decides to get a haircut at a local barbershop.

I grab the video camera and film as our friendly barber shears Brian like a baby lamb. Pulling back Brian's ear, he shaves a perfect arc, curls falling in clumps on the linoleum. Another man in the swiveling chair next to Brian tells us a joke. "You know why it's so windy in Iowa?" We all shake our heads. "Because Nebraska sucks!" We all hoot and holler as he leaves the shop. The barber says, "That's Sid. He tells that joke everytime he comes in here." To tell you the truth, I don't understand the joke, but it feels great just laughing with a crowd of men.

The electric razor zooms over the top of Brian's head and an Iowa crewcut is born. His head looks so tender and his eyes so big. The barber invites us out for a drink that night in a place where he tends bar. "The drinks are on me," he says, while Brian quips, "Okay, but don't expect another tip. I'm only good for one a day."

Brian drives the car while I look at the map and explain where the bridges are. In between my navigation, I adjust my remote-controlled seat back and forth, up and down, relishing the comfort. We stick a symphony tape in the stereo and cruise the dirt roads, finding bridge after bridge. The other tourists are gone and the bridges are all freshly painted and waiting, like gap-toothed grins across the streams.

Crickets call out over fading lovers' names carved on the Roseman Bridge. We park the car and play-act the scenes of Clint and Francesca, my hand running over the rough planks painted bright white as Brian jumps around behind me, snapping imaginary pictures. Gift shops sell sand from under the bridge for $5, cashing in on romance, selling the moment when time just stops and the world shines. They're closed now, hidden away in the trees on either side of the bridge.

Brian and I sit in the shadows of the bridge, our feet dangling over the edge, watching the stream ripple below as a leaf floats slowly downstream. We're reminded of the fortune cookies that we opened earlier, after lunch at the Chinese restaurant. Mine said, "You believe in the goodness of mankind." Brian's stated, "A handful of patience is worth more than a bushel of brains."

11

"Your trip will make a wonderful story for your children to tell someday. Most mothers have such dull pasts."
—Holdredge, Nebraska, newspaper, August 5, 1956

Brian

Riding west out of Winterset on September 12, I turn to Peggy and mention how odd it was to drive a car yesterday. "I almost forgot how to do it," I remark as we pedal off.

"It's great to be looking around at fields instead of at the back bumper of another car and to breathe fresh air instead of exhaust," adds Peggy.

"Yeah," I conclude, "and we haven't had to stop for gas once."

The weather has taken a remarkable turn from the unmerciful 90-degree days and accompanying humidity. Leaving the Village View Motel, we are greeted with a temperature that can't be more than 45 degrees. This, accompanied by a swift headwind, soon has us digging out all of our cool weather gear that has been buried deep in our bags for three weeks. I mention to Peggy that yesterday's thunderstorms were good for something besides our unscheduled stop and adventures in Madison County. They brought with them the cold front that has been promised for almost two weeks now. Peggy agrees, but suggests that maybe it just feels cooler because I got all of my hair cut off. I laugh and pull my knit cap on under my helmet as we ride off, layered in polypropylene shirts, tights, gloves, and nylon jackets.

Riding under puffy clouds and into a gusty northwest wind we make good time on a pretty good road. Highway 92 has a little shoulder for us to ride on some of the way. This is a nice change of pace from hugging the white line and looking into our rearview mirrors for traffic. And the road isn't too busy either, so all in all, we cruise along pretty comfortably, stopping at a diner in Greenfield for a lunch of French toast, bacon, and lots of warm coffee. Next to our booth in the diner a group of elderly gentlemen are gathered at a big round table and sharing the local gossip about feed prices, who is in the hospital, and why Iowa won't make it to the Rose Bowl again this year. "They ain't got no passing game," one man comments, "You can't win in the Big Ten anymore if you can't pass."

Peggy reads the newspaper and starts to give me a hard time when I pull out the cellular phone and call my work in Park City. She says that people are staring at me and my "highfalutin" ways. I tell her that even in Iowa, people use cellular phones. "Heck, I've read that farmers have digital tracking devices on their tractors that help them plow their fields more efficiently." Anyway, I'm just too lazy to get up and stand in the hallway to use the payphone and my calling card when I can sit in this comfortable booth, drinking coffee and taking notes as I discuss the projects going on with my co-workers.

Apparently, things are getting quite busy at the water company I manage in Park City. For that matter, Park City is busy all over. It's one of those sleepy mountain resort towns that has been discovered in the past 20 years. Dave and Rachael, my co-workers, say that they are bustling to keep up with all the development, bringing on additional water sources and hooking up new services to the $750,000 homes that are sprouting up all over the mountains and valleys. As it's the end of September in Utah, water demands are also very high. Our customers use eight times as much water in the summer as they do in the winter in order to keep their lawns green. Rachael says that the system is running at maximum capacity and if the weather doesn't break soon, they'll have to start rationing. I tell her that the weather has finally changed for us, so maybe it will for Park City. "I hope so Brian. It's really crazy around here," she says. I sign off from the heart of Iowa, telling her I'll check in again tomorrow, hopefully from Nebraska.

As I hang up our heaping plates of French toast and bacon are brought out. Oh, the diners of the Midwest! We dig in. When it's all over our bill comes to something like $7 for everything. We leave a good tip and pedal towards Griswald.

We make it to Griswald at about 2:30. We've covered 65 miles so far in the wind and Peggy is ready to stop for the night. I urge her on, saying that the wind is turning and coming more from the north now. Looking at the map I pointed out that most of the rest of the way to Red Oak will be south, so we'll have the wind at our backs. Peggy gives in, but I know that I'll never hear the end of it if I'm wrong. Thankfully, I'm not. Turning south we're able to cruise at about 18 to 20 miles an hour. It's great when the end of the day is easier than the beginning—a rare treat when you're on a bicycle for seven hours. We pull into the Super 8 at the edge of town and look forward to a dip in their hot tub and the use of their washing machines.

Red Oak is situated near the western end of U.S. Highway 34, the main east-west route for southern Iowa. Leaving town the next morning—our 22nd day on the road—it seems as if all the traffic in the state has converged upon this stretch of highway. Trucks and cars pass us in lines 5 and 10 vehicles long. Truck, truck, car, truck, car, car ... on and on. The only sound in our ears is the relentless rush of traffic passing in both directions. Most of the road is nothing more than two lanes, one going each way. Occasionally, a passing lane will appear if we are going up a hill. Slow-moving vehicles are supposed to stay to the right. We stayed to the right, often foregoing the anxiety of hugging the white line and instead just riding on the gravel shoulder. This slows us down considerably, but is safer. We travel 25 miles like this, spraying pebbles and rocks as we lumber along at 11, 12 miles an hour. At last, just outside of Glenwood, the road widens to four lanes and we have a shoulder. We turn southwest and head for the Plattsmouth Bridge.

Scouting our route via the maps at hand I realize that this bridge across the Missouri River is an unknown for us. Will bicycles be permitted? How busy is it? We don't have many choices anyway—the closest crossing options are either a bridge 15 miles to our north or 22 miles to the south. The map shows that this one is a toll bridge, so we just ride on and cross our fingers.

Upon reaching the rickety old iron structure, we see one-way signs and a traffic signal, allowing either eastbound or westbound traffic to cross in turn. We stop for a few minutes and survey the situation. One thing becomes readily apparent—this bridge really isn't all that busy. In the time we rest on the eastern side of the Missouri we watch the light turn from red to green about four times. Two of these times there aren't any cars coming from the other side at all. So we mount our bikes and wait for the green signal. When the light turns, we tuck ourselves in behind the only car heading our direction and look in our rearview mirrors—nothing. Crossing is a breeze; quite pleasant, in fact. We amble across the wide Missouri and pull up to the tollbooth on the other side. Vehicle rates are posted on the sign under the attendant: Trucks: $4, Cars with trailers: $3, Cars: $2, Bicycles and Pedestrians: Free. Hah! We ride on through and glance at the sign greeting us: "Welcome to Nebraska." You bet!

Pleased with our luck, we head into Plattsmouth. Signs near the city mention an upcoming detour. We ride on. As we get closer we see a Ferris wheel and other rides bopping up and down in the city. A "Road Closed" sign stops us at the city limits. The detour points left; the closed way is to the right, towards the rides. Since we are on bicycles, we opt to take our chances with the closed road and walk them around the barricades.

Soon we know what all the fuss is about. A parade is taking place right through the center of town, apparently to mark the start of Plattsmouth's three-day Husker Festival. We stop next to the grandstand and watch floats of cheerleaders and 4-H clubs go by, all with a corn theme.

As we watch, a fellow comes up to us with his wife and asks us if we are riding across the country. He proceeds to tell us all about this festival and how we should really stop for the night and enjoy it. "We get 20,000 people who come here for this thing—it's almost as big as a Nebraska football game," he says as he turns and walks toward the grandstand. His wife laughs and mentions that this is a bigger deal than a homecoming celebration. "Kids come home to visit cousins, friends ... Everybody comes back for this. It's a lot of fun."

All of a sudden we hear our names over the loudspeaker. The man comes back and tells us to go ahead and get onstage. We'd been on *The Today Show*, hadn't we? Why would 20,000 parade watchers scare us?

We shyly decline, more surprised than afraid, so they just announce our names again and tell us to ride through as the announcer says, "Hey folks, this young couple is riding their bicycles across the country. Why don't you all give them a hand as they ride on through." So we do, waving like festival king and queen, as people clap and take photos of us heading down Main Street behind the high school band. Peggy giggles at our fine welcome and says how much she likes Nebraska already. I agree even more when we find out that Nebraska roads are very bike-friendly.

It's almost as if we have entered a different country. We discover that Nebraska roads have wide shoulders like Iowa—only Nebraska's are paved. What a treat. Peggy and I ride side-by-side for the first time since Ohio. Soon we approach Lincoln and are ready for an evening at my cousin Cindy's house. Her husband Denny drives about 10 miles east to meet us and show us the way to their house. Once there, they treat us to a good old Midwestern feast of homemade beef stew, mashed potatoes, green beans, and apple pie. Afterward, Cindy gives us each a tee shirt with the University of Nebraska emblem so we can blend in with the locals. "Welcome to Nebraska," she says. You bet!

June

Saturday, July 28, 1956. A day off greeted Teri and me in Red Oak, Iowa. A well deserved rest it was. After the excitement and misadventures of the last couple of days we were ready to take it easy, and it was a treat to loaf in bed until 10:30 that morning. The anticipation of mail—the first time in five weeks—finally roused me. Teri's aunt and uncle lived in town and we had left their address with family and friends back home so they could write us on the road.

Teri came back a little past noon with an armful of mail for the two of us. I dove into the letters from my mother, my sister Adelaide, my brother Artie and sister-in-law Gert, and friends Lee Austin, Jean, Cecilia, Frank, and Jim. Home seemed so far away and it was all hitting me now, almost halfway into the trip. My journal recalls a deep feeling of joy and sorrow at the love that was accompanying me across the country: "I thought how lucky I was to have these wonderful friends who think of me and love me even though we are far apart. I got choked up and teary-eyed and thanked God for them. Friends are the real purpose in life and a trip like this would be meaningless without them."

Later on, we were picked up and driven down to the Shenandoah radio station for an interview. I recall taking the letters along so I could read them all again, in between looking out at the lovely countryside and sky. Back in Red Oak, we had dinner with Teri's aunt and uncle, who were quite old but very dear and charming.

The evening ended early as I tucked myself in, surrounded by the thoughts and wishes of those I loved.

We enjoyed another day off the next day, going to church and a big Foster family dinner. After that, we spent a leisurely afternoon sipping iced tea, telling stories, and taking naps. We also went to the home of another friend of Teri's family, Mrs. Olsen. I remember that she was the most interesting woman to talk to. And her books—what a library. I waxed philosophical in my journal that evening:

> Sometimes, you are inclined to forget the great adventure in the mundane tasks of the day—pedaling, eating, sleeping—and do not appreciate it to the fullest. I try to imagine how I will feel about this trip and remember it years from now when it is only a memory. I really am learning to appreciate each day and all that I have unearthed from the people met along the way. This really is the experience of a lifetime and once over, can never be recaptured.

Well rested, we left Red Oak early the next morning and headed towards Nebraska. Right away, I had more gear trouble in the hills. We found a mechanic who did his best to correct the problem and so we pedaled into Plattsmouth. Along the way we met Gene and Dick, a couple of nice young farm boys who invited us out for the evening. Pulling into Plattsmouth at about 4pm we called Margaret Molsney, an elderly woman who had offered to take us in for the night. After getting situated and cleaned up at her place, we went out for a little supper. Then we met up with the two young men who had asked us out.

They took us to Omaha for dancing, and then we got the biggest hamburgers and took them down to the Missouri River for a picnic. We all went swimming and then, later on, lit a fire and sat around telling stories of our trip. What fun!

But amidst all the excitement, we lost track of the hour. By the time the boys drove us back to Mrs. Molsney's house, it was 3am. She was very worried and had waited up for us. When we didn't show by 1am she called the police and Teri's aunt in Red Oak. It was just a simple oversight on our part, and we told her that we would have called, but assumed that she would be sleeping and we didn't want to wake her. It was very embarrassing for all of us, so we apologized and then hurried off to sleep.

Perhaps as a bit of retribution, Mrs. Molsney woke us up early with a big breakfast at about 7:30. We ate graciously, with our best manners. Then we packed up, thanked her the best we could, and headed towards town.

"More gear trouble!" is the only entry from my journal that made any reference to our bicycles that day. Resourceful as always, we called Dick and Gene to see if they could help us out. "Sure, we'll meet you at the park," responded Gene. Soon, the young men picked Teri and me up, bought us some lunch, and then took us to the beach so we could all go canoeing and have a swim. Then we went to Dick's farm for dinner.

Dick's folks were elderly Germans and couldn't do enough for us. His mother prepared a big chicken dinner while his father explained how the recent rains might save some of the corn. All in all, it was a most pleasant experience.

Since it was getting late and our destination for the day was supposed to have been Lincoln, Dick and Gene offered to drive us there. They loaded our bicycles into the back of Gene's pickup and we headed west. While admiring another beautiful sunset en route, I made up the story that the real reason that Teri and I wanted to travel from east to west was because we would be able to "ride into the sunset" instead of having it at our backs. Then Dick added, "We have the best sunsets here, though. Isn't Nebraska great?" I turned to him and nodded in agreement.

Peggy

Lincoln is a nice stop where we can feel like part of a family instead of part of the road. Brian's cousins definitely provide the homespun sleep we need on a bed that arches toward the middle, "That bed's the one we made all our children in," Brian's cousin explains as she shows us around their house. Surrounded by banners and posters for the Cornhuskers, we sleep smashed together for nine hours, exhausted from the tour of downtown Lincoln and triple helpings of Cindy's mashed potatoes.

The nice thing about Nebraska is that you can see your next watering hole. Water towers, like bigheaded billboards, advertise towns in the distance as we passed through fields flattened with slabs of green turning brown. The road is always straight and we just cruise, the wind behind us, toward Hastings.

It's a Saturday afternoon, and we pass cattle being auctioned from makeshift fences as farmers, cigarettes perpetually stuck to their lower lips, pile out of various American-brand trucks. The cattle blandly stick mud-covered noses between the slats in their pens, seeming to accept their fate as rib-eye, porterhouse, or T-bone. They watch us pass, their heads following us down the road.

Many towns lay silent, the only sound coming from the wind whipping American flags atop rusting grain storage bins. Clouds darken the day and drizzle falls over an old silo, birds twirling in figure eights above our heads. We stop to take photos of the shadows, watching the distance ahead.

Drizzle develops into sheets of gray rain as we enter Hastings, and we are overjoyed to see the Midland's Lodge, its neon light blinking fluorescent orange. Saturday night in Hastings, Nebraska—what better way to spend it than to order pizza and drink beer? We sit in tee shirts, chomping on greasy pizza and chips and garlic breadsticks as we launch can after can of Old Milwaukee at the trashcan. A bad movie runs in static on the TV, and we watch it, eyes glazed.

I'm tired. It has been 13 straight days of riding, packing up, and leaving each morning for parts unknown, and I really just want to hibernate awhile. When the alarm goes off the next morning, wind and rain whistle outside our motel room and Brian and I just look at each other, shaking our heads. "Let's not go today. Let's just be slugs and go out for breakfast and read the paper and not even look at our bikes or pack anything or organize anything." When Brian sticks his head out of the door to look at the sky, a piece of trash blows past his face. We decide to go to Andy's Café next door.

Brian and I enter a shrine for farmers. Andy's is the kind of place you go when your tractor's broken, your cow just died, your fields are flooding, or your wife just left you to visit her sister in Lincoln. You've got plenty to eat at home, but you just don't feel right making anything without the missus and it is Sunday and the boys will all be there waiting for you. Most of the booths are taken by men wearing flannel with caps on their heads advertising manure, chemicals, or machinery. The counter is completely full, as coffee cups clink and conversations rage. This is a place of locals; everyone knows each other, but nobody seems to notice us since we aren't decked out in our bicycle regalia. We sit in our booth and relish the obscurity.

"Hey, Bill, you want to go in with us on a paper? You got a quarter?"

"Hell, anybody see that new truck Sid's driving? He sure thinks it's somethin'. Don't let nobody touch it neither."

"You know Sam? Well, he just got him a John Deere with power steering. Thinks he's something special."

"Not much to do today but sit in here."

Brian and I each order a Hungryman Flapjack Breakfast, which someone should have cautioned us about. They come on platters, piled high with pancakes and butter and eggs and toast and bacon and sausage and ham. One platter might yield a week's worth of breakfast for us both, but since we don't have much to do today but sit here, we eat until our stomachs look like all the others in the place. The churchgoers come in later, wearing galoshes and windbreakers and a nicer brand of flannel underneath polyester sportcoats. They squeeze in with the farmers and talk about the sermons and the choir.

"Didn't hear much but squawking today from that choir."

"They all sounded like my chickens."

"Sermon ran much too long. Think God even got bored."

The waiting line soon runs out the door and we feel compelled to leave, our transitory booth really someone else's on a regular day. With our fluorescent yellow jackets we push into the rain. I turn to watch the café patrons staring back at us, wondering what they are saying.

Back in our warm room I figure it's a good time to give Mom and Dad a call.

"No, really, we're fine. We just needed a break for a day." Mom thinks I have a cold and that I'm getting burnt out from the trip. I'm not burnt out, I'm just tired, but Mom is worried about us not having energy.

"Why did you pick Hastings of all places to take a break?" she asks.

"Well, it's raining here and when we woke up this morning, we just felt it would be a nice place to rest up and stay out of the rain."

"Are you sick?"

"No, Mom. I am not sick." I've said this three times so far in the minute we've been talking.

"Well that's good, by your itinerary it looks like you're a little past half-way, so you still have a long way to go," Mom says confidently.

"Gee, Mom, how'd you know that?"

"Oh, your father and I have been going to the library and there's this pretty young woman named Jackie that helps us look up your bike trip on the computer."

"That's great, Mom."

"Well, I was going crazy between your phone calls," she says.

"You only called home a couple of times on *your* trip—we've already beaten that number," I add. "So what do you think of the web site?"

"Oh, it's fancy. That brother of Brian's sure has a knack for putting all those photos and stories together, but he could use a little more about my trip. Two young girls on their own in the '50s wasn't too common."

"Yes, Mom. You know that I'm in awe of your feat, especially riding that three-speed bike compared to ours."

"You know what I was thinking?" she continues.

I sigh because I know that she has something up her sleeve. Whenever Mom starts off a sentence with "You know what I was thinking ... " it is usually some crazy scheme she's cooked up.

"What?" I respond nervously.

"Your father and I would love to meet up with you and follow you around for the rest of the trip. Wouldn't that be nice? If you had a flat tire, we could drive you to the nearest gas station and..."

"Mom, we change our own tires and we have tools."

"Yes, and anyway ... we could give you snacks along the road and visit at rest stops and if you got tired, you could sit down for a while. It wouldn't be any bother. We'd stay out of your way."

"No, I don't think that's a good idea."

"But we don't have anything to do right now with our schedules. And I think you'd really like to have us along, wouldn't you?"

"Well ... "

"Now, we don't have to make airplane reservations tonight or anything, but I was thinking about meeting up with you somewhere in Colorado and we could all go together to the Utah Parks and then I'd be with you over Nevada and then it's California. Wouldn't that be fun?"

"No, I really don't think ... "

"But I worry about you on that road. I've been reading my journal and have been thinking that I was a little too trusting sometimes on the road and I worry about the same with you."

I try to make a joke. "You don't need to worry about us. We've got cellular phones."

"Why don't you and Brian sleep on my idea and we'll talk about it later."

Brian is laughing as I put down the phone. He has an idea himself. "I know. Let's just not check in with your parents anymore—then they won't know where we are to meet us."

"Oh, they'd find us all right. I thought you knew my mother better than that, Brian."

"Yeah, you're right. It was just a thought."

I'm proud of the way I handled my mother's suggestion. I realize that I'm finally pulling away, doing this on my own, without her help—without the safety of her laughter. For once I was able to hold my ground and say "No" to my mother and not feel guilty about it.

That night, I dream that Mom finds us hiding from her behind a grove of aspen trees and she gives me a motorcycle to ride along with a bulletproof vest. She and Dad are in a Mack truck following us across the desert, and she looks like Sigourney Weaver from *Alien*, shaved head and all.

June

Teri and I had a simple 42-mile day of riding from Lincoln to Friend. There, we took the opportunity to recover from all of the family, friends, and excursions of the last few days. My journal notes that we went to bed around 7:30 that evening.

The rest of Nebraska would prove to be a pleasant experience for us. We got into the groove of getting up early each day to beat the heat and were able to accomplish most of our riding by the early afternoon.

Following Friend, we stayed in Hastings at a tourist home for $3. After dinner we went out to the movies to watch *Anna and the King of Siam*, a re-release of the popular 1946 movie starring Rex Harrison. Whenever the opportunity presented itself on the trip, Teri and I would try to take in a show. Back then there wasn't a TV in every hotel room like there is today, complete with cable and movie channels. For entertainment, people usually went to the local movie house to see whatever was showing, even if it was a film that had been out for a decade.

The next day we pedaled against a difficult headwind for about 60 miles before a rainstorm battered us just outside of Holdredge. A reporter noticed us as we rode through town and flagged us down. He introduced himself as Jim Rippey, the local newspaper writer. After asking some quick questions he wondered if we had a place to stay for the evening. "Why, not yet, we were just trying to get out of the rain for now," I responded.

"Well, you can just stay at our place. That way you can get dry and comfortable," Jim said. "I'll finish the interview there." So, off we went.

Jim's wife and their four rambunctious children were very kind and let us get cleaned up before serving a huge dinner. I remember that two other children were visiting for the evening, so the place was very active indeed—especially when they kept asking if they could ride our bicycles and then took turns riding them around the house, ringing the bells. We ended the night by sharing stories and listening to some classical music. The next day, Jim's story appeared in the *Holdredge News*.

His article was much like many of the other reports that documented our trip: A few photographs with us and our bicycles with captions saying who we were, where we had come from, and why we were doing this trip. That was followed with some details about the bicycles and the gear we had taken with us. Then, some information about how we had prepared for the trip, including lodging and expenses. His article summarized that aspect under the heading "Paying Their Own Way":

> But for the most part, the girls have been on their own. They are paying their own way out of what they have been able to save. At many places along the line, they have been guests in private homes and they have arranged their trip so as to stay with as many friends and relatives as possible along the way.

His article continued, like most others, by including a bit of our upcoming itinerary. "They plan to stay in Arapahoe tomorrow, McCook on Sunday, Benkelman on Monday and to cross into Colorado on Tuesday." He concludes by asking Teri and me if six weeks on the road was getting old and making us homesick. "We've never regretted a bit of it," we responded. He added that "even the Holdredge drenching failed to dampen their enthusiasm for the road."

Upon leaving Holdredge the next day on our way to Arapahoe, I noticed a change taking place in the landscape. My journal mentions that "the country looked quite different today. Lots of hills and barren open country without a tree for miles. Cattle were grazing on dried up grasses and we crossed deep canyons with sharp cliff walls."

During one of his visits here to Virginia Beach, Brian and I were reading this journal entry when he got up and went over to my map. "Yep," he said to me.

"Yep, what?" asked Peggy.

"They were crossing the 100th meridian just then," he said, "That's the start of the West." He added that the 100th meridian is the approximate geographical boundary between the rich eastern lands of the Plains States, used mainly for farming, and the western, more arid stretches, where grazing is the major land use. The Rocky Mountains lie about 300 miles to the west, and this part of the country receives very little rain. Twenty inches will fall in a good year, five inches in a bad one. That compares with a normal rainfall of 30 to 40 inches in the eastern states.

Brian added that most of the West is dry like this. Without the mountains rising up to capture the clouds, rain, and snow, moisture would quickly pass the mid-section of the country altogether. And unless it is irrigated, most of the land in these parts will yield little more than enough sustenance for grasses and shrubs. Wind, dryness, and brown hues abound. Then, he pulled out a book by Wallace Stegner, a noted writer of the West, and read that "To know and appreciate the West, one must first get used to brown, for it is the prominent color of the land."

Well, both Peggy and I thanked him for the geography lesson but, facts or no facts, I read in my journal that I found myself extra thirsty on this stretch of the ride. "We used up all the water in our canteens and it started to feel just like being in the desert," I wrote. "I kept thinking of the song, 'Cool, Clear Water.'"

When Teri and I arrived in Arapahoe, the mayor and his daughter met us. He promptly invited us to stay at their house for the evening. We accepted the hospitality without hesitation. After a fine dinner and a game of bridge, we headed downtown since it was the big Saturday night out for all of the farmers.

Once there, we stepped into a local bar, and my journal recalls that one beer soon turned into "a few." Everyone was very friendly and we didn't have to bother with the bill—everything was on the house. "It's not often we get such pretty celebrities like you gals here in Arapahoe," the bar owner commented. One of the farm boys even gave me his hat to "keep that nasty sun out of your pretty little eyes."

The bartender started to talk about western Nebraska, where the land was harsh and often hostile to both body and spirit. He said that the dirt, dryness, and open space could creep deep into your bones. Saturday night gatherings at his place provided the locals with a needed break from the relentless "sameness" of the long, hot summer days. He said, "Bars, saloons, and cafés—whatever public place it may be— provide an oasis for the weary soul on the open plains." I looked around the bar and felt like we fit right in.

We paid the price for all of the fun we had the night before when we started out the next day. We didn't feel too sharp, and Teri got a little ill as soon as we started pedaling. But we kept going, because it was Sunday and we were invited to be special guests at the McCook Methodist Church.

We made it to McCook in time to sit in the front row seats they had reserved for us. I recall the uncomfortable feeling I had with all eyes upon us. Reverend Edgar, the minister, talked about us for five minutes during his sermon. We just sat there smiling and squirming in our sweaty shorts. I started to think that *The Today Show*, other television shows, radio interviews, and newspaper articles were fine, but to be the focus of a sermon in a full and quiet church was a bit overwhelming. However, the Edgars invited us to stay at their home that evening, so I reasoned that it was worth all the squirming. Besides that, the Edgars were a very nice and interesting couple.

We got a 6 o'clock start the next morning and rode sixty miles to Benkelman before it was noon. The day wasn't uneventful though— I recall riding west through Nebraska's wide-open spaces when all of a sudden, a car coming the other way *exploded*. By shear coincidence—or, as I like to say, divine intervention—a truck happened to be passing us at precisely the time the car exploded. We just happened to be all lined up when metal went flying everywhere. The truck blocked all but a tiny piece that hit my ankle. As we pulled over to the side of the road to inspect the damage I said to

Teri, "What do you figure the chances of all those things happening at once are? Here we are out in the Great Wide Open, with hardly any traffic, and that truck just happens to pass us at just the right time to shield us from the flying debris." I chalked up another one for my angels, always there when needed.

After that near mishap we spent the rest of the afternoon in Benkelman lounging, reading, and writing in the air-conditioned comfort of our hotel room. We really enjoyed it, too. In my journal, I noted, "It's funny—at home this would be a boring afternoon, but on a trip like this, it's delightful. Life's simple pleasures are all the more appreciated."

Another early start helped us reach Yuma, Colorado, by 10am the next day—a 60-mile ride. We checked in to the Yuma Hotel for $3.50. After cleaning up, we went out and ate a T-bone steak dinner, and met a couple of young men who bought us drinks.

It seemed that no matter where we were, our friendly personalities and sense of purpose attracted a lot of hospitality. In return, I guess these folks were treated to a bit of vicarious adventure themselves, as we shared stories of our trip with them.

We rode 27 miles before stopping in Akron the next day at 9:30 in the morning. The miles went swiftly as we pulled into Brush just before lunch. Then we rode 10 more miles into Fort Morgan, stopping at the Chamber of Commerce to see about accommodations. There, we hooked up with Helen Cudworth, the editor of the local paper. Helen was a charming woman, who, like Jim Rippey in Holdredge, offered lodging in return for an interview. I recall that we went to her house and rested and read until she came home. Then she took us to town for a delicious dinner. Quite a talker, she told us about her five-week press tour to Europe and Asia and about the history of Leadville, where we were going to cross the Continental Divide. She gave us the name of the owner of the Pepper Pod in Hudson, saying that he would put us up for the night when we got there the next day.

The next morning, Helen prepared a nice breakfast of fresh strawberries, eggs, bacon, toast, and coffee. Then we headed west towards Hudson and the Pepper Pod. There, we celebrated seven weeks on the road by having three Tom Collins drinks each.

We had ridden 500 miles in 9 days, averaging a little over 55 miles a day. We were really feeling good and in shape. But the Rockies, looming in the distance, were an unknown. 14,000-foot peaks and long, steady climbs were ahead. With that in mind, we lifted our drinks and toasted the road gone by, hoping that our bodies, bikes, and good fortune would continue long enough to get us up and over America's Great Divide.

Peggy

After an extra day of laying around with papers and magazines and Sunday afternoon movies, we are ready for a "big day," meaning lots of miles to make up for our day off. We decide that we'll just ride until we can't go anymore.

Riding west out of Hastings, we pass through tired towns that seem to have had their hearts taken out. Boarded-up windows and peeling paint adorn out-of-business Mom-and-Pop gas stations, while right next door stands a shiny new Mini-Mart. We search for little diners like Andy's in the tiny towns, but are forced to settle for expensive Fig Newtons and potato chips in overly air-conditioned gas malls. Riding through such places feels like turning the pages of a musty old book.

From Arapahoe, the manager in yet another Mini-Mart tells us that our time in the flatlands will soon be done. "You're in the hilly part of our state, next to the Republican River Valley." He's right. It's back to the unending hills, the ups and downs, the changing of gears. But there is a difference from Iowa. Within these hills, the West begins. We sense subtle differences: muted greens, rockier soil, the scent of sage growing in fresh pockets. The landscape changes as we head toward red rocks and the open sun-blue sky. Cattle seem to sense our direction and they stampede, following us along the hills, believing our black handlebars and white helmets to be their leader.

As we hit the 100-mile mark, Brian tries to talk to me, but I have withdrawn into a place of pleasant cycling psychosis. Oblivious to the hills, my mind floats out over the fields, into conversations I'll eventually have with Mom and Dad, into quiet spaces where I think of the death of Tim, or of my grandmother taking my hand on walks down by the ocean as a child, or of my brother singing songs with me. I think of Brian and me, sitting wrinkled in the sun, smiling in silence at each other.

When we finally get to McCook, Brian tells me we've ridden 130 miles and only have half a mile to go to get to our Best Western hotel. I can tell he's worried about me, but I pedal slowly down the pockmarked streets, blandly observing the stripper bars, the pawnshops, liquor stores, the fast food places that blink and smile in dismal neon. Downtown is boarded up here, too. "Out of Business" signs outnumber the lights of stores that still have a pulse. If you look carefully, you can see in the brick facades the memories of better times, of people strolling and shopping, of schoolchildren on bikes and skates. Now, at dusk, this downtown struggles for life as cars pass by to get to the Super Wal-Mart on the edge of town. With flags blowing on its castle and a wide asphalt moat, Wal-Mart has become the feudal lord of McCook.

We eat dinner and go to bed—nothing more memorable than that. We awaken the next day, ready to leave. It's amazing how differently my mother saw this town, all full of vim and vigor in its heyday, before the interstate took travelers 70 miles to the north. Her journal doesn't mention anything about boarded-up buildings, strip clubs, and rent-by-the-week hotels. No mention of Wal-Mart superstores, either.

*　　*　　*　　*　　*

You can usually pull off being a slug the day after a 130-mile ride—so I do exactly that, in a sneaky fashion. I ride behind Brian and just kind of meander along, stopping to adjust my bags, taking time putting on my rain jacket when it starts to drizzle, coasting down hills and humming miscellaneous tunes. Brian doesn't know that I have in my mind a 50-miler. I know that the tiny town of Benkelman is ahead of us and I know there is a motel there, waiting for us. As the rain gets heavier, my plan grows more specific: I plan to sit in bed after taking a warm bath, propped up on pillows, and watch Oprah, followed by an early dinner in the local diner.

With the wind blowing the rain across the hood of my jacket I feel like I'm in a tent, rain pounding upon the roof. Wiping my face occasionally with a bandanna, I listen to the lovely sound of my tire slicing through the water that cascades down the empty road. I watch the waterfall flying off Brian's back tire and up into the air in delicate arcs, the cottonwood and willow tree branches dripping across the prairie grasses, and feel my warmth underneath from the layered polypropylene. I feel clean.

By the time we get to Benkelman, my shoes are filled with water and my toes are swimming backstrokes in my socks. We stop for coffee in yet another Mini-Mart, and while in the bathroom blowing my hands warm with a hand dryer, I stare at my face—windblown, red, and smiling, with hair in dripping strands over my face. I look like a wild woman.

Before I can even suggest stopping, Brian says, "Let's stay here." Such a peaceful face on such a disheveled looking woman must disturb him. He probably thinks I'm having a relapse of cycling psychosis again and wants to get me off the road so I can recover inside after a hot shower. My plan has worked perfectly and I didn't even have to say a word.

In the evening we have the perfect dinner of tomato soup, toasted cheese sandwiches, and French fries accompanied by Happy

Hour Beer at the Circle B Diner next to our motel, the Circle B Motel. The owner's wife is so excited to see us—"I saw you both 40 miles before McCook and thought, *Wow! One of those bikers is a girl ... I think.* And now I know you really *are* a girl!" She gives us leftover yeast rolls, butter, and jam for breakfast, explaining, "You'll get up earlier than I will."

That night, lightning flashes as thunder pounds at our windows, which shake in the rain. I watch Brian's face light up, then recede into shadows minute after minute with the flashes, like a silent movie in freeze-frame. I lay there visualizing the black storm blowing off down the road to McCook, away from our destination in the West, right over to that Wal-Mart with its colorful flags, and just staying there.

"You're going to get caught in a storm worse than the one from last night," some kid says as he gets into a van with his parents. We stare out at the grayish-black sky. "I wouldn't want to be caught on those bikes if I were you." Then off he goes in the safety of his car with two bored parents. At least the clouds are mixed with some blue, and the wind—the strongest it has been—blows them away from us. We have no choice but to go on.

With the wind hitting us directly in the face, we can't go very fast, but it doesn't matter. We cross over into Colorado—the West! We take pictures of a fading, peeling, "Welcome to Colorado" sign. A derailed rusting train lay on its side, weeds growing up through the caboose, abandoned and left to the earth as a new train on the other side of the road flies past. We sit in the blowing grass and congratulate ourselves for being 10 feet within the West, surrounded by the strong smell of drying sage.

In Wray, we stop at a museum filled with Western memorabilia: rusted horseshoes, 100 versions of barbed wire, prairie dresses on handless plastic mannequins, a huge sculpture of a buffalo and a thumbnail history of Buffalo Bill, old desks, and a telephone operator's switchboard. We tell the tour guide what we are doing and she takes a picture of us and tells us to eat at the Riverside Café for a good breakfast.

French toast is usually the highlight of my mornings, when I can find it. At the Riverside, my French toast is like custard with whipped butter—a joy to eat. The café has little booths in three long rows and waitresses with wide smiles and lots of coffee. Brian calls up places to stay in Yuma, Colorado, while I scrape my plate. A woman comes up to me and asks, "Are you the couple who was on *The Today Show*?" When I say yes, the whole place turns to look at me—old men in suspenders, women with babies, and a whole table of men in plumbers' outfits—as if just waiting to hear my answer. "Well, then you're celebrities! I need to call the paper and have Beverly get her butt down here for a story on you two!" We soon have people asking questions and looking out the window at our bikes; I drink too much coffee and become hyperactive. Beverly, the reporter, comes in the door and asks two boys if they are the bikers from New York. "*Hell* no!" they say, flicking their thumbs back at me, "It's the girl in blue." The whole place erupts into laughter.

People watch us from the diner as we get our picture taken in front of the Riverside. "Don't know why I'm advertising for them," huffs Beverly, "they don't buy any ads in our paper." We wish we could stay here for the night—Beverly says we can sleep at her house with all her dogs. I suddenly miss our dog, Miss Lulu.

The next day, from our Yuma hotel room, Brian films me refusing to get out of bed after watching sagebrush and branches fly past our window. The wind must be blowing at over 40 miles per hour and cars are barely making it down the road. I hide my head under the covers (as if that will make Brian go away with his camera), but it only makes him more insistent on getting me up and going.

We set out, having to lean left and then right on our bikes, depending on which direction the next gust of wind decides to strike us from. Wind hits us in walls, pushing us first toward the fields, then suddenly switching direction and sucking us back toward the road. I feel like I'm in a typhoon, the wind battering us like waves. Sagebrush is flying everywhere, just like in those old western movies. It gets caught in our spokes and on our packs. One piece smacks me in the face and attaches itself to my helmet. I can't get it off for fear of removing my clenched hands from the handlebars and flying off into a ditch or in front of an oncoming truck. Holding my handlebars really doesn't make that much of a difference anyway, as I find out just as we enter Akron, 28 miles down the road.

We've been fighting the wind and the road for five hours now, including a stop in a tiny diner for refueling with French toast and coffee. This is like riding on a stationary bike in a wind tunnel. Six miles an hour is practically standing still—if we had these kind of winds back in Nebraska, we'd barely be to McCook. All of our training rides in the Salt Lake Mountains, the Pocono Mountains back east, the hills of Iowa—nothing had prepared us for this. But it is kind of amusing being encrusted with weeds of the West from head to toe.

As we enter Akron, the windbreaks of the buildings and trees seem to offer us cover—or so we think. Suddenly, a gust strikes us like a sledgehammer and for half a second, we are airborne, only to slam down haphazardly in the middle of the road. Luckily, we seem to be the only people stupid enough to be on the road, and we don't become victims of a traffic accident. Brian and I stop by the corner of an out-of-business gas station as a tree branch flies past us and bounces off a gas pump. Eyes red from the wind, we stare at each other, speechless. "Let's call it a day," we seem to say to each other, and we head into town to barricade ourselves in the Yorka Café.

Eating our second helping of French toast that day, we listen as people come in for late lunches and early dinners.

"It's so windy out there it blew the blooms off the flowers!"

"Glad I'm not a toupee man in this wind!"

"Well, the wind's back. Better get ready for winter."

Elderly couples with kind faces and canes walk over to us, asking us about our bike trip. "You're the couple from *The Today Show*. Where's your mother?"

"It's a good thing you stopped here, it's too dangerous to be on that road to Brush. That's the windiest stretch of road in the whole state. Two cars a week get blown into the ditches."

We decide to call Paul Brannigan in Denver for rescue. He offers to pick us up with his Jeep, a bike rack, and probably beer in a cooler, and can whisk us on to Denver in comfort and safety. I can tell Brian feels a bit like a dog with his tail between his legs by stopping at 28 miles, and getting a car ride, but I really don't care. We had planned on making it to Fort Morgan to meet Paul there, so 20 miles doesn't mean anything to me. Brian agrees. Besides, the lobby of this café has stories to tell.

After our meal we sit on musty sofas facing an old player piano, dusty with disuse, as people walk by for a quick sandwich or for an afternoon of coffee and conversation. The lobby has high ceilings, and a chandelier full of crystal swings with the gusts of wind let in from the swinging glass doors. We sprawl out, our legs on the backpacks, reading the news of the town by the light of tasseled lamps with pull switches: cattle sales, farm sales, gas prices, garage sales, church suppers, and obituaries. Names and faces of the dead filled the news: "a husband, father, grandfather, and great-grandfather loved by all who knew him ... a dedicated volunteer on the altar guild ... successful farmer for 50 years ... " Marriages and births seem to be the news in other places, but not here.

Brian starts playing with the video camera, rewinding the tape to the sagebrush stuck on the spoke of his tire, tree branches arching in painful contortions. Then, he finds the button to switch from color to black and white. In an instant we are transformed back to my mother's time, a time when this was the lobby of a swank hotel. Looking through the viewfinder of the camera, our surroundings are layered in shades of gray, black, and white. Everything looks to be of another era—the '50s. Again, I think back to my mother and her ride.

Part of my mother's unique style is her sense of adventure—she picks life up and spins it around in front of her, expecting it to be good, knowing it can always be fun. The bike trip was the adventure of a lifetime, "but there was always room for more," she says. "Sure, I was like everyone else in the '50s I guess. I wanted a husband and children—but I wanted to see places and do things first."

On the surface, my mother fits the mold of the women of her times. A Girl Scout growing up, she went to college and earned a respectable degree in teaching, but what she really wanted to be was a stewardess so she could travel. She often tells the story about her long-awaited, but ill-fated interview with an airline. "I failed the knee test. You see, in those days they required you to lift your skirt to show your knees. Well, a week before the interview I had broken my kneecap while skiing. When it came time to stand up and shake the interviewer's hand, I fell flat on my face and screamed!" She didn't get the job, but found other ways to travel and find adventure.

As a 23-year-old living with her parents and no marital prospects, Mom felt like "everyone had a home but me." Her friends were getting married, moving to the new suburbs, away from the big city. Mom remembers feeling displaced, rootless, "like the future had arrived and passed me by."

When Mom told her mother that she wanted to ride her bike across the country, she remembers her mother laughing, thinking the trip to be just another of June's frivolous ideas. Her stepfather thought it was "not the thing to do," but knew that he had no power over June and her decisions. Mom felt like the country would be one big Girl Scout camp and all she had to do was ride across it and enjoy. She didn't express fear of attackers, of men in cars knocking her off the road. She didn't carry mace, or have the luxury of help being a 911 cellular phone call away. Instead, she slept in parks and in stranger's houses, trusting that everyone would treat two women on their own with kindness and respect.

Before our trip, we drilled Mom with endless questions in order to know what to expect in retracing her path. She acknowledged that it wasn't all wine and roses and expressed fear and anxiety about our safety and well-being. But whenever I asked how she really felt about our trip she'd respond, "Do it—I've never regretted it a minute."

Singing at the Chuckwagon Dinner

12

"Wanderlust got the best of these two young women who are bicycling across the United States this summer."
—*The Denver Post*, August 14, 1956

"When my mother rode across the country, they ate steak and potatoes and had lots of parties with farm boys," Peggy says with a smile. "They'd smoke cigarettes, drink Manhattans and skinny-dip with the farm boys." Lifestyles have changed. For sure Peggy and Brian won't be smoking any cigarettes—"yecht," says Peggy. And partying will be held to a minimum. Skinny-dipping? Who knows?
—*The Mountain Times*, August, 1996

June

Four days of rest and relaxation awaited Teri and me in Denver, but first we had to ride from Hudson to Lakewood, 32 miles away. The going wasn't too smooth as I was feeling a bit of the after-effects of our previous night's indulgence. I wanted to kick myself for such a premature celebration, but my hangover did the job well enough. I felt pretty awful when we mounted our bicycles, and it didn't help that Teri kept telling me how bad I looked. Bumpy roads with lots of traffic added to my discomfort.

Happily, we made it to the house of my sister-in-law Gert's parents after a few hours of riding. The Mores gave us a hero's welcome and treated us to a wonderful lunch, after which we settled down to our second batch of mail for the trip. Letters from home, families, and friends—I wrapped myself in their good words and took a nap as my hangover became a distant memory. Later on, Gert came over and her parents drove us all up to the Red Rock Theater and Lookout Mountain. It was our first real taste of the high and mighty Rockies and the biking that awaited us; "Wow!" was my journal entry for the day.

On Saturday, *The Denver Post* sent a journalist and photographer to do a story about us, entitled "Pedaling from Coast to Coast."

> Cyclists leave comforts at home: Traveling wardrobe and transportation reservations are the least of worries to two sun-tanned Denver visitors. The pretty travelers who have been providing extra highway scenery for automobile travelers are Teri Foster, 25, and June Meyer, 24, both of New York. They left Rockefeller Center June 22 and other than "hitching a few rides" they have cycled over the Poconos and Alleghenies, the rolling hills of Iowa and stopped in Denver before tackling the Rocky Mountain ranges.

On Monday, our third day off, my brother Artie took us up for a backroads tour of the mountains. We went to Central City, a typical old western mining town full of taverns, hotels, and banks, all spread out like the set of a John Wayne movie. Then we went up to the Glory Hole—an open pit mine just outside of town. There, Artie took us to a hidden stream he knew about so we could pan for gold. It wasn't long before I found a few gold leaves. Artie informed me that I really hadn't hit the mother lode. He joked that I'd be better off sticking to pedaling than panning. And so that's just what I did.

We started south again on Tuesday, August 14, making it to Castle Rock, about 26 miles away. We had a late start, since it took awhile to say goodbye to Gert, Artie, and their three children. That was okay—I was soaking up all the love I could to keep in reserve for those big Rocky climbs.

After the break, getting back on and riding *Ali* for the first time in four days was almost effortless. I don't recall much else on that day other than how good it felt to be with family.

The next day, with the Rockies still over our right shoulders, we rode south towards Colorado Springs. About halfway there, a man pulled over and flagged us down. He invited us to his home, saying, "I suppose you think that I am just another masher, but by the looks of your tans and your loaded saddle bags, I know you are on a long trip." He introduced himself. His name was Phil Palaski. He went on to tell us that he and his wife, Audrey, were avid bicyclists and had taken two years from 1948 to 1950 to ride all 48 states. He offered to put the two of us up for the night at their house.

That was all that Teri and I needed to know, so we didn't hesitate to take him up on the offer. Instead of serving us dinner at home, the Palaskis arranged to have us be honored guests at the Garden of the Gods Chuckwagon Supper. It was a good ol' western hoedown, and when dinner was over, the band invited Teri and me up to join them in a song. Well, I certainly couldn't turn down that invitation, being the good Girl Scout that I was. I lead everyone in one of my favorites: *"When it's twilight on the trail ... and I jog along ... please plant this heart of mine underneath the lonesome pine on the hill ..."* On my way back from the stage, a woman slipped me a dollar bill "for some hamburgers along the way." I was touched deeply by her sweetness. People seemed to keep doing little things like that throughout our trip. And it's the little things that really matter, especially when you're so far from home and the places you're familiar with.

Back at the Palaskis', Phil and Audrey pulled out their scrapbook and told us stories about their own bicycling experiences. I was quite humbled and wrote in my journal, "Their two-year trip made ours seem kind of puny." But the Palaskis didn't boast of their feat; they simply enjoyed sharing the camaraderie and opportunity to support and encourage a couple of fellow tourists on their own journey.

Forty years later, I wrote in my memoir, "Being with the Palaskis was another special moment in time—one that could never be recaptured, because recently my husband and I were in Colorado Springs and I tried to locate them. There were three Palaskis in the phone book, but none of them were the 'pedaling' ones."

After a day-off sidetrip to visit Pike's Peak, we headed southwest from Colorado Springs to Canon City. A few hilly climbs gave us a taste of the mountains we would soon face. Four hours later and 40 miles down the road, we stopped at the Shanty Café and were treated to a free lunch. Within minutes, Larry Williams, the local news reporter, arrived, as well as the Canon City Chief of Police. He told us we could stay in Rudd Park that evening and that he'd put his officers on "double duty" patrolling the place to keep us safe.

Mr. Williams' article appeared in the next day's paper with the headline: "Two Girls Crossing Nation on Bicycles Stop in Canon City." In his story, he asked Teri and me about bicycling on the open road, especially about the trials and tribulations of two women out on their own:

> "We've had amazingly few problems. Lonely and sometimes amorous truck drivers are the hardest on the nerves. They pass too closely and hoot airhorns with nerve-rendering blasts. We don't mind it too much though. It's usually all in the name of good fun."
>
> "People tried to warn us of the dangers of our trip. Actually there are no particular dangers involved. We don't just throw our sleeping bags off to the side of the road and sleep as some people seem to think."

In my journal, I wrote about our evening in the park. Of course, first I had to mention our night on the town with 10 geology students that we'd met in the café. "They sure were cute and very funny. We went drinking and dancing and then they escorted us back to our camp in the park."

Back at the camp I settled down and snuggled into my sleeping bag out under the stars and slept like a log until 3am, when I awoke and looked up at a dazzling array of sparkling stars. I saw my old friend Orion and for the first time this summer saw Mars. It was tremendously large and bright, a beautiful sight to behold, especially framed by the leaves of the surrounding trees. I sighed deeply and then rolled over and went back to sleep.

The next two days truly gave us a good taste of the Rocky Mountain sights, sounds, and weather. Our route took us west along US 50. Without a doubt, this had to be the most spectacular stretch of highway I had ever seen. Riding from Canon City to Salida, we had the Arkansas River below us on the right and a great view of the snow-capped peaks of the Sangre de Cristo Mountains on our left. We spent the night in Salida and then headed north the next day on Highway 24, still following the path of the Arkansas River. My journal entry describes those two wondrous days of riding:

> *Saturday, August 18, 1956:* Rolled out of our bags at 6:30am and got on the road. Pedaled 8 miles straight up, to get to the entrance of the Royal Gorge Bridge. We left our bikes and hitched a ride to the bridge with a man and wife from Texas, all four of us in the front seat of their pickup truck. Teri and I walked across the suspension bridge and up a cliff, taking pictures all the way. We rode on the steepest railway in the world to the bottom of the Gorge. As we left again on our bikes after lunch, it started pouring rain with 50 miles still to go to Salida. Then it hailed! It really got chilly going downhill, but then we warmed up when we started climbing again. Even though it poured for a couple of hours, I thoroughly enjoyed every minute of it, as the sky was so dark and interesting and the mountains so close, and towering and majestic—a new and beautiful scene changing every minute with every bend in the road. I'm sure that people in cars thought we were crazy. But such crazy fun. One time after cresting a hill, we looked down into a lovely valley. It reminded me of the song, "Suddenly There's a Valley." We rode 2,000 feet up and

hardly noticed it as we were riding right in between mountains and a swiftly flowing river. The road was winding and gorgeous. We neared town as it was getting dusk and I sang, "Twilight On the Trail," "Perfect Day," and "Now the Day is Over."

Sunday, August 19, 1956: It was sure cold when we left the hotel and it had snowed on the mountain peaks during the night. The sun was hot and when the wind blew, our sweat froze. I felt the altitude a bit — like a rubber band around my chest. We got to Buena Vista at noontime for a BBQ, which preceded an old western rodeo. It sure was exciting, especially the bucking broncos. In town, we had a couple of Rock and Ryes due to our dampness and wet feet. We camped in a field under a pine tree and I got a fire built and watched it in the rain. Rolled into the bag and got to sleep pretty fast despite the rocky ground. The weather is crazy here: sun, clouds, fog, rain, snow, and all within an hour. What a change from Iowa!

A change indeed—snow in August—but Artie had warned me that we should expect this in the mountains. He gave me a book to read on Colorado and the West that said, "the climate of the Mountain States is mixed, to put it mildly. At best, it is superb ... at worst, the weather is so terrible that Westerners never tire of boasting about the challenge it presents." My journal for those two days told the same tale. In the corner of each day's entry is a box to check what kind of weather occurred: clear, cloudy, rain, snow. I had checked off all four boxes for both of these days!

Our next day's ride from Buena Vista to Leadville would not be the longest of the trip, at 40 miles, but would prove to be one of the most challenging, for we had to ride up to 10,000 feet. I knew that because Artie's book told me so: "At 10,200 feet, Leadville is the highest incorporated city in the United States."

Brian

When quizzing June about her riding in the mountains, I was very curious about the fact that she had only three gears to choose from. Knowing also that she had experienced gear trouble on her trip, I wondered if they gave her trouble on these big climbs. "Oh, no, by that time all of the bugs were worked out and they were functioning pretty well. I remember that day to Leadville too. I was determined to ride all the way up and not get off and walk or thumb a ride." I asked how she got that determination. "Oh, it was sort of like all the other days on the trip. I did like I would always do ... I focused on a loved one or a family member who had passed away. I am sure I thought of my father that day and felt his strength carrying me up the mountain."

June hit on a point that I certainly related to regarding bicycling. "You know, even though you're out there with someone else as I was with Teri, you're really alone because seldom do you get the chance to ride side-by-side and talk. So for six, maybe eight hours a day, it's just you and your thoughts to keep you company. I liked that though, it was very meditative and it gave me time to daydream and pray." I whole-heartedly agreed with her, adding how the rhythmic up and down cadence of pedaling and deep breathing brings about a wonderful peace of mind. You don't get to that point without a little bit of effort though.

Riding 65, 70, or 100 miles a day, day after day, is tough. You get up early to sore muscles, pack your bags, load them on the bikes, check the tires, adjust your helmet, fill your water bottles, check your map, and fight the traffic for a place on the road, all the while trying to avoid potholes and other dangers. Your legs resist those first revolutions as you plod down the road early in the morning. Then, after an hour or so, you look at your odometer and the mileage reads 12, maybe 15, miles. You've still got a long way to go. But as the day wears on, you get into a groove. You forget you are even pedaling. You take a drink from your water bottle without even noticing that you were thirsty. Riding becomes automatic, like breathing. Your mind drifts into a steady state and your body feels good. You don't realize that you still have 25 or 30 miles to go. And you don't care.

Upon reaching Leadville, June wrote that she had finally made it to the highest city in America. "I had weak knees, but a feather in my cap because Teri and I had made it all on our own." That evening, they celebrated their feat in their own patented manner—over T-bone steaks and Manhattans.

Peggy and I keep joking that we are going to eat steaks and drink Manhattans on our trip, but we always settle for lighter meals of pasta and microbrews. We have plenty of both during our three days off in Denver.

While staying at Peggy's cousin John's house, we finally have the chance to log on to the web site that my brother Phil had been busy updating for us back in New York City. So far, we have been sending him our film once a week so he can develop it, scan the photographs, and then post them on our web page. We have also been updating him with telephone calls most every day so he can keep a running log of our progress. It's a great way for our family and friends to keep up with us as we travel east to west. My sister in California, Peggy's brother and sister-in-law in Oregon, Jane Sweet in Buffalo, the Hodgkins in Maine, Peggy's cousin in Florida, and my uncle in Tennessee are all able to dial up our site and see how things are going for us.

Looking at the site, we admire how Phil has composed photo collages of our trip so far. He has arranged the trip by week, so all you have to do is click on a week and you can view some of the photos he has developed and scanned into our page. We sit at Cousin John's computer and click on a few of these weeks. There we are, riding past a "Pocono Mountains" sign in Pennsylvania. There we are on the deck of the *Jiimaan*, crossing Lake Erie on a perfectly clear blue day. And here is a photo of Peggy standing next to the mayor of Winterset, Iowa. A couple more photos of that day show before-and-after shots of me standing next to the barber pole in front of the shop where I got my "Iowa Buzz Cut."

The highlight of the site is a little song snippet that Phil and Andy composed as the theme song for the trip. The song is called "Saint Rita" and lasts for about 25 seconds—somewhat like a commercial jingle. However, it's much better produced and arranged than most of the commercials I have heard lately. We sit there and click on the song icon a number of times, wishing that the song was a bit longer.

Back in Findlay, Dan Sheaffer is kind enough to print out our updates and give them to my mother, who considers herself computer illiterate and isn't wired to the digital world yet. She and Dutch eventually go down to the public library, and they are both amazed at being able to surf through the photos that Phil so artfully arranged on the screen. Even Bob and June get into the act in Virginia Beach when they log on at the library.

Reading our e-mail in Denver, we feel a new sense of togetherness on our trip. It's heartening to see that all of these people are interested and supporting our venture. In a way, I guess it helps us gain strength for the mountainous roads ahead.

Riding south from Colorado Springs is somewhat unusual. On our left, we look out over a flat and barren desert landscape, while on our right sit the lush green mountains, waiting for us. We have a few healthy climbs through the foothills until we turn west on US 50 and a good tailwind pushes us forward. Dark, low-lying clouds encourage us to ride faster toward Canon City.

Once in town, we look for a cute old western motel to put us up for the night so we can sleep like Calamity Jane and Wild Bill

Hickock. As fate and the reality of the 1990s has it, we have to settle for a Best Western by the highway. We turn around and start to ride the mile back to the hotel when Peggy notices she has a flat tire. And just as I'm starting to change the tube, the clouds open up. Peggy tries to shield me from the wind and pelting drops as I rush to slap a new tube on the back of the rim and pumped up the tire. This isn't the sort of Wild West we had in mind, but it will have to do. Later on, we can't even locate a local diner for dinner—we end up eating at Pizza Hut.

The next morning, we are greeted by a crisp, clear day—perfect for riding. Today is one of the rare days that we will be riding the exact point-to-point distance that June did in 1956—60 miles from Canon City to Salida. Two miles out of Canon City, I gain a new respect for June and her three-speed bike, as Peggy and I gear down for a 6-mile, 1,200-foot ascent. It reminds me of the road from Dansville, New York, to Letchworth State Park—minus the 90-degree heat and accompanying humidity. My watch/thermometer says it is 70 degrees. Knowing how dry the West is, I figure that the humidity can't be more than 30%. So even as we lumber past the state prison and start up the road at 6 miles per hour, it feels just fine.

We see billboards and signs advertising the Royal Gorge Bridge, but we decide to skip the side trip and not worry about checking it off our list of "been there, done that" attractions. Instead, we just continue west along the Arkansas River. Soon, the Sangre de Cristo Mountains appear on the southern horizon in all their glory.

Fall and winter arrive early in the mountains, and our vista gives us a taste of both. Hunter green pine trees line the lower parts of the mountains while orange and yellow aspens highlight the slopes. A new dusting of snow caps all the mountain peaks. Peggy and I feel as if we are on a *National Geographic* assignment, picture-perfect as it is. We take our time and do our best to get it all on 35mm film and Hi-8 video, knowing that these images will only do faint justice to the scenery that spreads out before us.

Judging from the license plates on the cars that pass us, we aren't alone in our admiration of this gorgeous landscape. I count 21 different license plates in all—Colorado, British Columbia, Nebraska, Iowa, Indiana, Illinois, Iowa, Maine, Pennsylvania, Missouri, Oregon, Washington, California, Kansas, Ohio, Arizona, New York, Texas, Arkansas, North Carolina, Nevada—representatives from nearly half of the United States. That isn't altogether surprising, with Colorado being the popular tourist destination that it is. What *is* surprising is that we don't see any of them pull over—not even for a minute—to let the drivers and their passengers see, smell, and feel this beautiful place. From the out-in-the-open position we have on our bikes, we pity them for missing out on a more direct experience this day.

In the evening, we eat at the Windmill Restaurant, recommended by the Comfort Inn receptionist. Peggy and I continue our pasta and microbrew habit, since it has proven to be the perfect complement to a day in the saddle. As our waitress brings out our food, she asks where we are from. When I finish with the basics of where we live and where we are going, she says, "Oh—so that was *you two* on the road from Canon City. I thought so. I drove past you, one in front of the other with your packs and all. You looked like you knew what you were doing. That's neat—you don't see a married couple doing something like that very often." We thank her for the beer and the nice compliment, and silently forgive her for not stopping along the way to look at those beautiful mountains—she sees them every day.

Cousin John shows up at our room around 9pm. He's taking a couple days off to be a support vehicle for this mountain leg of our journey. He also says that it gives him a good excuse to get away himself, even if it is behind the wheel of his Ford Explorer. He arrives with bags of groceries full of Powerbars, Tiger bars, granola bars, Fig Newtons, raisins, Gatorade, water, bananas, and pretzels. He wants to make sure we have all the fuel we need to get over "The Pass," as we have come to call it. He also has a couple copies of satellite weather reports he has pulled off the Internet earlier in the day. "Looks pretty good tomorrow," he says, "but they say a storm may hit us the following day. Snow." We shrug and turn on the Weather Channel for their opinion—snow. I give a confident thumbs-up while keeping fears of unpredictable weather in the mountains to myself. After all, June experienced snow in August and this is the end of September.

The next day starts out well enough. We put on our sunglasses in the parking lot as we go over our route with John. He takes our video camera and says that he'll just drive ahead a few miles and wait for us. He is looking forward to the chance to do some reading and air out his thoughts, so we don't worry about him being bored. We know that with his stockpile of provisions he won't go hungry either, so we clip in, start pedaling, and head north.

We're able to go a little faster without the packs adding weight and wind resistance. This is good, for soon the wind begins to blow and black clouds assemble. Wind, rain, sun, rain, flurries, wind, calm, wind—we experience a little of everything between Salida and Buena Vista. Clouds continue to pile up over the mountains when, suddenly, a rainbow appears and cheers us up as we stop in the Evergreen Diner in Buena Vista.

The diner is packed with locals drinking coffee and reading the paper, so we sit on three vinyl padded metal stools at the counter. The diner was probably there when June passed through; again, we feel like we have been transported back to the '50s. We sit and drink coffee, reading the paper and waiting for our French toast and homefries. John orders the Lumberjack Breakfast with eggs, toast, homefries, bacon, sausage, and a pancake. He's really getting into the spirit of the trip.

"I could get used to this. What a life—eat, travel, relax." We remind him about the riding part of our trip and of all the calories we burn over the course of 6 to 8 hours of cycling. "Oh, yeah, you're right. Maybe I'd better use Sweet & Low in my coffee— Nah!"

We ask other customers for their opinions regarding the weather. Some say it will blow over, most shake their heads. When we tell the waitress that we are going to Leadville today and then over Independence Pass tomorrow, she says convincingly, "Oh, I'd definitely do the Pass today. They say the snow will probably get down to 6,000 feet tonight. That'd probably close the road and you'd have to go another way."

Well, that settles it. Without much discussion, we decide that "The Pass" is more important than seeing Leadville. Peggy doesn't mind at all; she's seen more than enough of it on vacations with her parents. Besides, we don't think Leadville has any microbreweries, and we know that Aspen has one. So, "The Pass" it is. Leadville will have to wait for another trip.

13

"A car whipped past, the driver eating and a passenger clicking a camera. Moving without going anywhere, taking a trip instead of making one. I laughed at the absurdity of the photographs and then realized I, too, was rolling effortlessly along, turning the windshield into a movie screen in which I, the viewer, did the moving while the subject stood still. That was the temptation of the American highway, of the American vacation. A woman in Texas had told me that she often threatened to write a book about her family vacations. Her title: *Zoom!* The drama of their trips, she said, occurred on the inside of the windshield with one family crisis after another. Her husband drove a thousand miles, much of it with his right arm over the backseat to hold down one of the children."

—William Least-Heat Moon, *Blue Highways*

Peggy

I feel like I'm in *Monty Python and the Holy Grail* with my black balaclava pulled down over my head, mouth, and neck. "It's going to keep you warm," Brian says as Cousin John laughs at my expression. John says he is traveling with us on this portion of the ride because he is worried about snow in the mountains and our safety, but mainly he's with us because it gives him an excuse to take some time off work and continue the fun we had during our three days off in Denver. On those days we lived like traveling bohemians, eating friends' food, drinking their beer, having dinner bills paid for us, and sleeping in. We didn't once look at our bikes during this extended time off—well, maybe Brian did, because he likes examining gears, oiling things, and checking brake shoes. Those three days made me feel normal again, and without spandex encasing my legs, I could kind of ignore that we were going to ride over the Rockies—the "Big Guys."

We can see that a storm is coming in over the mountains as we bundle up in Twin Lakes and ready ourselves for the 18-mile, 3,000-foot climb ahead. (I throw these numbers in for Brian's sake; all I really know is that I can look up and see some pretty darn tall mountain peaks disappearing into the clouds and know that we have to ride up and over them). Expecting snow in the higher elevations, we put on all the clothes we have in our bags. I'm happy we're going to Aspen and not Leadville, because where would you prefer to stay if you got snowed in: The rocky barren place of Leadville—where my dad got Rocky Mountain Spotted Fever—or Aspen, the land of glamour, of Arnold Swarzenegger and Don Johnson, of hot tubs and champagne? The choice is not difficult. With fleece, polypropylene, my *Holy Grail* hat, layered mittens, and three pairs of socks, we are ready to finally face the peaks.

John reminds us of Aunt Gert's comments about Independence Pass. "Mom says that the road up there is so steep, and so narrow ... but it sure is beautiful." John is always one to look at the bright side of everything that looks ominous, like this day. The wind swirls over us from the Twin Lakes and we watch as a fully loaded biker cruises down the road from the other direction. He stops at the posh Twin Lakes Resort, known to have feather beds and hot chocolate and fireplaces. He's done, we haven't even started, but dammit, if he can make it up and over, we can too. This is the one thing we wanted to accomplish—Independence Pass. Brian mumbles numbers, checks gears, and resets his altimeter watch before he looks at the map one last time—manly tasks that fill him with a sense of purpose and importance. He reminds me again that this is the road we've been waiting the whole trip to do.

We hear distant thunder past the mountains and the clouds engulf the peaks, making them look like dirty ice cream sundaes with black whipped cream. I decide to be a Pollyanna and think saccharine-sweet thoughts. *I'm really not cold. We're really not riding into a snowstorm. The weather report didn't actually say thunder and winter warning with intermittent hail.* I envision my mother climbing this mountain with only her three gears, smiling and saying to me, "Make it an adventure."

"Aren't the aspen beautiful? Look at all the bright colors! Oh, this is so exciting!" I smile back at Brian, who looks perplexed by my sweet voice. "Is John checking on us every 15 minutes or every half hour?" is his only reply.

At least with the winter warning, people are not driving around for the scenery. The road is ours and yes, as Aunt Gert stated, it is narrow and it is steep. And very beautiful. Orange and yellow trees close in on the left and right as moss peeks through the cracks in the road. It begins to rain and I suddenly fall in love with my Grail hat because my head stays nice and toasty even as the rain mixes with snow and sleet. Icicles start to form on the spokes of my wheels as I pull the *Holy Grail* hat over my runny nose.

Like clockwork, John drives ahead and waits for us every half hour as we plod forward through the snow-dusted yellow aspen meadows and up toward the granite pass. Sometimes we go right past him waving, but as we get closer to the top we become moving snowpeople, sliding in the slush around the cliffs on our way to the top. As they pass us, people shout from their cars, "What are you, crazy? You're going to ride off the mountain!" A nice man in a pickup truck offers us a ride to Aspen but we are going to do it— make it to the top. I have my sights set on taking a picture with Brian and me up there in the blizzard.

The sign reads: "Continental Divide, Elevation 12,095 feet." John takes a picture of us standing in front of it as the snow covers our bicycles, but not our grins. I look down at my feet and notice a condom lying between my shoes, bright orange in the white snow.

Some people must do more than take photos to celebrate making it to the top of this landmark. Looking around we really can't see any kind of view at the top, other than our faces bright red and smiling through the storm as clouds hover low in black layers, spraying snow in our faces.

Passing over the Continental Divide and into the last part of our trip, I have mixed feelings. To be done, to attain one of our goals, is sad and glorious at the same time. We may go over these roads again by bike or car in the future, but standing here, shivering in the wind, this moment is everlasting. Time stops for once while we stand in it, together, looking out. As I reach over to grab Brian's mittened hand I know that I married the right guy.

The ride down to Aspen is quick and cold and we feel like Yukon Jacks riding into town as fur-coated, sunglass-wearing celebrity wanna-bes drove around in the storm in open convertibles. It's an alpine haven full of wealth and glamour as we count the Mercedes and Landcruisers zooming past us. We stop in a bike store and ask about inexpensive lodging and we're directed to the Lamplighter Hotel for the night. "It's cheap, they let you bring your bikes inside, and they have a heated pool and hot tub. It's where all the bikers go."

John buys a six-pack of beer and we all proceed to become increasingly silly, the jokes worse and worse, yet funnier and funnier—at least to us. I think our weariness has made us slightly psychotic. Stories of the day are repeated as we sit in long johns, our feet propped up, wet hair from hot showers plastered to our foreheads.

" ... and so John is eating those energy bars, one after the other right along with us, and then he looks at the caloric intake and freaks out—'*Four hundred fifty calories in one bar* and I've already eaten *three* and I'm just sitting here on my butt!'"

"Remember when John was filming us coming up the pass and he zoomed in on Brian peeing by the side of the road?"

" ... and what about that orange rubber!"

We spend the next day being disheveled tourists, eating muffins with the bus tour group in the hotel's lobby, drinking entirely too much coffee, and sitting in the hot tub every other hour. Eight inches of new snow reassures us that we made the right choice in doing The Pass yesterday and staying here today.

We try to interest the local paper with our story, but since we're not biking with Arnold or Don and we haven't sold any movie rights to our life stories, they aren't too thrilled. The woman that Brian speaks with basically says, "Well, good luck," following the synopsis of our trip and purpose.

Later in the day, the snow clears and John drives us up to see the Maroon Bells. We hike from the lower parking lot, thinking we'll be alone in the wilderness, and walk along through golden aspens while their leaves sparkle and fall on our faces. But at the lake, we notice lots of people milling around with cameras. They've all driven to the upper parking lot. Like cows at a feeding bin, we angle in for better positions so we can capture the scene of the three identical "belled" mountain peaks reflected in the water. Children run around and throw things in the water while photographers wait for the perfect light. We take seats on the rocks and giggle at the activity. It's the kind of day to pay attention to nothing and everything at the same time.

With our day off gone, we wake to the sounds of irate senior citizens on a bus tour. Their bus won't start up due to the 20-degree morning and the tour is supposed to go to Leadville, Vail, and the Coors brewery. Women in groups of three or four, suited up in matching knit pantsuits and sensible shoes, gather in front of the window staring at the bus. Men pace, their crossword puzzles put aside for this morning. A few brave souls monitor the lack of progress with the bus repair, shaking their heads as Brian and I ride past on our human-powered machines.

The road on which we leave Aspen, Highway 82, must have been designed for Mario Andretti or celebrities quickly zooming back to Hollywood—there is no shoulder and cars arcing around turns almost on two wheels force us to the side of the road every 10 minutes. Bundled up as we are with so many layers of gear, we look like black and yellow roadworkers on bikes. If a car or minivan does hit us, we'll probably just bounce safely off our bikes, saved by all the padding. We finally hit Basalt, where a kind road designer included a bike lane all the way to Glenwood Springs. We eagerly strip back down to our usual spandex Spiderman suits as the sun melts the snow and warms into a perfect day.

Nearing Carbondale, Brian points to the mountains of Crested Butte, or at least the backside of them. A year ago, we did a mountain bike ride from Marble to Crested Butte with Jenny and Tom Day and some of their friends. It's a ride that they all do every year, camping in Marble, riding the singletrack trails the next day to Crested Butte, and then staying in a condo for the night before riding back the next day. The roundtrip is only about 60 miles, but on steep, dirt trails, it is easily as challenging as any day we have done so far on our cross-country trip. Beautiful too, riding on high singletrack trails through evergreens and aspen that eventually open up to Crested Butte's picturesque valley. I remark to Brian how it seems like it was only yesterday that we were sitting around the campfire telling everyone about our upcoming cross-country ride. "Look at us now," I say. How quickly a dream can become reality once you put your mind to it.

"Hey, didn't we see you on *Good Morning America*?" the owner of the Daily Bread Restaurant says, smiling at us as we wheel our bikes to the back of the place. We didn't have the energy to explain that it was *The Today Show*, so we just let it fly. She invites us to stay at her house in Rifle that evening, but we decline because we want to get closer to Grand Junction. But we do enjoy her food—

sandwiches piled high with every sort of vegetable and cheese, all between slices of thick, fresh wheat bread. We eat every last morsel and even have seconds of the fresh soup, knowing that we will soon be heading through Glenwood Canyon on the only road available—Interstate 70.

Riding on the interstate is actually a pleasant experience. It has wide shoulders and the traffic usually stays far left. You also get to watch people in cars staring at you, their bored faces lighting up for just one moment. At first I'm nervous riding in the breakdown lane with all the tire scraps, paper cups, and cigarette butts, but it feels safer than the Mario Andretti Highway out of Aspen. We spend the night in Parachute and try to guess why this highway town has such a colorful name. I ask the cashier at the gas station attached to our motel about the town's name. Without looking up, she shrugs, "Don't ask me."

John leaves the next day after a large trucker breakfast at Hungry Mike's restaurant. He doesn't want to take the remainder of June's brown flowers home with him, so we say goodbye to my birthday arrangement and leave it for the Super 8 maids to enjoy. Leaving the hotel, I recall the telephone conversation that Mom and I had the day she had them delivered to me in Denver.

"So, do you like the flowers? I thought that they would look lovely on the front of your bicycle—Happy Birthday!" Mom had sent a large assortment of flowers to John's house because, as she said, she thought that I'd like some flowers to brighten things up for our long ride over the Rockies. Large purple flowers, cascading vines, and pink daisies sat on John's kitchen counter in a large wooden basket. I thought to myself, *Where am I going to put this on my bike?*

"I'll just put the flowers in my hair and behind my ears," I laughed. Mom always lives by her heart—she's not exactly practical with her ideas. When I was a child, it was always fun to pick strawberries instead of going to school or to look for driftwood on the beach for family Christmas presents. One year for Christmas, my aunt couldn't quite understand what June had made for her. "It's a woodland creation?" she asked. Mom and I shook our heads "yes" at the mushrooms, sticks, rocks, and dried leaves all glued onto an odd-shaped piece of driftwood. So even though John and Brian didn't understand the practicality of a floral arrangement on a cross-country bike trip, to me, it made sense. It was from Mom.

"Why don't you just tape them to the front of your bike? You can smell the flowers as you push up the mountains," she continued.

"Well, that's a good idea, June." Brian had popped into the conversation. He was unsuccessfully trying to stifle his laughter. "But then where'd we put our winter gear, since it's supposed to snow over the pass to Aspen?"

"What winter gear? You two have too much fancy equipment."

So the arrangement came with us across the Continental Divide—in John's truck. I selected a few flowers, pulled them out of their basket, and tucked them into my bicycle bag. They were a fitting compliment to Tim's scarf and the guardian angels that I was carrying across the country. My front handlebars were becoming a bit of a rolling shrine.

Riding up the divide I watched as the purple became brown, the pink faded to white, and the ivy fell into the blowing snow. But when we got to the top of the pass, there was John and his Explorer—and that flower arrangement. We all thought that it was a great idea to put the arrangement between Brian and me as John snapped photos of us in front of the Continental Divide sign. In her own way, Mom was with us. Once again, she wasn't trying to be practical, but creative and loving in her own way.

Perhaps it made sense for Mom to send me tropical flowers for the Rockies. Every time I got discouraged or tired, I'd look down at those ridiculous dying flowers and start laughing. I guess I need to give Mom some of the credit for helping me make it over the mountains.

*　　*　　*　　*　　*

We ride on the interstate again. I hate driving on these roads—in fact, I hate driving long distances anywhere. I get so bored with the sun on the dashboard, my legs don't know what to do with themselves, I can't read because I get carsick, Brian won't talk to me because he's in the "driving mode," and you pass things so quickly, nothing makes sense other than the distance you've covered. If I sleep in a car, I wake up with a messed-up neck, drooling on myself, and I scare Brian if I sing along too much or too loudly to Bonnie Raitt or the B-52s. Bicycling beats a car trip hands down.

On a bike, you're free to ignore traffic, and you notice how weeds push themselves up from cracks in the road. You can hear a bird and watch it fly above your head, following it as it follows you. Your legs know what to do and you really can't fall asleep. On the highway to Grand Junction, we get to ride on our own bike path that goes around a mountain as the interstate tunnels through it. Our path is covered in weeds, which tickle our kneecaps, as it follows the flow of the river. Sagebrush and cottonwoods layer the banks as butterflies skim the sides of the red canyons. A fox, surprised by our silent wheels, runs with its toenails clicking on the deserted road. We hear echoes of cars in the mountain.

We meet Mark, our next companion on the road, at the train station in Grand Junction. He has taken the 3am train from Salt Lake City so he can ride with us across Utah. He's asleep on a high-backed bench, his bike fully loaded and ready to go. Brian films him rubbing his eyes, his crew cut neat and fresh, as I chase him around the empty marble-floored waiting room.

Mark is a flight attendant who longs to be a monk, and like us, this trip is a time to reflect on pathways to himself. Before our trip he stated over and over that he could barely wait to get on the road and just ride with his thoughts—no choices, no decisions, just him, his bike, and the road. He threw us a going-away party a week before our trip, complete with a custom cake that said *Good luck Peggy and Brian*, spiked punch, and his special onion chip dip. All of our friends came to see for themselves that we were really serious about riding across the country. My parents were there to celebrate, too, and everybody toasted us time and time again as Brian played his guitar and we sang John Prine and Bonnie Raitt songs well past midnight.

Mark worried more about our trip than we did—how many miles a day we were going, should he bring two pairs of bike shorts or more, what about a rainjacket, did we know where we were going to stay each night, what if he got a flat? Brian made him promise to learn how to change a tire before the trip and Mark became quite proficient at the whole process. He's a map-watcher, mileage-computing kind of guy, too, and I really think Brian is excited that he now has Mark to compare numbers with at the end of the day.

Mark also has energy that surpasses the Energizer Bunny. I was looking forward to his jump-start as we head into our long stretch through the desert. I need his occasional silliness and jokes. As much as I try to push the thoughts aside, I have a lingering fear of that desert, of brown and red and silence hanging in the middle of nowhere. What if one of us gets hurt and cars don't come around? What if we run out of water? I keep these thoughts to myself, but they remain, sometimes shaking me.

Brian
Tuesday, August 21, 1956. June's journal reads:

> The Stoners took us to the Golden Burro for breakfast where we met the mayor and were on the daily radio talkshow hosted by a charming old man called "Grandpa." Then we went on a grand tour of Leadville: To the Healy House, the Matchless Mine, and St. Joseph's Church. Had a nice lunch and then we were ready to take off, but first, Sylvia Stoner bought us each five packs of cigarettes.

I've read a few other accounts of cross-country trips and researched others. June's is the only one that mentions cigarettes as part of this type of physical endeavor. I'm also aware that this was the '50s and smoking was more of the thing to do, but these two women were at 10,000 feet! I guess they figured the ride would be all downhill from Leadville, so they might as well light up and celebrate. Steaks, Manhattans, and cigarettes—what a training regimen!

June and Teri rode up to Tennessee Pass and took a few photos of the Continental Divide sign that said "Elevation 10,042 Feet." An arrow pointed to the east and the "Atlantic Ocean Watershed," while a second arrow pointed to the west and the "Pacific Ocean Watershed." A simple lesson in geography will enlighten anyone to what that means: Rain and snow that falls to the east of this dividing line ends up draining into tributaries, streams, and rivers that eventually run east and south to the Gulf of Mexico and the Atlantic Ocean; moisture that falls to the west of this line travels west and south to the Pacific Ocean. Though this divide is somewhat past the halfway point between the Atlantic and the Pacific coasts, crossing it is a milestone for any trip.

There are a lot of debates about where the West begins. Some say that it is anything west of the Mississippi River; others, west of the 100th meridian; still others, the Continental Divide. One thing is for sure, though—when you have to use your own power to pedal a bicycle up and over this point on the map, you're not worried about where the West really is, because you are fully enveloped in the moment and the task at hand: getting to the top.

June wrote, "Climbing that very steep incline to reach the Continental Divide at Tennessee Pass was a very sweat-wrenching challenge. I made sure that I did not walk my bike one step because I was doing this one for my father. He was the motivation in my thoughts and the will to reach that goal. It sure did feel good to reach the Divide because we kind of had our doubts about making it all this way on our own." She didn't mention this, but I bet they lit up a smoke there at what was to them "the top of the world."

They were rewarded for their efforts with a long stretch of road that went downhill through "great pine trees and gorgeous scenery." Then, they hit Battle Mountain and another three-mile climb to a summit that sent them immediately down through hairpin curves at breakneck speed. June wrote, "We had to brake real hard because we almost passed a couple of trucks on the way down." Thinking about her riding that three-speed, I know that she did not have the center-pull brake technology that we have on our bicycles. Her brakes were the old-style cantilever side-pull type that required a lot more muscle to depress and slow the bike down. Top that off with the fact that she didn't have a helmet to protect her from a fall and her accomplishment is all the more impressive. "We didn't have helmets back then, nobody did," June said before our trip. "I guess what we didn't know didn't hurt us." She added that she was glad that Peggy and I would be wearing helmets. "We wouldn't go without them," I responded. I then told her why I first got a helmet.

It was the fall of my second year of college and I was home in Findlay for a weekend of Mom's homecooked food and laundry services. We were eating dinner on Sunday night and she mentioned a friend's son who had been in a bicycle accident. Apparently, he was riding his bicycle to work and was pulling into the parking lot when he hit a speedbump. His front wheel struck the bump and it caused him to flip over the front handlebars. The first thing to hit was his head. He ended up being hospitalized in the intensive care unit for a few days with a serious concussion. He wasn't wearing a helmet.

"Do you have a helmet, Brian?" Mom asked.

"No, I just don't have the money right now for one," I responded.

"How much do they cost?"

"Oh, 50 or 60 dollars."

Later that evening when I was loading my stuff into the car for my trip back to school there was an envelope on top of my neatly-folded and fresh laundry. I looked inside and there was a $60 check from Mom.

"What's this for?" I asked.

"To buy a helmet," she responded.

I went out the next week and bought a new, black Bell helmet for my rides. I've worn one ever since.

June

Teri and I spent the night at the Sante Fe Railroad "YMCA" in Minturn. I underlined the "M" in my journal to emphasize the fact that there were a lot of men staying there that evening, too. However, the manager let the two of us have a room of our own for the night and didn't even charge extra for it. I wrote how wonderful it was to meet and get to know people so fast and to have them treat us so kindly. We would soon find that kindness and good fortune would prevail again for us the next day.

We rode west on a stretch of road that is now Interstate 70, which cuts through Glenwood Canyon. Forty miles from Minturn we stopped at a ranch/café for lunch. Soon, the manager asked us to be guests on a horseback ride through the canyon. Never ones to pass up an adventurous sidetrip, we took him up on the offer.

Jack Roberts was our guide and to this day, I have nothing but great memories of this man. He was a cowboy's cowboy—rough, handsome, and talented. He was the kind of man who lit his cigarettes by striking a twig across a rock. Every time I see the man on the horse in the Marlboro ads I think back to that time with Jack.

Our day started with a ride through aspen groves, pine trees, and up to Hanging Lake, a beautiful, aqua-blue mountain lake. Later, Jack invited us up to his studio in the mountains. Apparently, besides being the model cowboy, Jack had another, gentler side—he was an artist. I was surprised to find that his studio was a cave cut out of a mountainside. I was not only impressed by his art, but by the fact that his bachelor pad was so neat and clean. I remember that he even had fresh flowers on his kitchen table. Jack showed us his paintings and then made dinner. My journal recalls the rest of that evening:

> Around a blazing campfire, nestled deep in a cave, we shared a bubbling aromatic pot of beans with a cowboy artist. This was Jack Roberts' home, where we shared stories and songs around the campfire surrounded by his colorful oil paintings of cowboys, horses, and buffalo. Later on, Jack made a self-portrait sketch for me to put in my scrapbook. It capped off a great day. Earlier, we rode horseback up to Hanging Lake, which seemed to be suspended in space above the canyon. The water was so blue and clear we could even see fish swimming. It was so beautiful that we took the same trip the next day.

After going for another trail ride the next day, Teri and I treated Jack to lunch and then started riding again at 1:30 in the afternoon. I remember that this wasn't the best time to start riding because it was hot and the sun was straight ahead, shining in our faces. However, my spirits were lifted when I looked down and noticed my odometer had surpassed the 2,000-mile mark for our trip. Certain moments—like hitting that milestone—had a way of making our long trip all the more worthwhile. It seemed that anytime things started to drag, something would happen—a nice, neighborly person might offer us a cold lemonade or some kind words of encouragement, a rainbow would appear in the horizon between dark banks of clouds, or the wind would shift to give a needed push late in the day.

We spent that night in Rifle, Colorado, where we had supper, an ice cream soda, and went to bed at 7:30 in a hotel for $3.50. The next day we started early and headed towards Grand Junction. The green mountains of the Rockies were now giving way to high, brown plateaus and deep canyons, carved by rivers that ran brown with sediment.

As we rode through these varied colors I noticed that the day was getting quite hot. It was a different kind of heat than that of the east, though. With clear, blue skies, the sun was beating down and started to bake everything in its reach. To cool off, we had lunch at an umbrella-table that consisted of root beer, two barbecue beef sandwiches, a milk shake, and an orange drink. Fortunately, we weren't far from Grand Junction by this time, so all that food didn't hamper the rest of our day too much, and we made it to town all right.

Reaching the western border of Colorado was certainly a time for me to reflect on all that I had accomplished so far and to look forward to the road ahead. In the spirit of the trip and the moment, Teri and I went with the flow of things and ended up hanging around Grand Junction for a couple of days. That was fine, for the itinerary that the American Youth Hostels had prepared for us had scheduled our arrival in Grand Junction for Sunday. From there, we were to catch a train to Salt Lake City for a few days off. By arriving Friday afternoon, we had a couple of days to kill. As always, it didn't take long to find a way to occupy our time.

We met some "Uranium men" on their way into town who asked us out for the evening. We took them up on the offer and they treated us to a big roast beef dinner at a night club. My date was named Bob and he reminded me of the movie star, Douglas Fairbanks, Jr. As the evening wore on he revealed that he was the president of some mining company and was worth $47 million. With that, we all piled into his pink Cadillac and headed to a striptease bar. And so began my initiation to the new "Wild West."

A couple more days of off-bike adventure were to follow. The manager of our hotel asked us if we would like to go to see a concert in Aspen. "Sure," we said, and off we went in his car for an evening in the mountains. What we *didn't* know was the fact that the concert was on Sunday, not Saturday. The men suggested that we get some rooms at a hotel. We agreed, but when it came time to bed down for the night I remember that I didn't agree with the sleeping arrangements. Apparently, my date had his sights set on sleeping in my room. Later, I recalled that event in my journal: "He showed up at my door later that night. I straightened him out real quick as soon as I figured out what he had in mind. He was quite embarrassed, but pretty nice about the whole thing."

Despite the awkward moment the night before, I recalled that the next day was an enjoyable one: "We went swimming in a pool surrounded by immense mountains. I felt like a movie star vacationing in my contour chair by the pool." Later, we went to the concert, which was mostly chamber music, and then drove back to Grand Junction into a blazing sunset.

We got back on schedule the next day, Monday, when a family offered to drive us to Salt Lake City in their station wagon. The wagon was stuffed to the gills even before we got in, but we managed to get ourselves and our bicycles to Salt Lake around eight o'clock that night.

Having a few days off in Salt Lake was fine with me because I had developed the cold that Teri had just gotten over while in Colorado. As always, the local news media was interested in interviewing two women doing a novel thing like riding bicycles across the country. We took it all in stride, happily sharing the stories of our adventures and accomplishments so far on the trip. What lay ahead for us was still a bit unclear though, for we were now faced with some wide-open and desolate country. AYH had set us up with train rides to remote places like the Grand Canyon, Bryce and Zion National Parks. We would ride our bicycles some too, but with civilization, water, and shelter spread out over such great distances, we had to resort to alternative means of travel. Resourceful as always, I knew that we would figure out ways to see these grand places. So, that in mind, we enjoyed the city for a few days and didn't dwell on the future.

14

"Much of the [Southern Utah] region will never have anything to offer but scenery. But scenery it has in superlative degree and extravagant forms ... Here geological and human history have at least a poetic similarity. It is a perfect paradise for anybody—still is."
—Wallace Stegner, *Beyond the Hundredth Meridian*

"What slowed down traffic were the massive motor homes lumbering up and down the mountain passes ... That, alas, is the way of vacationing nowadays for many people. When the urge to travel seizes you, you pile into your 13-ton tin palace and drive 400 miles across the country, hermetically sealed against the elements, and stop at a campground where you dash to plug into their water supply and electricity so you don't have to go a single moment without air-conditioning or dishwasher and microwave facilities."
—Bill Bryson, *The Lost Continent*

Brian

Packing up our bicycles this Sunday morning, we are ready for our next state and the next phase of our trip—Southern Utah. I call it "Southern Utah," because it is different from Utah itself. Utah is one thing; Southern Utah is something else. Its deep canyons, red rock boulders, high buttes and alpine landscapes are like nowhere else on Earth.

My first exposure to Southern Utah was when I read Edward Abbey's *Desert Solitaire* when I was a college student in Northwestern Ohio. In it, Abbey wrote about the two summers he worked as a park ranger in Arches National Monument (now Arches National Park) around 1957. He wrote about the desert in ways that evoked a place teeming with life and beauty where I imagined there was neither. Later, in *The Journey Home,* Abbey further recounts his deep feelings about this place:

> Despite the best efforts of a small array of writers, painters, photographers, scientists, explorers, Indians, cowboys, and wilderness guides, the landscape of the Colorado Plateau lies still beyond the reach of reasonable words. Or unreasonable representation. This is the landscape that has to be seen to be believed, and even then, confronted directly by the senses, it strains credulity. Comprehensible, yes. Perhaps nowhere is the basic structure of the earth's surface so clearly, because so nakedly, revealed. And yet—when all we know about it is said and measured and tabulated, there remains something in the soul of the place, the spirit of the whole, that cannot be fully assimilated by the human imagination. The land here is like a great book or a great symphony; it invites approaches toward comprehension on many levels, from all directions.

Having been born and raised an Ohio "flatlander," I found his descriptions of this land hard to imagine. Vistas as far as the eye could see. Colors the depth of a rainbow. Knowing little about this part of the nation, I pulled out my trusty Rand McNally atlas to get a little perspective.

Turning my sights to Southern Utah, I found Moab just below what was then US 50 and is now I-70. Just above Moab was Arches National Park, Abbey's ranger home. Then, I scanned the rest of the map, west and south of Moab. I found Canyonlands National Park just southwest of Arches, Natural Bridges National Monument below it, and then, Glen Canyon National Recreation Area below that. All around these parks and monuments, names of other natural features like Cataract Canyon, Waterpocket Fold, Kaiparowits Plateau, and the Vermillion Cliffs dotted the map. There were more "points of interest" than towns or roads. Moving my eyes further west I located Capitol Reef National Park, Dixie National Forest, Bryce Canyon National Park, Cedar Breaks National Monument, and Zion National Park. My imagination started to race. I looked at the towns and at the roads and realized that both were few and far between. Knowing that this was the country that Abbey had described in *Desert Solitaire*, I knew that the flatness of the page I was poring over was deceiving. With names accompanied by descriptions like plateau, mountain, canyon, and cliff, I knew that this part of the world must be something else to see and visit. I was looking forward to doing just that one day. Little did I realize that ten years later, I would be married and living in Salt Lake City, only a few hours away from these wonders.

When we married in 1993, Peggy was just finishing graduate school in Salt Lake City and I was working in southern Indiana. We had a choice of she moving to Indiana or me moving to Salt Lake. We chose Salt Lake. Excited to get to know some of Abbey's country, we started to explore Southern Utah.

On our first trip south, we went to Moab and hiked on red rock trails high above the Colorado River. I remember sitting on a cliff overlooking Canyonlands National Park. We could see forever—breathtaking. During that same trip, we got ourselves lost in the Fiery Furnace and the red sandstone formations of Arches National Park.

On our next trip, we went to Bryce Canyon to cross-country ski on trails above splendidly eroded spires of red, orange, and yellow sandstone. On our way back to Salt Lake we took the scenic route past Calf's Creek, north of Escalante, and hiked through its magnificent canyon, passing petroglyphs along the way before reaching a sparkling waterfall at the trail's end. Above us was the "hogsback" road, Highway 12 on the maps. It's a winding, cliff-hugging, spine-tingling labyrinth of a road, if there ever was one.

In the spring of 1996, prior to our bicycle trip, we drove through the midsection of Capitol Reef National Park on the only road for miles, a dirt road called the Burr Trail. We traveled its many switchbacks down into the Waterpocket Fold. The National Park brochure that we picked up described this fold as a "spectacular, eroded jumble of colorful cliffs, massive domes, soaring spires, stark monoliths, twisting canyons, and graceful arches." The aerial picture that they show of it in the guide looks like a surreal watercolor painting of a long, long row of green, brown, gray, and red dominoes stacked on end for miles and miles. Later, we hiked through "the Narrows," an amazing canyon that closes in between 1,000-foot sheer cliff walls. It was like walking through downtown Manhattan, minus the traffic.

Between these southern excursions we enjoyed the anticipation of exploring more of this measureless place. Of getting ourselves lost in its vastness. Of getting away from it all.

During the summer of 1996, President Clinton was gearing himself up for a re-election campaign. Unknown to all but a few of his staffers, the president had been busy planning a "Grand" announcement. On September 18, 1996, while we were focused on riding the Rockies, he and Vice President Gore announced the creation of the Grand Staircase-Escalante National Monument, a 1.7-million acre tract of canyon lands in Southern Utah. Using the powers of the Presidency and the Antiquities Act, Clinton declared this place a national treasure, saying, "Our parents and grandparents saved the Grand Canyon for us. Today, we will save the grand Escalante Canyons and the Kaiparowits Plateau of Utah for our children." With the stroke of his pen these beautiful lands were now protected for years to come. They were also "on the map." A new place to visit and say you've "been there." No doubt, this national attention aroused a lot of curiosity over these lands, once billed as "desolate," "inhospitable," and "barren." Much like "Wall Drug," "Rock City," "Disneyland" and "Six Flags," this place has now become a destination.

Tom Till, a photographer who specializes in canyon landscapes, described Utah as "the world's most beautiful place," in the epilogue to his book *Utah, a Centennial Celebration*. He adds, however, that in proclaiming it "the most beautiful place," he may be doing a great injustice to the land "because of the hordes who may be drawn there by such talk."

And so, Peggy, Mark, and I ready ourselves for six days of riding through the exceptional beauty of Southern Utah. Checking our map, I note that, even though we had planned our route months before Clinton's announcement, we will be riding through the northern boundary of Grand Staircase-Escalante National Monument, along Highway 12 outside of Escalante. I imagine Rand McNally is already busy updating their maps, sandwiching this new "point of interest" between Capitol Reef and Bryce Canyon National Parks.

Mark is about to crawl out of his skin. He's been up since 6am, dressed, packed, and ready to go. He's excited to finally have an opportunity to get on the road with us. Yesterday's eight-block ride from the railway station to our hotel didn't do much to calm his anxiousness; it only served to intensify it. Peg and I—the veterans of the road—lag behind, but we are looking forward to this leg of the trip, too—a week of riding through the canyons of southern Utah. Besides that, today is Peggy's 33rd birthday, and we have our sights set on a celebration at Eddie McStiff's microbrewery in Moab. So we pull ourselves out of bed and start day number 38 of our trip.

Ten miles out of Grand Junction, we stop for breakfast at the local diner in Fruita. It's Sunday and this place is definitely the spot to be. We know the food will be good because the parking lot is full of both beat-up old pickup trucks and brand-new Cadillacs. The local diner—one of America's last great melting pots.

Peggy and I sit down and order our usual—French toast, coffee, and orange juice—without even looking at the menu. It takes

Mark longer to decide what he wants. We joke about the fact that we should have told him to go out for breakfast a few times before the trip so he would know what a biker's breakfast was all about. Anyway, he settles on a waffle, coffee, and juice. We eat up and check the map to see what our day will bring.

Fruita appears to be the last real town on the map before we reach the end of Colorado, about 20 miles west. Mark wants to see the rest of our route, so I give him a hard time because that means I'll have to go out and dig the rest of my Utah maps out of my panniers. He has my curiosity going, and even though I've looked at the Utah segment of the trip dozens of times, I figure another look is in order.

Besides calling me "Sweatboy" and "Gadgetman," Peggy has given me another nickname for the trip—"Mapman." She loves to tease me about all the maps I'm carrying and how I'm always looking for a better one. Before the trip, I searched high and low to get as detailed a map of every state as possible. Road atlases and the maps that the states give you are fine if you are in a car, but on a bicycle, you're always looking for an alternative route, something paved that will take you off the beaten path. I was able to purchase DeLorme maps of quite a few of the states we would be traveling through. DeLorme maps are great because they are on a scale that shows you every road in every county, even the dirt ones. Using them came in handy when we were riding through upstate New York, Ohio, Illinois, and Colorado, the four states they had available before the trip. For the rest of the country, we've had to rely on highway maps and whatever local maps we could find.

DeLorme has a map available for Utah, too. I bought one and shipped it ahead to Jenny and Tom's in Colorado. There, I cut out the pages we would need for the Utah segment of our trip. However, the thing about Utah is that an atlas *is* good enough if you're touring on a bicycle, because the roads down south are so few and far between. Rand McNally even shows the dirt ones on their map. I still like the DeLorme maps better, because they show elevations and contours, unlike an atlas. The contours give a cyclist some idea of the grades and climbs ahead. Big atlases don't do much in the way of letting you know what kind of terrain you will be going through. The editors of these maps probably don't worry much about that anyway, because, to people in cars, steep grades and high mountain passes only mean that they'll have to do a little downshifting, brake a little more, and possibly get a little worse gas mileage. Long, steep grades mean a whole lot more to bicyclists.

So we look at the Utah map. Adding up the mileage between the dots on the map I count about 90 miles between Fruita and Moab, and not much in between but dry desert. Realizing this, we drink one last cup of coffee and head west. Fortunately, it's late September and the weather is fairly cool for this part of the desert—cool enough that as we leave the diner at about 9:30am, we're all still wearing our windbreakers to keep warm.

We ride old US 6, which parallels Interstate 70 to Utah. We're not totally sure, but from the looks of our map, it appears that we can almost ride all the way to Cisco, Utah, and Highway 128 without having to get on the Interstate. Mark is worried about riding on the Interstate and keeps asking me if I'm sure we won't have to get on it. I'm not sure, but we do the only thing we can do—keep riding.

The old road we're on doesn't have much traffic, which is nice because we're able to ride three-abreast at times. But minus the traffic, it's also minus the maintenance. Not long ago, this road was the main east-west route through western Colorado and eastern Utah, at least until the interstate was put in. Now it's just a remnant of what it was. Its white and yellow lines are now all faded gray, barely distinguishable from each other, while most of the road signs are shot full of buckshot. The shoulder has gone to seed. With grass now growing up between the cracks, we have to ride more towards the middle of the road to avoid the bumps. It's an interesting thing to see, this road being reclaimed by nature. We figure that in a few more years the highway department is either going to have to break down and re-pave it, or they'll just close it off to traffic. We figure the latter is more likely, since the Interstate can handle the locals just as well as this road. Later, I read a good description of this stretch of road in Peggy's journal:

> The road is lizard skin. You can see how the asphalt has been scaling off season after season on this extinct road, drying and falling in chunks in this desert. Arid plants grow only knee-high as the earth splits open for the sun to bake. I feel like I'm on a cookie sheet.
>
> No one passes us and we see nothing but sky and brown, our bikes the only things of color in any direction. I wonder what we might look like from the air, red and blue dots lost in a vacuum while Matchbox cars parallel us a few miles away on sleek highways.
>
> The old highway takes itself back to its beginning, of dried prairie and red soil, letting go of technology, of direct routes to places other than this, and pushing over, on top of itself. The road is proud to be here, rather than over there as we ride, motorless and silent.
>
> We see an eagle, sitting like an old cloak-covered man, shoulders hunched, in the grass. As it flies from awkward beginning to smooth line, the sound of wings is louder than wind blowing through the weeds. It circles twice above us as if giving us a road blessing, then disappears behind a mountainous mound of dirt. We can barely catch our breath.

We stop at a faded old concrete monument that has cracked letters spelling "Utah" engraved into it. We take photos and a break to celebrate our ninth state of the trip, listening only to the silence. If there ever was a West, this is definitely it. Riding slowly across the country, we've had time to assimilate ourselves into places like this. Just like people have to acclimate themselves to altitude, our minds have been given the chance to get used to the wide-open, brown expanses of the West. I can imagine people who just land in a place like this, feeling as if they've been dropped off on the moon. Peggy and I hug next to the monument as Mark takes a photo with a backdrop of brown fading to blue that goes on forever.

Utah's maintenance of US 6 is even less than Colorado's. We find ourselves getting closer to the interstate, too, as our road becomes one lane and then, dirt. We figure that if we have to, we can get over the barbed wire fence and on to I-70. However, the dirt is packed hard and smooth by whomever is still using it, so we keep riding because it's really not that bad. Finally, we wind our way around a hill and are led towards an onramp—the end of the road. We've got no choice but to get on the highway and ride in the breakdown lane. It's not that bad and Mark's fears are subdued.

After about 10 miles of riding along the side and being passed at 80 miles an hour by semi-trucks, motorcycles, cars, vans, and RVs, we pull off at exit 212 and head for Cisco—or at least, the Cisco that is on the map. Another 10 miles and one flat tire later, we are disappointed to discover that Cisco is nothing but a bunch of deserted buildings, windows broken out or boarded up, and an old train stop that is no more. So much for a cold Gatorade today. We check the map and see a sign, "Next services 50 miles." It is getting warm, so we quietly turn south, toward the Colorado River and Moab.

Suddenly, we find ourselves amongst a lot of fellow bicyclists. People with shiny new mountain bikes are passing us and waving. The only thing is, they aren't riding these bikes; they're driving Volkswagen vans, Honda Civics, and Jeeps, all with their bikes attached to racks. We figure that they are all coming from a weekend of riding the mountainbike trails around Moab.

Moab is the self-proclaimed mountain bike Mecca of the world. The popularity of its Slickrock Trail has lead 120,000 riders to attempt to do its 12.7-mile loop over Navajo Sandstone each year. I note to Peggy and Mark that we're on mountain bikes ourselves, but the only "slicks" we'll be seeing in Moab will be our tires, not trails. It's a strange dichotomy, seeing all of these bicycles pass us, but we're the only people actually riding them. But, even though everyone else is driving a vehicle instead of riding their bicycles, we feel their camaraderie as they move over to give us more room and honk their horns as they pass. Peggy says, "It's great to be in bike-friendly country."

Without much notice—other than seeing its cliffs in the distance—we find ourselves amidst the red rock canyons of the Colorado River. We proceed to ride through 30 miles of the most spectacular scenery we have witnessed yet on our trip. The road follows the river, and I get worn out filming video and juggling the camera in and out of my bag. Mark and Peggy ride on ahead, discussing in awe the sites all around. Later, Peggy illustrates this segment:

> Monuments of rock, like prayers cast out to the blazing sun, rise into wrinkled hands. The river is a liquid snake through the rock, sliding south on its brown belly, shedding skin on its sandy banks, where two sets of footprints walk off into the cottonwoods.
>
> The canyon walls pull us deeper into the earth and we are covered by frozen tidal waves on either side, cooled in their shade. We stop to take lots of photographs of the snow-capped LaSalle Mountains in the distance, fronted by the red spires of Fisher Towers, all next to the raging Colorado. We immerse ourselves in the splendor.

Despite the beauty, we feel a bit down by the time we hit the 90-mile mark. We are getting baked by the heat of the sun, magnified by the canyon walls. Even Mark's enthusiasm is a bit hushed. Fifteen miles later, we pull into Moab and dive into the coolers of the first convenience store we come to. Then it's off to our hotel and to McStiff's for dinner and some brews. There, we toast Peggy and her birthday, while the staff brings her a free cake and sings "Happy Birthday." We also toast Mark for his first century ride, our third of the trip. Totally spent, we sleep about 10 hours that night and take our time hitting the road the next day.

In the morning I turn to Peggy and make a comment about how well we broke Mark in yesterday. "Yeah, he's in no great rush today, is he?" Peggy says with a laugh. That's fine with all of us. Yesterday was such a treasure and a workout anyway, we're ready for something light. Our destination is Green River, only 55 miles away—at least by the map. Mark drills me at breakfast. "Fifty-five miles—are you sure?" he says, grabbing the map from me. Now I know he's definitely in the groove of the trip.

After breakfast, we amble back to our hotel and sit in the shade of the patio to write some postcards and catch up on a few things. I do my daily check-in with work. When I call them at about 10am things are in full swing. Apparently, a few projects have gone awry over the weekend and I find myself making half a dozen work-related phone calls before we finally hit the road around noon. We bicycle to Green River in the heat of the day.

My mood isn't so great from the touch of reality I've been given by work, and the heat doesn't help. Green River is a welcome sight and we treat ourselves to a room in the brand-new Super 8 with its whirlpool and washers. Even though we are decked out in our cycling regalia, the clerk asks us for our license plate number as we check in. I suppose she is used to seeing a lot of cyclists pass through, but most of them are probably like the ones who passed us going into Moab—"destination" cyclists, who drive hundreds of miles to ride a certain trail or terrain. Anyway, Peggy responds to the question the way she has done so many times before on this trip: "Schwinn."

Peggy

A sign just like the one we saw heading to Moab says, "No services for 60 miles," as we leave Green River, heading toward Hanksville. No 7-Elevens, no Quick Stops, no Circle Ks, no conveniences of any kind, anywhere, as long as we're on this road. In a car, you think vaguely about flat tires and radiator problems; on bikes, you just deal with it. We're single-file nomads, spacing ourselves along the breakdown lane of I-70 as we coast over the asphalt waves of highway with our heads down, our thoughts our own. Mark has his rosary beads out on his handlebar ahead of us and I watch as he says his prayers for the day, the beads swinging as trucks pass us. He says his prayers every day, touching each bead in succession, and I think of his dedication.

This is the perfect place to pray. Not out of fear, but for the space that surrounds you in muted browns and grays. I've never liked to pray in church, those rote prayers that everyone mumbles along, the same words that occasionally make sense, but usually feel robotic, turning the pages all together and kneeling and standing on cue. There, I just go on automatic pilot and my prayers seem not my own. Praying for me is more like a tuneless song, humming along to the flashes of pain and happiness that flow in and out of a person's life, and directing the notes inward. Out here, on this unserviceable highway, I think about Mark's description of Saint Rita—the patron saint of the impossible—and I try to picture her, sitting in a dried-out garden along this road, trying to make flowers grow. I start talking to her—or at least have a one-sided conversation with her. I'm praying, I guess.

"It seems almost impossible, Rita, that we're already in the West and we haven't been hit by any cars. Thank you for watching over us—that is, if you do watch over people riding their bikes across the country."

I look back at Brian and he's filming us riding ahead of him. He smiles at me and points ahead.

"And Rita, if you had anything to do with me meeting Brian ... maybe you were playing bridge with my Grandma Margaret or Brian's Grandma Bea up in heaven one day because you were bored and you all decided that Brian and I should meet in Chicago ... thank you for letting me meet Brian."

In the distance, it looks like the world was flipped upside down for one second, then flipped back up again. Fins and spikes appear in the rocks, looking like the backs of dinosaurs. I guess that's what Brian is filming and pointing at—the San Rafael Swell. I've driven past this place many times on this same highway in the car, but I never noticed how beautiful it is, like a glimpse of history outside the pages of the book. In that car, I was probably road blind, not seeing anything on the sides of me, only what was in front. Winnebagos and trucks hauling gasoline speed past us through the center of those rocks and I wonder if the people in them know that they are driving through a visual time line. Rocks seem to walk toward us as the clouds cast shadows on and off the layers of red, yellow, pink, and brown, creating the illusion of movement. A hawk soars above one of the ridge peaks, then disappears behind the sculpted back of the Swell. This place is silent to the ear, loud to the eye.

"Thank you, Rita, for making this view possible and for making me slow down on the bicycle so I can appreciate it for once. Maybe you can convince the 'big guys' up there in heaven to start a gas crisis so we all have to walk and ride bikes more and notice things instead of rushing around getting there, going fast, passing through..."

Mark stops up ahead and I pull up next to him. His rosary is still out. "Did you finish your rosary?"

"You can never be finished with your rosary. That's why it's in the form of circle," he explains.

I guess the rosary is like this land. To people who don't know the land, who aren't familiar with it, the rocks look finished, passed over, having no purpose. But to others, this land is a circle of time, never finished with itself. Rocks come up from the earth for a little air, only to be eroded and knocked back down by the endless cycles of wind and rain.

We eventually turn south from the Swell and off of I-70, onto Route 24—a road that looks like the one the Roadrunner *beep-beeps* down when he's running away from Wile E. Coyote. It's straight, it goes on forever, and we are all alone. I can almost see Wile E. hiding on top of a butte with dynamite. I start singing the Roadrunner Song as Mark pops up and down on his bicycle seat, shouting, "Beep! Beep!" Too much talk with Saint Rita and the rosary makes a person need to blow off the steam of solemnity.

We ride in the middle of the road since we can see for miles in either direction. The only signs of humanity we see are bungee cords, sprung off in various bright colors along the side of the road. Brian says they must pop off of all the tarps that people strap on their boats on their way south to Lake Powell. He starts picking a few up because "you never know when you can use them."

The road goes over a butte and we stop to eat some cookies we bought way back in Green River, when we had stores and people around us. Without any warning, another biker passes us, waving. He's a tiny Japanese man on a racing bike. Everything is tied onto the back of his bike—sleeping bag, tent, various items of clothing, water bottles, hats, books, maps. He's also wearing a large backpack.

"He doesn't have any granny gears!" Brian is amazed as he describes the kind of bike the man is on. "That's a racing bike—look at how thin those tires are. I bet he gets a lot of flats."

"He doesn't have anyone with him."

"He looks like he's 12."

We eventually catch up with him again on another butte. Through broken translations and hand signals, we find out that he flew over here from Japan, that he's all alone and wanted to see desert. He's been riding from Flagstaff and is heading to Cedar City where he is going to catch a train back to Los Angeles and then a flight to Japan. Brian asks him if he gets any flats and the man doesn't understand but smiles and shakes his head, as if in agreement, nonetheless. We all smile at each other and look around, eating Power Bars. We're amazed that he's here all alone, cannot speak English well, and he's on a racing bike. He must know Saint Rita very well.

Temple Mountain, Factory Butte, Henry Mountains, Gopher Rock, Goblin Valley—we peer at them through viewfinders at one of those scenic lookouts along the highway. Brian gets the video camera out and zooms in on each point of interest. Then, he pulls out his map and rattles off the distances we can see counterclockwise, all around us— the red-rock hoodoos of Goblin Valley, 10 miles to the north; the castle-like brown turret of Factory Butte, 30 miles to the west; the green and yellow aspens of Boulder Mountain, 55 miles to the southwest; the snow-capped granite peaks of the Henry Mountains, 60 miles to the south; and what looks like a big mound of dirt, but is actually Navajo Mountain, 100 miles to the southeast.

I peer over Brian's shoulder at the map to get some perspective on what he is talking about. The map is full of names of places like all the other maps we've been using on our trip. The difference is that names like The Big Flat Top, Table Mountain, Bull Creek Pass, Coyote Benches, Purple Hills, Waterpocket Fold, Ragged Mountain, and Impossible Peak aren't for towns, but for prominent features in the landscape; places to use for orientation in this Great Wide Open. Turning away from the map I look again at the sights. To tell you the truth, I'd rather just look at them without knowing the names. Names only try to describe what is really indescribable. Looking out, I realize that the only thing separating me and the great distances between these natural wonders is the wind.

We get back on our bicycles and start south again. I feel like we're riding on the bottom of the sea; it's been drained and we are the only things left beside the hidden treasures inside the mountains around us. We are lone fish, out of our element, separated from our school. I can see how people become crazy in the desert—your mind becomes loose and wild.

When we get to Hanksville, it's an oasis of shade. Three motels beckon us with their shaded porches; we choose the most modern one, since the other two have chained-up dogs barking within pens that used to surround swimming pools. The only convenience store is built inside a huge rock and is creatively called the Hole in the Rock Store. Tee shirts advertising the store's name are the priority purchase here, as we grab large Gatorades and Mark photographs us coming out of the rock.

We relax in the shade of the motel's porch and swig beers, glad to be out of the sun. After a few minutes two English women drive up and are in the room next to us.

"This is where I belong," one says as the other agrees. "The sun just soaks into my bones." We sit on the porch together, five people staring at the sun reflected on hot rocks, as cars with boats headed toward Lake Powell speed past.

There's nothing better than finding the only restaurant in town and getting there before the Winnebago crowd. All three of us order the pork chop dinner for $4.95. We eat the kind of yeast rolls we haven't had since grade school cafeteria lunches. With melted butter on the rolls and on real mashed potatoes, we are in desert heaven. Brian notices our Japanese friend paying for dinner. His costs $8.95. He must've had the steak dinner—big spender. We wave at each other, and as he crosses the street to his campground, he almost looks like he's skipping, his feet light as his arms wave back and forth with carefree ease.

Later, Brian and I stand behind our motel as a sunset spreads over us like a psychedelic tablecloth, pinks swirling into purples as the sun melts into distant Boulder Mountain. As quickly as it comes, it goes, but we stand there anyway, as the drying grasses blow. Back in the room, Mark tells us that he just found out that there have been three deaths in his family this week, two unexpected: an uncle, a baby niece, and a cousin. We give him some time and space so he can make some phone calls home to his loved ones. He eventually joins us outside and we all sit and look west, our faces holding the last of the light, our thoughts turning to the heavens.

Capital Reef is one of Utah's national parks that is often overlooked. Most people think of it as a place to drive through between their tours of Arches and on their way to Bryce and Zion. It's a long park; it's boundaries stretch over 80 miles north to south, but only about 15 miles east to west. The main highway through the park takes the east-west route along the Fremont River, so going through in a motor vehicle can be done in a short time. But in doing so, you can easily overlook some of the pockets of beauty hidden just off the road. On bicycles, our view is unrestricted by windshields and blind spots, so we are able to notice these treasures while the traffic whizzes by.

The beauty of Capital Reef is in its uniqueness, from the moon-rock grayness east of the park where silence is so loud it rings your ears, to the sounds of waterfalls ricocheting off its towering inner canyon walls, to the green splendor of the Sulfur Creek Canyon just past the west entrance. In a car, you curve past these secret pockets and miss the surprise of rounding a corner to find dripping green oases, or sliding lizards following the moving shadows.

We stop our bikes at almost every other turn on the road, finding these secrets thanks to our slow pace. A sunken waterfall, hidden from the road, sprays its triangle of blue over moss-covered rocks. We hike down to the spray, our heads the only thing visible from the road. A Winnebago cruises by and the driver has a video camera in one hand and the steering wheel in the other. He films the road and probably our mist-shrouded heads while his wife sleeps, her cheek smashed against the passenger window. These people are witnessing life through a viewfinder, capturing only the images directly in front of their camera, experiencing nothing. What's their hurry? Maybe they are late for a tour of Arches and are cruising with that "Gotta go, gotta get there" attitude. Sometimes I wonder why they don't just rent the video and save the hassle of driving.

"I know what kind of business I should get into," Brian quips. "I'll hire myself out to people and they can give me their video cameras and I'll go to faraway exotic places like Yellowstone and the Grand Canyon and I'll shoot the film for them. Since they don't see these places till they get home anyway, it would sure make vacationing a whole lot easier." Turning my gaze down to the water, I notice a fish as it's scales shine in a patch of sun and think that maybe it's better to see life sideways, rather than straight on. You can miss a lot by just seeing what's ahead rather than what's next to you.

We have a hefty, long climb out of the park, and when we finally get to Torrey, the sky is looking bruised, black and blue, as the wind files through the huge cottonwoods. Luckily, we are near the Chuckwagon Motel. The owner of the motel likes to tell stories of the road as he checks you in. We know, because Brian and I have stayed here before when we've come down to do some exploring in the area.

"In the '60s, hitchhiking was the way to go. If you had to take off, you just did, just started walking and sticking the thumb out and off you went, wherever you took yourself off to. Didn't have any responsibilities, just myself, and I met some wild cats along the way, most of the time in parks or just off the highway when I'd crash for the night. Thinking back to then, I guess I'd have to say I was happiest, learning from the road and taking what came..."

Even with the ominously blackened sky, we sit in the hot tub as leaves and branches fly into the water and the wind blows waves along the sides of the pool. Mark and Brian buy a 15-pack of Stroh's because it's cheaper than any of the 12-packs and we sit, bubbles massaging our backs, three heads visible in the water. The owner walks past, smiling broadly, shaking his head. We give him a beer and ask if he wants to ride along with us through Utah. "Where would you put me?" he laughs. "I'm a hitcher you know—I don't drive."

That night, we are awakened by thunder and rain leaking in through the windows. At dinner, people had been talking about snowstorms and hail in the forecast and how they were going to drive over Boulder Mountain. "But the colors will be so beautiful... we can't miss them—we'll just bundle up in the car and deal with it," we heard one woman say.

Looking ahead to tomorrow's ride up Boulder Mountain's 9,500-foot summit and the weather report I think back to last week's climb over Independence Pass. I tell Brian and Mark that mountain passes must like to test us.

The next morning we stock up on Gatorade and Fig Newtons and Snickers bars at the Top Stop in Torrey. The day is blustery and a group of Winnebago drivers in plaid polyester pants look nervous. And angry. The line to the gas pumps is long and tempers are short.

"What? Are you stupid? Move this car! We gotta get gas!" One Winnebago man shouts at a perplexed German couple with a baby in backpack. "Marge, can you believe how stupid people can be?" he shouts to his bright pink-lipped wife, who ignores him.

The German couple moves their car and drives off, looking over their shoulders.

The Winnebago men smoke cigarettes and throw the butts—still lit—on the pavement. "We gotta get moving. We gotta make it to Zion before all the good camp sites are taken. Can you believe that stupid idiot, taking all the time in the world to pay for his gas?"

"Can you believe how *rude* people in Winnebagos can be?" I had to say something—I guess I get a little feisty with a lot of coffee.

The Winnebago men look at me, scowling. They probably don't trust me, since I don't wear bright pink lipstick and I'm not buying gas. It's too bad our Japanese friend, who we saw ride into Torrey late last night, isn't here. He'd be able to see some modern-day gunslingers; the only difference is they're riding Winnebagos instead of horses.

The sun illuminates the canyons of Capital Reef below us, as Boulder Mountain remains dark. A sign says "8% grade next 10 miles" as we ride past scrubby oak, their roots exposed on crumbling rock. "The Winnebagos are coming—*over*," Brian commands. Like bandits holding the road for ransom, the Winnebago Men blaze past us, three in a row. We ride on the white line, our hands holding fast to our handlebars, the sandy breakdown lane our only other alternative. A lawn chair strapped to the back of one Winnebago almost knocks me off my bike, but I persevere, my water bottle ready to shoot at the rear window if I have to. The air is filled with electricity and exhaust as the Winnebagos shift down to get up the mountain grade and they are gone. Everything is good in our world again.

Spinning up the hill in tiny granny gears, we hear some distant tinkling of bells and some crashing in the brush. An angry "Moo!" explodes from behind a tree and we are suddenly in the midst of a roundup. Bulls saunter around as their hefty heifers follow. Cowboys shout in Spanish as Australian shepherds bark; the cows look pissed. They'd rather be munching up in the high meadows than down on this road with a bunch of bikers. We pass the cows, noticing how much nicer they are than the Winnebago Men—and not in nearly as big a hurry, either.

The aspen are the color of Halloween pumpkins and the leaves wave in the stiff breeze coming up from the desert floor. Capital Reef looks surreal, the multi-hued rocks shining like jewels. The sun seems to light the Reef from within as it hides from the storm brewing above our heads. A low-lying cloud covers the road ahead of us and within minutes we are getting pounded with hail. We hide in a cattle cart, left open to await the cowboys and their cattle drive. The hail explodes on the roof.

After the hail stops and the rain begins, cowboys in chaps and dripping 10-gallon hats laugh at us as our shoes leak rain. I really can't see, but we point our bicycles upward toward the summit as Brian insists on stopping for photos, then downward, sprays of water fanning out behind our rear tires. It's freezing as we descend the mountain, even with polypropylene layers, but I have a smile on my face. There's something about your cheeks being frozen that makes you smile crazy clown smiles while your eyes tear up.

Near the bottom of the mountain we run into the biggest cattle drive of them all—there must be 500 cows ambling down the highway. Cars are backed up waiting to get through as we squeeze past them. A guy who looks every bit the Marlboro Man waves us through, saying, "Don't worry 'bout these cows, they won't hurt you. They're dumber than your thumbnail."

So we weave ourselves through the mass of bovine. When we finally arrive in Boulder, we resemble frozen Frankensteins, our arms stiff in front of us, our legs squeaking and leaking water, our crazy red faces and white lips. The Boulder Lodge gives us a huge room and we spend what seems like hours warming the cold out of our bones in the shower. We use their laundry machines and drink the rest of our Stroh's as the sun powers back into the sky and all clouds disappear. We feel like the storm was just a figment of our imagination as the ground dries up and we walk around in shorts and tee shirts.

I wait out by the entrance to the Lodge. Karen, our friend who has kindly been housesitting for us during our trip, is driving our 4-Runner down here to accompany us the rest of the way to San Francisco. She's also bringing Miss Lyla Lou Lou, our yellow Labrador retriever, and I can hardly wait. When I see our red truck pull in, Lyla is in her usual position, sitting in the passenger seat, her nose out the window. She jumps out and runs around, doing circles, wagging her tail and sniffing us. As she piles into my lap, Karen pours us some wine. Through all of the commotion, a warm feeling emerges, and again, I have a crazy clown smile on my face. This time, it doesn't take hail and rain to make it appear—I've found another moment of perfect place.

The next day we find ourselves riding on the "Hogsback" road. We ride breathlessly as we hang on a ridge between Escalante's deep canyons. Any type of order to this land is taken back by the harshness of solid rock ridged into deep crevices, the earth tucking itself into creases and pockets. The windblown ledges on either side take your breath away and fling it across to the trees that are barely hanging onto boulders. My skin prickles as I imagine sliding off this butte, this tiny strip of asphalt over mountain, my bike and I in flight, like the hawks that soar and disappear above. The sun rises along the waves of rock and Brian rides with the camera clicking away, recording Clinton's new monument. This place makes a huge statement in an elder's voice; with its newfound federal protection, perhaps its words can be heard.

Winnebagos arrive—they are scenery vultures, trying to capture the monuments and parks in quick bites, scavenging through images from one scenic overlook to the next. They edge us off the road, but they can only stop where the road allows them. With our bikes, we stop on the edges of cliffs, where the scene is secret and silent and uniquely ours.

We ride through the valley of Dixie National Forest and stop at a sign describing Native Americans in this region. In the distance, we see our Japanese friend pedaling along, his neck craning up to look at the cliffs and evergreen trees on red rock. We invite him over for a snack and begin our haphazard conversation.

"Beautiful ... " I wave my hands over my head and smile.

"Yeah ... " He waves his hands over his head and smiles. He looks at the sign and the picture of a Native American weaving a basket. He looks confused because there aren't any Native Americans weaving baskets in the fields around us or in the woods.

"They lived here a long time ago." Brian tries to explain the sign to him, but our friend just looks past us to the woods.

"Where are you going today?" Mark asks, pointing down the road.

Our friend points at Bryce National Park and wipes his forehead in mock exhaustion. We all laugh as we share Power Bars and Fig Newtons.

We take off again as he lies down in the grass, his face a picture of contentment. The west must seem so open, so quiet to him, but he doesn't seem worried or fearful. He fits into the land, laying down and exploring the space around him by closing his eyes.

Just as we are getting used to the flat, rolling valley, we start to rise again as we head toward Powell's Peak. Our granny gears click in as we slowly wind ourselves up the incline and at the top, we sit on wooden railings and stare at the exposed precipice in the distance. Red layers fall into yellows, pinks, and whites as time whittles her designs in gray rock. Our Japanese friend arrives and we all wave our hands around over our heads and smile.

Leaving Dixie National Forest, we shoot down a long canyon into what we call Mud Meadow—everything is brown, parched, and thirsty looking. The river is melted chocolate, trees are brown and dead, and dirt blows around in our faces. This land probably holds the remains of dinosaurs, buried under layers of crusted earth; it's like a graveyard without any tombstones.

In Tropic, we begin to see green again as red sand castles above us designate Bryce Canyon. Our Japanese friend huffs next to us, his lean body spent from a day riding high elevations and staring full force at kaleidoscopic beauty. When we tell him we are heading up to Bryce, pointing directly overhead to the ridge, he shakes his head and says, "No more!" I could stop here too, but I know that we have a cabin inside the park and I just want to sit on the front porch and stare at one object, mesmerized.

We have one final climb on the way into the park. How do I know? Gadgetman has his trusty altitude watch and computer odometer. By the time we make it through the traffic to our cabin in Bryce, my head is reeling from his numbers, but Brian is grinning from ear to ear over our accomplishments for the day. "Even though we didn't do any summits," he says, "we climbed 6,000 feet today—and we did 81 miles, too." Okay with me; I'm just happy we had the foresight to reserve a cabin by the rim of Bryce Canyon.

Our cabin reminds me of the family cabin we had in Maine—wooden beams, stone fireplace, polyester bedspreads with bright yellow and orange flowers, a dripping shower—a perfect place to throw your legs up and lean into a chair as you watch squirrels on pine trees. In Maine, we had a lake to jump into. Here, it seems, we have a landscape to leap into. With the melting sun as the paintbrush, deep reds and golds are lightly stroked by translucent pink, the canvas a moving sunset causing rock to slide slowly into shadow.

The next morning, we watch the sunrise. Not at Sunrise Point, but at our own little place along the canyon rim. People race to pull sleepy-eyed children up to the designated point of land where you are "supposed" to watch the sun rising up while we nurse cups of steaming coffee, witnessing the same event from a different angle. The sun arches over Powell's Peak and the tops of the Hoodoos, dislodging the shadows. If Mom were here, she'd be standing by the rim, cigarette in one hand and coffee in the other, singing "Morning Has Broken" or some Girl Scout song.

June

Bob and I figured that we should make one last trip to the library to check up on Peggy and Brian's progress before our flight to California. When we got to the library we found out that our friend Jackie wasn't there to help us out. Another assistant in the computer department said that she was out taking an exam for one of her college courses but that he would be happy to help us. To my surprise I declined, suddenly confident that we could manage on our own. Bob and I sat down at one of the available computers and were able to get all of Peggy and Brian's trip up on the screen without anyone's help.

We spent most of our time looking at all of the new photos, especially the ones of Colorado. There were a lot of pictures of Peggy holding the flowers I sent for her birthday.

"Look at that, Bob—even at the Continental Divide," I said, pointing to their photo by the sign on Independence Pass. "See, I told you that she would like them."

Bob just mumbled something under his breath, like he always does when I do something impractical that works out. Later, coming back from the bathroom, I caught him chuckling at that same photo again and he finally agreed that I was right. Then he clicked on their itinerary. The map showed that they were heading into Utah.

"Utah," I said. "Boy, I remember that state well. How beautiful it was. We didn't do much bicycling there, but we sure found other ways to get around to see a lot of it."

Back home, I pulled out my journal and photos to reflect on that portion of the trip.

Teri and I spent three days relaxing in Salt Lake City. While we were there we did our best to take in all the required tourist attractions: We visited the Mormon Church's Temple Square; floated in briny Salt Lake; rode roller coasters at the Saltaire and Lagoon amusement parks; took in a couple of movies, including the Disney classic, *Fantasia*; and listened to the Tabernacle Choir practice on Thursday night. The choir practice was a highlight for me. I just sat there in the pew, closed my eyes and drifted on the melodies of all those voices singing in unison. It was so good it brought a tear to my eyes. But that didn't deter us from enjoying some of life's wilder pleasures, for later that evening Teri and I went dancing at the Saddle Club with a couple of men who worked in a silver mine. We didn't get back to our hotel room until 5am the next morning.

We started riding south again on August 31. Our AYH itinerary read: "Either take train from Salt Lake City to Cedar City or take Routes 89 and 67 down to Grand Canyon." Then, they had a gap of five days to allow "traveling time to Bryce, Zion, and the Grand Canyon." We opted to try and ride our bicycles out of Salt Lake instead of taking the train. It wasn't long before we hit a major construction zone. A truck driver picked us up and gave us a 40-mile ride to Springville where we spent the night camping out in the City Park.

We made it to Bryce the next day thanks to another ride from another truck driver and then one with a Navy pilot who drove us all the way to the entrance of Bryce. It was late by the time we settled into our campsite, so we hadn't even seen the canyon itself yet. What we did see was a beautiful clear sky full of stars. They were so lovely we decided to sleep under them right out in the open.

That night turned out to be a chilly one, so we didn't have any trouble getting up early to catch the sunrise. It was worth it, as my journal describes:

> *Sunday, September 2, 1956:* We got to the top of the canyon just in time to sit down and watch the sun peak over the distant hills and light the beautiful formations in the canyon. What a feeling to see it this way, for the first time—all alone in the park at sunrise. It was breathtaking. We hiked about 5 miles down

through the red cliffs and formations and it was really a thrill. After that, we packed our gear and rode through the lovely Red Canyon.

From the Red Canyon, we hitched a ride with a couple from California all the way to Zion National Park, about 65 miles away.

We didn't stay long sightseeing in Zion because we got a ride with the mailman early in the morning to the Grand Canyon's North Rim. Most people are familiar with the Grand Canyon from the south side, with its red rock and wide-open vistas. Across the way is the North Rim, a more remote place and about 1,000 feet higher in elevation than the South Rim. It's a whole different kind of place, and a lovely one, too. I wrote in my journal how surprised I was to see so many trees during our long drive into the park. I wrote, "The park road was lovely, we drove through green pinion pine trees, white birch, and aspens, some of which were changing color. This wasn't the landscape I had expected from photos I've seen of the canyon. It didn't look like a desert at all."

The mailman dropped us off at the North Rim's Bright Angel Lodge, one of the beautiful log lodges with vaulted ceilings built during Franklin Roosevelt's administration. Despite its size, being inside this lodge, with its grand fireplaces and stone deck, one has the feeling of cozy comfort, like that of a small cabin. It reminded me of Girl Scout camp.

We hadn't even looked out at the canyon when we walked into the lodge and talked with the manager about getting jobs. He immediately hired us as cabin maids. So, after a quick tour of the building and some lunch, we reported to the linen cabin for duty. I remember that we didn't do much more that first day than fold a few blankets and sheets. Other than that, we mainly sat around until our shift was over and got to know the other cabin maids, who were mostly girls on break from college.

The big bonus of our jobs was the fact that they came with free room and board. Finally, after settling in and having dinner with the other employees, I took off by myself for some quiet contemplation by the canyon's edge.

"At the moment I am sitting on a big rock jutting out over the canyon and the sun is beginning to set," I wrote in my journal. "The clouds in the east are faintly colored in long, narrow strips. As the sun sets, it is surrounded by hazy circles of yellow, orange, and red. As it disappears, the canyon takes on a misty effect and I notice stars faintly coming out. This has certainly been one of the nicest hours I have spent on the trip." And so ended the first day of my weeklong tour of duty as a cabinmaid. The week ahead would prove to be a relaxing, pleasant experience, far away from the rush of packing up and riding to a new destination each day. I really enjoyed it, especially the part where we all got to sing. I fondly recalled that time in my memoir:

> Every morning at ten and every afternoon at two, the bus would beep its horn and we'd drop our toilet brushes and put on our maid's costumes—with the little frilly hat, a green and white gingham and a little white apron—and go out and sing farewell songs to the tourists: "Come back again to Grand Canyon ... "
>
> You know, Bob and I were back there a few years ago and they don't do that anymore. I thought that was kind of sad.

Brian

It was never in our plans for Peggy and me to ride to the Grand Canyon on this particular cross-country trip. We decide to save it for another tour. However, we continue on our way to Zion from Bryce. On our way, we cycle through the red rock tunnels of the Red Canyon, just outside of Bryce, and see some more great sights while riding south on Highway 89. The road follows the Severe River, narrowing at places to form a beautiful canyon with green meadows. The fall colors are starting to come out in all of their splendor, so we enjoy our final day riding with Mark, as he plans to meet some friends in Mount Carmel, just before we reach Zion.

Mark is a bit melancholy about leaving us, in part because it's time for him to go home and be with his family to grieve their lost ones. I try to cheer him up at the hotel where he is meeting his friends by complimenting him on being able to assimilate himself into the ride so well and for doing it all through some of the toughest terrain of the ride. All in all, Mark has ridden 450 miles and climbed nearly 15,000 feet in 7 days of riding with us—no small accomplishment. Nonetheless, we can see it in his eyes that he is ready for more. Maybe another trip, we say. "We still have to make it to the Grand Canyon, you know," we remind him as we pull away from the hotel, our bicycles on top of our 4-Runner.

Since it's late in the day and we want to be sure to get a campground in Zion, we choose to load the bicycles up and drive the 20 miles into Zion with Karen. That's fine with us; we make up for it the next day by riding back into the canyon to see what we missed on our way in.

After camping out under a beautiful clear desert sky, we wake up early and ride all the way back up Zion's canyon to the Narrows in the freshness of the morning. We've beaten the tourists, and it's great to see the park and its high, sculpted cliffs, with so little traffic ... almost solitude.

Zion is the most popular of Utah's national parks. Nearly 2.5 million people visit the park each year, and there is only one road to carry the throng of visitors that descends upon it during tourist season. At the height of this season, traffic lines can extend for miles outside of the park and parking spaces are at a premium. So popular are this and other national parks that the National Park Service is considering a reservation system, or a shuttle service to get people into the park. Apparently, their idea is to bus as many people in as possible, but if someone wants to drive in, they'll have to make a reservation. Fine with me—I think it can only encourage bicyclers like Peggy and myself. To be honest, I think there are a whole lot of people who would like that. An elderly gentleman who passes us in the parking lot of one of the trailheads confirms this thought. "What a great way to see the country," is all he says as he walks by with a smile.

Zion is an awesome place. Unlike Bryce, where you look down at it's beauty from the canyon's edge, in Zion you enter into the bowels of time, surrounded by the high cliff walls cut by years of weathering and the eroding action of the Virgin River. Our two-hour bicycle tour up and down the 10-mile canyon road only touches the surface of what is to be seen.

Brooke Williams is a man who knows this place well, having been a park ranger here in the mid-'70s. He writes, "When I think of Zion, this rock is where my mind takes me: Navajo Sandstone in every color of orange and sometimes white. How solid I feel when I stand there and look out on a world where I feel alive, the wonder and the wet air in my face, the swift breeze cooling my sweaty back and blowing air through the bottom of my lungs." Feeling a bit of Brooke's emotion riding through Zion's misty morning breeze, I tell Peggy that we definitely have to come back. She agrees.

It's about 10am when we reach the park's entrance on our return trip and the tourists are lined up and ready to descend on the park. Riding into Springdale for a late breakfast, we stop counting the number of buses, cars, and RVs that pass us. We'll just call it "lots."

Leaving Springdale, we find ourselves thrust back into the hot, dry, red desert of the west. Complementing the western theme is a real Wild West movie set—or at least that's what the sign says as we pass by this Hollywood mock-up of a small western town outside of Virgin, Utah. Here, for a few dollars, passersby can stop on their way to Utah's national parks and do a bit of play-acting. Visitors can strap on a six-shooter, spurs, and a 10-gallon Stetson hat while doing their best John Wayne or Clint Eastwood imitation. We aren't interested in re-living this myth of the west since it might spoil the week we just spent passing through the real thing, so Peggy and I just pedal by with only my video camera zooming in to visit the dusty brown Main Street. While shooting, I try my best Jesse James impersonation, saying to Peggy, "Don't worry Sheriff Stewart, we'll be outta here by sundown."

Approaching St. George, we are met by Peggy's friend Janet Brown, who lives here. Her boyfriend, Bob, has driven Janet and her daughter Elizabeth out to meet us about 15 miles east of town. Janet is keeping her promise to Peggy to ride with us today. After exchanging hugs and some small talk, our entourage of cyclists is now three again. Janet doesn't quite get into the groove of riding as much as Mark did, but her energy and enthusiasm are certainly his equal. She and Peggy laugh and talk their way to Saint George as I hang back and enjoy the leisurely pace.

That evening, Janet treats us to a wonderful barbecue, fit to please any cyclist: chicken, beef, pasta, potatoes, salad, fruit, corn on the cob, you name it—she had all of the food groups covered. In addition, she provides all the wine and beer we could want to drink. Janet, Bob, Karen, Peggy, and I all sit around until it's very late, reliving the trip so far and celebrating a marvelous week in Utah.

"It's been everything we hoped for and expected," says Peggy when Janet asks how this portion of our trip has been. "Yeah," I add, "If we were doing a documentary, southern Utah would definitely be a whole episode unto itself."

"Yeah, but what about that Monument stuff—weren't the local people down there hostile to tourists?" someone asks.

"You know, I didn't hear one comment about it—no billboards, no protests," I respond. "Come to think of it, from the looks of towns like Escalante and Torrey, you'd of thought they were embracing the idea of another tourist attraction on the map. They had new hotels, shops, and restaurants with menus in English, Japanese, and German."

The conversation shifts to what's ahead for us during the next segment of the trip. We talk a bit about Nevada and California, and about our plan to stray from June's route. We decided long ago that we want to finish our ride in San Francisco, because my sister Andrea lives there, instead of Los Angeles, where June finished in 1956.

"I can't see why June would have gone that way anyway," Janet remarks. "Did she ride her bicycle across the desert to get there?"

"No, they took a train from Las Vegas to Barstow, California," I answer, "but it wasn't much of a fun ride."

"Really, how come?" Janet wonders.

Peggy jumps into the conversation and proceeds to tell the tale of how a near tragedy struck her mother in the desert on the 84th day of her trip.

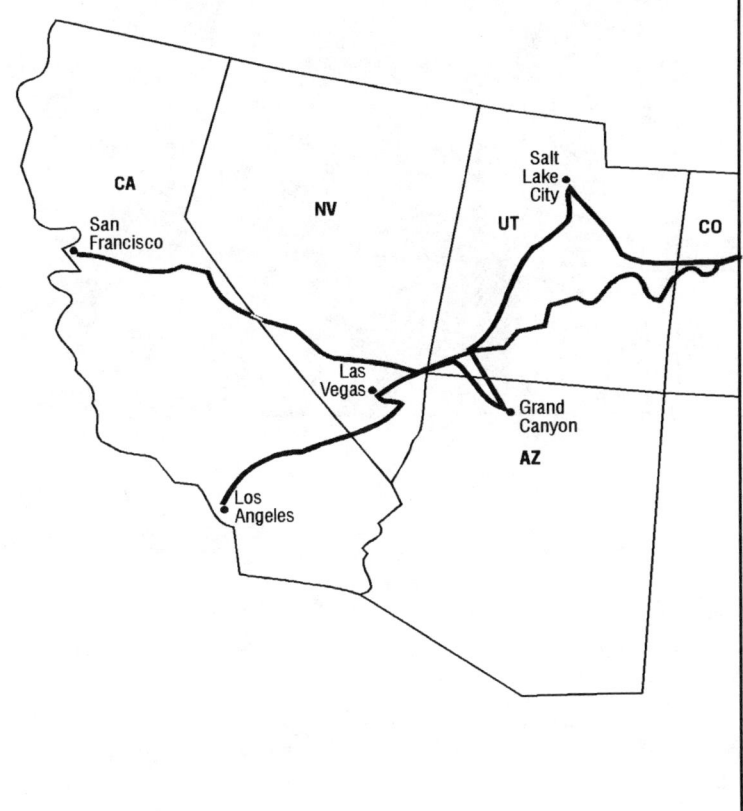

The Adventure of Two Lifetimes
Western Section

━━━━━ 1956 Tour

━━━━━ 1996 Tour

CA

NV

San
Francisco

Salt
Lake
City

UT

CO

Las
Vegas

Grand
Canyon

AZ

Los
Angeles

15

" ... I have been shipwrecked; a night and a day I have been adrift
at sea ... I never lose heart."
        —Paul's letter to the Corinthians 11: 21-33 (from a
prayerbook that June took with her in 1956)

June

After our week as cabinmaids, Teri and I hitched a ride out of the
North Rim on a 5am delivery truck. We stopped at a diner in Kanab,
Utah, for breakfast and then headed up to Cedar Breaks. The beauty
of Bryce's colored spires and the Grand Canyon's awesome depth
had already overwhelmed us, so it was with much surprise that
Cedar Breaks was the loveliest of them all. After a day of wander-
ing and relaxing in its splendor we caught a train from Cedar City to
Las Vegas. We never intended trying to cross Nevada on our bicycles and were quite happy with the alternative transportation,
especially when we looked out the windows and saw nothing but
burnt green-brown hills full of tumbleweed and the occasional cattle
ranch. People? Well, I don't remember seeing any signs of them.
We had plenty of time to look, though, because for some reason
the train puttered along slowly. Teri and I entertained ourselves by
taking trips to the ladies room and smoking.

Finally, we pulled into Las Vegas at 8pm and rode our bicycles
down a great white way that resembled 42nd Street and Broadway.
We stayed in the La Cortez hotel, where we splurged on the package deal of a room, dinner, cocktail, breakfast, and lunch, all for
$15. We didn't know it at the time, but it also included a free pass
to a stripper show. Later on I mentioned to Teri how quickly we

had left the natural wilds of southern Utah and exchanged them for the glossy, glittery wilds of Las Vegas.

We spent the next day hanging around the Vegas strip, going to the Showboat Hotel, and swimming in the pool in the heat of a 109-degree day. After riding uptown to do some errands, we took a nap. I was looking forward to calling my friend Ann Finnigan, but I had a dilemma—should I put all of my quarters in the slot machines or use them to call my best friend? I chose my friend because, even if I won at the slot machine, I knew the rewards of conversation would be much better. And I was right—it was so refreshing to hear Ann's voice and share a laugh and some stories with her. Later, I watched a beautiful sunset dissolve over the desert and then went out to dinner and caught a show. I wrote in my journal that evening that I sure felt good. Little did I know that my good fortune was about to be shattered.

Thursday, September 13, 1956. My journal reads: "Got up too late and started through the desert to Boulder City anyway. We stopped for a drink of ginger ale in the Ranch House and I wish we had never done that. Today was a day I would like to forget."

That was it for that day's entry, one of the shortest of my trip. Turning the pages of my journal, they got even shorter. September 14: "Was shook up." September 15: "Miserable day." September 16: "Swam and then started on that road in the desert to the Ranch House. Jack had to work until 6, so from 12 to 6:45 we sat there. I was furious, tired, and disgusted."

Forty years later and with the distance provided by time and space, I was finally comfortable reliving that horrendous day when I described it in my memoir:

> September 13, 1956, was the worst day of my cross-country bicycle trip and most certainly, the worst day of my life. It started out in the desert between Las Vegas, Nevada, and Lake Mead. It was the 86th day since we had left New York City. Only five more days were left

before reaching our anticipated goal of riding into Los Angeles, California, to complete the trip. This dream almost ended on that September day.

That day the desert temperature was a sizzling 120 degrees. The heat drove us to seek water for our canteens at a bar called The Ranch House. Two men warned us about the dangers of riding in the desert heat and offered to drive us to Lake Mead. We agreed and had a few drinks with them. After touring Hoover Dam, they took us to the Lake Mead Campground for a swim. Teri got out of the car, leaving me alone. Before I had the chance to get out of the car, my "date" pulled the car around and sped down the road. He kept saying to me that he was going to f— me, and that if I tried to jump out I would be killed as he was doing 90mph. When he passed another car I screamed *"Help!"* It seemed like the thing to do, as I felt I was in a horror movie. *This can't be happening now,* I thought, but it was. Then he punched me in the face. I was terrified.

He pulled far off the road after we were deep in the desert and stopped. He then proceeded to attack me. I resisted, and he tried to knock me unconscious with blows to the nape of my neck with the flat of his hand. I was determined to stay conscious. He sat back for a minute and I said that I wanted a cigarette. He lit two cigarettes and said that he would burn my eyes out if I tried anything. My thoughts raced from reality to fantasy, as I couldn't believe that this was happening. I talked constantly: "I'm a Sunday school teacher. You don't want me. You can get anyone you want in Las Vegas. I'll meet you tonight at a motel." Nothing worked, so at that point I made a run from the car. As I ran, I knew that I was in the middle of a barren, empty desert with nowhere to run and no one to run to. He caught me, dragged me back, and threw me against the car. My teeth went through my lower lip and I slid down the side of the car. I looked at the hazy, yet glistening mountains in the distance and wondered if this was the last thing that I was ever going to see. I cried aloud, "Oh, God help me!" in the most heartfelt prayer I ever uttered.

He pushed me back into the car and the struggle resumed. He was exposed and I instinctively knew not to kick him there, as I had been taught. Instead, I kicked him in the face. We were both bleeding as he took out a knife and started to slash me. He cut my bathing suit off and discovered my sanitary napkin and belt. This also was cut off and flung into the desert. Immediately, he lost interest and said, "You didn't tell me you were sick." Strangely enough, it was the last day of my period and I almost didn't wear the pad and belt. I'm glad I did—it saved my life.

He drove me back to the campsite and dumped me there. I couldn't stop shaking. I knew I had to make a decision about going to the police. I re-read the letters I had received from friends and family. I read the Bible and prayed. Even though I wasn't a social worker at the time, I knew that I would be made the victim again. I had voluntarily gotten into the assailant's car. I drank alcohol with him. We had gone sightseeing. If a trial came up, my physical wounds would have healed—but would the inner ones ever heal? I was also aware of the "sin city" reputation of Las Vegas. I was a case of attempted rape and murder, but neither had been accomplished. I had to take responsibility for my involvement.

I decided to accept this terrifying experience as a tough lesson in life and be thankful that I was still alive, but terribly shaken. Therefore, Teri and I continued the last five days of the bicycle trip.

Peggy

Mom never told me about the actual rape. She talked about the desert and sky and feelings of not having control and about it all being her own fault. In high school, I remember reading her cross-country journal for the first time. I laughed at her Pollyanna attitude about singing the national anthem and carrying on about sunsets and flowers while riding in the Midwest. I was amazed by the distances she covered across the nation and how she camped out under the stars and in city parks. But I became confused when I read about September 13 being "the worst day of [her] life."

I remember Mom sitting in her lawn chair, smoking a cigarette, when I asked her about that "worst day" entry. She almost dropped the cigarette into her lap. I watched as her eyes became opaque, far away, and blank. She looked down, biting her lip. I was confused, because usually when questions about her trip would come up, my mother's face would be full of animation. She'd act out singing her Girl Scout songs in Michigan or imitate Dave Garroway with his microphone while she calmly answered his questions on national TV. Now, she just sat quietly, as if figuring out just what to tell her 17-year-old daughter.

"It was all my fault. I got into a bad predicament and was almost killed in the desert. I really don't want to talk about it right now." Mom's voice was monotone, like when people speak into a tape recorder and try to act naturally, but don't do a very good job of it. I remember not wanting to press the issue because if I tried, I felt that Mom would simply dry up and blow away. So I didn't ask anymore about Nevada, the desert, and that journal entry. I just thumbed back and re-read entries about the happier times of her trip like when she and Teri drank cold iced teas given to them by farmer's wives in the 100-degree heat or when the hotel in Des Moines made such a fuss over their arrival. I also looked over the many newspaper clippings in her scrapbook—clippings that included pictures of her and Teri wearing their dresses and pearls in the *Des Moines Register*; an article talking about them being greeted by the Simcoe, Ontario, mayor; photos of her and Teri riding bicycles in downtown Detroit; an article from McCook, Nebraska, with the headline, "Pair Cycling America Stop Here For Church"; or the Colorado Springs *Gazette Telegraph* article with the caption, "Tanned, Pretty New York Girl Cyclists Visit Region." These were the images that my mother evoked and wanted me to know about her trip, so I left it at that. September 13, 1956, would remain a question.

I finally got the whole story about Nevada when my mother brought her self-published memoir to Salt Lake City just before Brian and I left on our trip. After reading her frightening descriptions of that day I was able to finally ask her questions. "How come you stayed there after the attack? How come you didn't go to the police? What did Teri do?"

Mom talked to me for two hours, explaining that they stayed in Las Vegas after the attack because Teri wanted to go on a date with the bartender she had met earlier. She told me how fearful she was sitting in a motel room alone while Teri was away. How she shook and cried by herself, wishing that she was done with the trip and back home. How she blamed herself. How the police wouldn't have believed her because, as she told me, "it was 1956, not 1996." How she worried that the man would come back to kill her. How she had a hard time trusting men again. How she had nightmares and flashbacks of that night in the desert. How painful it had been to keep that memory inside for so many years. How wonderful it felt to tell the story and finally let it go.

Now that Brian and I are about to go through Nevada ourselves, I keep seeing images of my mother pleading and screaming as that man smacked her face and sliced at her with his knife. I worried that he or someone just like him may be out there in a truck waiting for me, that someone would grab me and kill me while Brian watched. I have crazy dreams the night before we are supposed to ride into Nevada, of people shooting at us, of Brian dead, of me in the back of a truck full of screaming fraternity boys with guns and knives. I wake up and lay in the dark, contemplating how fate could replay my mother's attack on our trip, and realize how dangerous our trip really is.

Nevada is a state I want nothing to do with. To me, it's a state to just ride past or around, to get through as quickly as possible. I can't see past my own fears; I feel suddenly small, a child hiding in a back closet from noises I haven't heard yet. I wish that I felt stronger and could get past the images I have of my mother alone out in this desert, but I can't. I want to drive across the desert in a car—fast—stopping only for gas and to throw anger over the landscape. I rationalize that taking a ride in our 4-Runner through the desert will heal my mother's pain.

Another subtle factor influencing our schedule is the daily calls that Brian is making to his work back in Park City. Apparently, things are getting no better with the water situation and the projects that are going on. His co-workers are doing a commendable job of keeping the water flowing, but they need his help. He's almost tempted to drive up there from St. George for a day or two and then start across Nevada after he has put out a few fires at work. I mention that skipping Nevada will enable him to get back to his job sooner, but he just shrugs. "We can do it," he says.

"I know, Brian, but that's not the point. Why ride three days through nothing when you need to get back to work?"

We still haven't decided what to do the next day when, by some quirky twist of fate, Brian wakes up sick and dizzy with something like a stomach flu. He still wants to ride, so he pulls himself out of bed, puts on his cycling clothes, and tries to balance himself on the bike and ride. He almost falls over a few times—he isn't going anywhere. I suggest that we drive some of the way across Nevada and he agrees. I can tell that he is depressed, like he has failed somehow by making the decision to load the bicycles on top of the 4-Runner instead of riding. I don't rub it in; I'm just relieved to know that Nevada's desert will soon be behind us.

As we drive across Nevada, the wind seems to push our truck through the cactus on either side. As the miles click by into monotony, I become mesmerized with the rhythm of the road instead of the landscape. With my face pressed on the window, my eyes half shut, I realize that this road is like my mother's near-rape experience—endless and barren.

Towns occasionally interrupt the stretches of nothingness. In Caliente, we stop at a gas station where nameless people pull the handles on slot machines inside. Men sleeping alongside shaded buildings raise bottles at me as I take Lyla for a walk past them. A car with tinted windows and a loud muffler idles past, and I'm very glad that we aren't riding our bikes through here.

When we were planning our bicycling route, we decided that maybe we would stay in Warm Springs for the night. On the map, it's the halfway point across Nevada, so we figured that there would at least be a motel there and a place for dinner. But as we come upon the town in our truck, there is nothing but an intersection and two abandoned buildings. Windows are boarded up and cracked; there is nothing here but the residue of a town. Brian takes photos of the falling-in-on-itself gas station, its pumps long abandoned and vandalized. Our truck's idling engine is the only sound we hear besides a trickling stream. We amble over and stick our feet in the warm spring, still running though its namesake town is gone. We zoom away.

I find that my thoughts have a way of rambling around loose inside my head as we ride deeper and deeper into the confines of Nevada without any radio station to listen to. Brian starts to sing Glen Campbell songs for some reason. He runs through renditions of "Rhinestone Cowboy," "By the Time I Get to Phoenix," and "Wichita Lineman" as if he'd written them himself. "You know that your trip is dragging on when you start singing Glen Campbell songs," he laughs, driving into the red sunset as Karen, Lyla, and I look out across the brown distance.

We drive, slouching over like rag dolls, taking turns behind the wheel while the others stare back into darkness, silent. When we cross into California, there is a sense of relief. Our butts are sore, our moods irritable, our clothes crumpled and sweaty. There is no sense of accomplishment this day—only a new desire to finish the trip on our own and on our bikes.

Brian and I sit in a Denny's that night in Bishop, California, sipping beer and eating pie, discussing why it was okay to drive, not ride, across Nevada.

"It's our trip and no one else's." I made this same comment to Brian on our first day in the Delaware Water Gap and it seems appropriate again tonight. "Sometimes I think premonitions, nightmares, and sickness are not just excuses, but reasons to look at other paths."

Brian looks at the map. "There really weren't any cities across Nevada for us to stay in safely, were there?" He calculates the mileage between Caliente and Tonopah. "195 miles," he says, "and nothing in between but Warm Spring—no water, no stores, a vast space of nothing."

Brian and I talk about "should haves," "could haves," and "next times," like maybe another route across Nevada would have been better—maybe even the interstate, which at least has gas stations. Then, in a moment of madness, I grin at Brian, knowing that I have blueberries stuck all over my teeth. We laugh and drink another beer and it all feels right again. This trip is ours, and what we are creating together and taking with us is all that matters.

16

"They spoke less and less between them until at last they were silent altogether, as is often the way with travelers approaching the end of a journey."
—Cormac McCarthy, *Blood Meridian*

Brian

It's good to be back riding our bicycles again. Traveling around in our 4-Runner seemed too easy and detached from the places we drove through. But if there was one place on our trip to zip through, Nevada was surely it.

With the sun rising up over our right shoulders, we ride north out of Bishop. We can see the remnants of the western edge of Nevada's dry desert on our right as we ride past the Owens River swiftly cutting through the brown/green sage. On our left stand the Sierra Nevada Mountains and their 13,000-foot granite peaks welcoming us to California. It's a beautiful but foreboding reminder of what lay ahead: one last climb before we finish the trip. We mapped our route to skirt north to San Francisco, rather than south to Los Angeles like June did. We are more interested in crossing the mountains of central California and in going through Yosemite National Park than sweltering across the Mojave Desert. Surveying this beautiful scene, I tell Peggy that it looks like we made the right choice. She quickly agrees.

The aforementioned climb will be on tomorrow's agenda. There is only one road into Yosemite and it consists of a 17-mile, 2,500-foot climb to 10,000 feet via Tioga Pass. We're psyched up for that pass, but 12 miles out of Bishop we start up a long graded climb, which takes us out of the river valley we are following. A sign reads, "Avoid overheating. Turn off A/C next 10 miles." It's about 11am and the sun is beginning to heat up the road as we notice other signs that say "Radiator water one mile," and "Steep grades—difficult for trailers." I grab my CamelBack straw and drink some water as I glance down at my watch/altimeter/thermometer—5,800 feet and 90 degrees. I don't say anything to Peggy, but I figure that we're in for a tough stretch of riding.

We lumber up the road admiring the view of the valley below on our right and the jagged gray peaks on our left. We also pass more radiator stops designed for people whose cars and trucks are overheating. As we hit the first of three summit markers, this one at 6,000 feet, Peggy wonders, "What about us bikers—where are the water tanks for us?" About a half-hour later, we hit the next marker, which reads, "Sherwin Summit - 7,000 feet." After spinning our lowest gears and drinking the last of our water, we hit the 8,000-foot mark, ominously named "Deadman's Summit." I pull out the camera and take a photo of Peggy, grinning and pointing at the sign.

Peggy and I don't feel any great elation or reason to celebrate this climb like we did two weeks ago for Independence Pass or last week riding over Boulder Mountain, but we have completed a chunk of riding that is equally tough—10 miles and 2,500 feet, all in 90-degree heat. Perhaps the reason for this is the fact that we were taken by surprise by this stretch of road. There weren't any markings on the maps showing this climb, and even though my DeLorme map of Northern California is covered with contour lines, I was deceived by what looked like a simple day of cycling from Bishop to Mono Lake. Sometimes, no matter how detailed your map is, your perception of what you see on paper can be far different from what you actually encounter. You find yourself misled by the roads, which always look straighter than they are, and by marked contours that look far gentler than the real elevations. And a printed map is always flat.

We run out of water near Mammoth Lakes, but fortunately, there is a rest stop five miles further where we take a welcome break and refill our water bottles. While we are resting, a gentleman comes up to us and inquires about our ride. He tells us that he is a college basketball coach for some team in the Sacramento Valley and that he is out recruiting. "I travel these roads all the time, and if you're going that way, just up ahead is the turnoff to June Lake. You just *have* to go that way—it's the prettiest road in all of California." He wishes us well and waves as he drives out of the parking lot.

Peggy asks me to show her where June Lake is on the map, apparently thinking the same thing I am. "Oh, it looks like another 10 miles, that's all," I respond. "Well that's it then," she decides. "We'll stop there for the night. I could sure use a dip in a lake and besides—it's *June* Lake." I can't argue with that logic, but I also remember that we are planning to meet Karen and Lyla in Lee Vining, which is another 10 miles down the road from the lake. We decide to just ride until we meet up with Karen, then backtrack to the lake.

Karen scouts out a cabin, which is down by the water. The owners of The Big Rock Lodge are friendly folks who let us use their washer and dryer so we can powerwash all the salt out of our cycling gear. Between changing loads, we all gather down on the beach as Lyla runs circles around us and in and out of the lake. Peggy describes the view we have looking out over the lake and towards the mountains as being "like the misty morning boatrip we took through the Norwegian fjords on our honeymoon—men are out in their fishing boats wearing flannel while women wave to them from the docks." Peggy has a knack for transforming what could be a mundane scene into something of near-epic proportions. I like that in her; it provides a welcome diversion from my facts, figures, and statistics.

Day 48 takes us up and over our last major summit of the trip—Tioga Pass—and into Yosemite National Park. The climb up the pass is on another steady 5% graded road. Tioga started at 7,500 feet and topped out at 10,000 feet, all over the course of 12 miles. Peggy and I stop to gather ourselves at the bottom of Tioga, each eating a Powerbar for some energizing carbohydrates, and we drink some Gatorade. Then we start cranking uphill—slowly.

It's a perfect day for riding. Yesterday's heat has given way to a crisp, clear 75-degree day. And unlike yesterday's surprising climb, today we know what to expect—it's no mystery since we can see all of the road laid out before us. There is no mistaking how far and how high we will be riding when we keep our eyes on the RVs and buses that gear down and pass us going up the mountain. They fade into the distance as the sound of their straining engines and their trail of black smoke slowly dissipates, but they never disappear from sight until they crest the top near the park entrance. When we reach the entrance I checked my altimeter for the details: 2 hours, 12 miles, and 2,850 feet. *Not bad,* I think. I report the ride statistics to Peggy, who replies, "Gadgetman!" Oh, well. It's an accomplishment anyway and a pretty ride. Riding the next 45 miles through Yosemite will be a different story.

I don't know what it is about national parks, but two things that I have noticed, especially in the ones we have ridden our bicycles through, have been: One, the roads get narrower and almost always lack any kind of shoulder; and Two, the traffic speeds up. Now, why is this? There is usually more traffic in a national park, so why don't they make the roads a little bit wider, or at least build them with a little bit of a shoulder? And why do people drive faster amidst such beauty? These observations trouble me as I tuck myself in behind Peggy and keep my eyes glued more to my rearview mirror than to Yosemite's beautiful scenery. It seems as though I yell "Over!" a hundred times to warn Peg of approaching cars. In jest, I remark that they should rename this place "Yosemite National Racetrack." Peggy, on the other hand, thinks that this road through the park is one of the best stretches of riding we have done. Her journal describes our ride through the largest subalpine meadow in the Sierra—Tuolemne Meadows—past the craggy gray rocks of Cathedral Peak and the rounded chalk-like Fairview and Medicott Domes, past Tenaya Lake's deep blue water, and through groves of giant Sequoia trees:

> The beauty drains me as it winds up the mountains and pushes me into places I didn't know I had. Then, descending, I fly past the red-barked trees with pinecones larger than my thighs. I feel that I can't make it up another hill when suddenly I find myself gliding to lower places. Riding past the Sequoia trees, I see only green and shadows, as the wind whistles in my ears. My eyes adjust and then open to see cliffs, falls, and impossible peaks, jagged all the way to the sky. I look at Brian and am amazed at how easy this whole trip really has been and how deeply it has touched both of us and brought us closer together. Even as our views are filled with car exhaust and our riding is made difficult by noisy engines and no shoulder, I find myself in a space where hushing sounds begin to take over.

Peggy

I envisioned Yosemite Village as a quaint mountain town with quiet hiking trails full of wild flowers and that famous waterfall cascading in a hidden pocket in the park for Brian and I to enjoy alone. We'd heat up hot dogs using sticks that we'd find in the woods and sit in the shadow of Halfdome.

As we ride in, the tail end of a slithering snake of cars, the image is shattered. One after the other, the sounds of pines trees and water are replaced by beeping, revved-up Winnebagos, stopping and starting at photographic spots, the sightseers clicking away like wild animals. There is a rush to stand in line at reservation counters for campsites and motel rooms. While Brian stands in line, wiping his forehead, I watch people piling out of cars, picking at shorts that had been previously stuck to car seats. No one looks happy.

When we finally get the key to our ramshackle tent-camp room—which is basically a hut with three single beds and four windows—I feel like I'm in an old mining camp, the miners living one atop the other. Dinner is the same, as we stand in line with trays, ready to pick up gourmet spaghetti in a cafeteria. Children scream, parents pull them along, and we sit and drink beer in Formica booths as the radio plays soft rock. We're not in a national park, but some sort of Disneyland created not for rides but for accessible wilderness sights. I wonder if sights like this should be so accessible—it probably diminishes our appreciation of them.

As the evening cools, Brian and I sit on rocks with Halfdome reflecting in the river. The Dome wavers, disappearing in and out of the ripples and for once, the quiet is real, the cars gone from the road. I watch my toes in the clear water until the light leaves the sky. The full moon becomes our direct spotlight to the ledges; rocks shine brilliantly white, like bones in the night.

The next morning, I can barely breathe. Or see. The canyon is covered in smoke, all the sights invisible. The Winnebagos have nothing to do as they drive around, searching for places to pull over. I really don't feel sorry for them. A ranger tells us that a controlled fire has become uncontrollable and that the smoke won't clear very well that day. So we load up our gear and head out of the park. We coast most of the way and I feel like I'm on a motorcycle, hugging the curves, almost wanting to lean my feet on the handlebars. It's mid-afternoon and the heat between the trees is starting to scorch them a bit. I want to ride quickly to a motel with a pool and continue this lazy day after yesterday's elevation/image overload. I speed past Brian.

I pretend that I can see the Bay, looking over the drying hills to the blue water, San Francisco, and us on the beach, finished with the trip. We have one of those nice bottles of Chardonnay and we sit in the sand, toasting and re-toasting each other. I see Mom and Dad around us along with my brother and Brian's sister and I can hear Tim's and my grandmother's voices over the waves, crashing onto the shore, clapping for our accomplishment.

"Peggy—Peggy, stop!" Brian is yelling at me, back in the distance. He is staring across the road, waving at me to come back. He probably has a flat tire. I ride back up the hill toward him, somewhat irritated that I have to actually pedal the bicycle.

"Look at this ghost town." He points down a lonely-looking street, the houses bleached in shaded wood tones, weeds growing out of windows and down the sides of fences. A faded sign says "Visitors Information." "Maybe they'll have places around here to stay," he says as we park our bikes on a wooden boardwalk.

The screen door tinkles, a rusted series of bells on its handle, and a man leaning back and reading a historical novel sits up in his chair. "Welcome to Chinese Camp," he says, standing up.

"What is this place?" Brian asks.

"It's older than you and I and gonna stay that way." The man introduces himself as Buzz. He's the "information man." "I know everything there is to know about this place and probably more than I need to." Buzz describes how Chinese Camp was a "rough and rowdy town, full of prostitutes and bars. Men living to find the gold coming down off the mountains. Searching for dreams that usually remained in the mind when this land got through with them. Some success stories, mostly ruin.

"This town is owned by a lady who refuses to sell out. Convention centers, hotel chains, and developers trying to cash in on a piece of past that's not theirs to grab, keep offering her more and more money for it but she won't sell for anything. They all want this little shred of history and they call it 'quaint' the way it is now. But I'm telling you, they'd change it, sure as I've got eyes to see, to an amusement park or some theme-parked ghost town, full of actors out of San Francisco shooting at each other and falling off the roof. Seems that people with the money to buy this all up just want to turn real to plastic. This is the real thing." Buzz explains the history of the buildings and how a bank had turned into a jail and back again, "depending on the needs of the town."

"Tell me more about the lady who owns the town." I picture her like my mother, wearing a mashed gardening hat, a pink and purple sundress with red sneakers, and smoking a pack of cigarettes while watching the sun set.

"Wouldn't come up much past your shoulder, but she's tough as nails. Family came here with the Gold Rush and stayed after the crash. She owns this street 15 feet under and 15 feet above and she won't ever give an inch of it to anyone. Sure frustrates all the developers, but not enough to stop them from trying."

"Why develop this?" I ask. "It's a hidden place that needs to stay this way. We almost passed it on our way out of here."

"Some places are better off staying hidden and discovered occasionally by those who see than made into a well-seen place that people pass through and forget."

We talk to Buzz for over an hour. He's the kind of man that rambles on while you sit listening, enjoying the threads of stories that emerge. Buzz tells us to stay in Jamestown that evening. "You could go to Oakdale and stay in a motel built in a parking lot or you can go out of your way about seven miles and stay in a place that has some character." We opt for Jamestown.

As we leave Chinese Camp, Brian turns around one more time to look back at Buzz. "He reminds me of a guy who I worked with in Indiana. His name was Dave and he died five years ago because he had Lou Gehrig's Disease. Buzz is the spitting image of him. The way he talks, walks, his clothes, his eyes. It's strange."

I think that maybe our friends and family who have passed on come back occasionally for us. They melt into hidden towns like Chinese Camp and give us inspiration to stop and have conversations with people in the most unlikely situations. Like history, maybe we pass our loved ones by because we're not looking hard enough on the fringes of life.

Brian takes picture after picture of the Chinese Camp buildings.

"Tim would've loved this place," he says, knowing that his brother was always looking for out-of-the-way places to take photographs.

Jamestown is a spruced-up, unpretentious old Western town. We ride through Main Street passing renovated saloons, mom-and-pop supermarkets with swinging screen doors, and candy shops. Buzz had suggested the Railtown Hotel and it's perfect. We meet up with Hal, the manager, and continuing the synchronicity that seems to pull us from place to person, he could be my Uncle Artie, the geologist.

"I remember you—you were on *The Today Show*. I saw you there with your mother." Hal has a crackled face, deep with lines, half from smiling and the other half, probably, from sitting outside by the pool drinking Old Milwaukees. "Look at those tans. Never seen tans like that, except on truck drivers passing through." White hands, white ankles, white upper arms, white thighs and the rest, a deep brown. "You two look like you could use a beer."

"So, what are the names of your bicycles?" he asks.

"This whole trip, you're the first person to ask that question," Brian responds. "Don't you want to know where we're from, where we're headed, how far we ride in a day, or how many flat tires we've had, like everyone else?"

"Heck, that stuff's boring. People used to name their horses, you know, so I figured you must have names for those shiny bikes."

"Well, as a matter of fact, we do," I respond. "Mine is named Miss LuLu after our dog."

"And yours?" he asks Brian.

"Steinbeck II, after John Steinbeck," Brian replies. "The original Steinbeck is back in the basement of our house."

"Well that's great. You know you're in Steinbeck country now— he lived out here most all his life," Hal adds.

"Yeah, I've read all of his books," says Brian. "They're full of Monterey, Carmel, San Francisco, and the Sacramento Valley."

"Great country," says Hal.

"Great books too," Brian concludes.

So we drink with Hal while he sits in his chair telling us how the world is too fast sometimes. "What's the problem with slowing down to let people pass sometimes? No one these days wants to be last, they all want to be first and to me, life isn't a race to finish. We all know what the prize of finishing life first is, don't we?" We talk about traffic patterns and how he doesn't see his grandchildren as much as he'd like and how he finds sitting here at the pool lets his mind wander back and forth over his life.

As we get ready to leave the pool, Hal suddenly shoots up from his chair. "You wait here. I don't usually share much about my hobbies with people, but I will with you." We wait in the shadows of the building for Hal. When he returns his face is serious, over-lapping his smiling eyes. "The lady picks the right hand, the gentle-man the left."

I open his right hand and a silver bullet key chain is crunched up inside. He gives Brian a gold-tipped bullet key chain. "These are for you because you both bit the bullet coming across the nation on bikes. Hang these on your handlebars and nothing bad will happen to you on the road."

We place the key chains on our handlebars and head out for dinner in a genuine old saloon restaurant. The gaslit dining room is empty while we drink a bottle of wine by candlelight in our high-backed stuffed chairs. I feel like I'm on Gunsmoke. I have my lady-like silver bullet for luck, my trusty Schwinn back in the stable, and my cowboy wining and dining me late into the night. When we walk around town that evening, a man even tips his baseball cap at me as we pass by and for a moment, I imagine myself as someone from the Old West named Miss Kitty. Brian is Marshall Bob, or some other gun-toting, peacekeeping fellow out to save me from lawless types.

In the morning, Hal is up again, making us some fresh coffee. "You got those bullets on?" We show him the keychains dangling from our handlebars and he looks satisfied. "Now, you got to see Cricket's Grave at about mile 24. He's a horse that used to stand by the fence along the highway and watch cars pass by and now there's a memorial for him by his place on the fence. I used to bring him apples and that horse would scoop them out of my hand. That horse knew a lot about the world."

When we reach Cricket's Grave, we find stuffed animals, fruit rotting in the sun, real and fading plastic flowers, American flags, pine cones, and wooden wreaths. A path through the brown grass worn by trampling feet shows the dedication people had for an animal that stood around watching life pass by. There are a couple of pictures of people with Cricket before he died, and it sure looked like that horse had a smile on his face.

The flat roads to Stockton curve through fruit trees and tiny towns, all with fruit stands. Men balancing on top branches of trees throw apples and pears down into crates on trucks while women nurse children in the shade. We pass like shadows through the groves of trees, listening to the muted sounds of Mexican music coming from distant radios. Traffic is sparse until we pass closer to Stockton, where the sounds of a highway overpass bring back the blaring of truck horns and the sound of tires on hot pavement overhead. Riding past the airport, we are suddenly thrust back into humanity as we land in a rundown industrial part of town.

Men in pickup trucks careen past us, drunk, with hands out the window. People exit shabby, industrial-area bars and lay in the street. Brian whispers, "Just look straight ahead. Don't look at anyone, and act like you know where you are going." But we are in a wave of color, of noise, of staring eyes, and it's difficult to turn away from the ripples of shouts, music deep with bass, and slow-riding cars with flashy mag wheels.

We stop at a Best Western in Stockton, east of the highway, but the chained doors, barred windows, and graffiti slung along repeatedly-painted white walls turn us away. People whistle at our shiny new silver bikes and we grow skittish, our eyes darting up and back over the crazed road. "There has to be a better area than this. We've got to get away from all this action." We decide to keep going, heading west. I keep tabs on the silver bullet dangling from my handlebar and thank Hal under my breath.

Two minutes later, after riding under the highway, we come upon a newer hotel with three or four police cars parked outside an Applebee's Restaurant next door. Another police car drives in as his colleagues wave from the window. We quickly wheel ourselves into the Motel 6, taking a second floor room, and lock the door—our stockade in Stockton.

That night, like moles up from our hole in the ground, we eat the dinner special at Applebee's with yet another group of policemen on break. Brian and I drink two frosted mugs of beer, eat a big dinner chosen from the pictured selections, and then enjoy our free pie. We look out the window and notice a bicycle rider, loaded down with packs, pass the window heading east, his expression one of confusion and longing. We watch silently as the flash of his red pack and white helmet disappear under the highway overpass and into the chaos we had left only an hour earlier. We are ending and he is starting and we imagine his route: Yosemite, Nevada, Southern Utah, Colorado. Will he see the smoke in Yosemite? How will he make it across Nevada? Can he cross Independence Pass? What about the wind in Nebraska? The hills in Iowa? Thunderstorms in the Midwest? Will there still be humidity in the East? He's on the flip side of our trip, a quarter flying in the air, heads to our tails, spinning toward fate, landing someplace other than here.

Roads lead and go past places seen and unseen. We see what we expect we may not find. Ending his cross-country journey, William Least-Heat Moon described this feeling in *Blue Highways:* "I can't say, over the miles, that I had learned what I had wanted to know because I hadn't known what I wanted to know. But I did learn what I didn't know I wanted to know."

"So, when do you think you'll be here? Can we meet you halfway? Maybe we can find you ... " Mom is still trying this angle with me, of finding us, searching us down, finishing the trip with us, but I dissuade her. I can just see Mom driving around the streets of Oakland with Dad looking at crumpled maps on his lap, yelling and pointing to exits as she drives 45 miles per hour in the breakdown lane. She'd eventually find us, somehow, with the help of guardian angels banding together for miracles, and I could see her beeping and singing and throwing confetti and flower petals. She might even have a blowhorn to announce the finish of our trip, shouting out our names and her name and why we were on bicycles. Brian and I would have headaches at the party at Andrea's because of all the noise and commotion.

"No, Mom. We want to do it on our own. It will be better if you wait with Dad and everyone else for us at Andrea's."

"Well, I guess I understand. It's just that I'm so proud of you. Can you believe that you're almost done? How do you feel about finishing?"

"It's happened so fast and so slow at the same time," I say, "like time had no consequence—its own way of letting moments pass."

"Are you happy?"

"I don't know if happy is the word for it. *Full* is more like it. Full of so many images in my mind. It's like I have so many thoughts mixed in with memories and I just would like some more space to keep it all close like it is now." I almost start crying, but if I start crying then Mom will cry and we'll just hold onto the phones and sob. Mom and I are like twins with tears; if one cries, the other joins in soon after. We react to each other and with each other. Mom is mixed inside me, like sand between toes.

But I am happy. Happy to know that my mother is so close.

"When I finished, I was confused, like I'd left something behind," she recalls.

We are both thinking of Nevada, of leaving things behind and going on—but always coming back.

"Nevada?"

"Yeah, Nevada. Sometimes I feel like the trip ended there and began again when I met your father."

"The fairy tale ending—a blind date with a cute boy. Where did you go on that date again?"

"A strip joint!" Mom laughs. "I'd never seen a stripper before that trip, you know. It opened my eyes up to a lot of things. I guess you could say I started the trip out as a naive Girl Scout and ended it a bit wiser about the world."

"And got a husband to boot," I add.

"Oh yeah, I guess that was important too."

Brian

June's memoir recalls the last days of her bicycle trip:

> The bicycle trip officially ended as we rode into San Marino, California, on September 18, 1956, our 89th day on the road. We stayed at Teri's aunt's house. There was no great feeling of exultation, as I was still suffering the physical and emotional effects of the devastating experience in the desert.

> We were on the TV program "Today in the West." The actor, Vincent Price, sat right next to me as he was appearing on the same show. He sneeringly asked what we had done to get on the show. When I told him that we had ridden bicycles across the country he said, "Why did you do such a foolish thing like that?" Since his haughty attitude annoyed me I replied, "Next time we're thinking of crossing the country on roller skates."

Forty years later, I asked June more about that ending. How did they get to California? What were her plans? How had she been able to keep herself together to finish?

"It was tough, but after thinking it over for awhile there in the desert I decided that I wasn't going to let that awful man ruin what had been, to that point, a great experience. I wasn't very happy with Teri, though. She wanted to stay there for a couple of days after my ordeal so she could spend time with a gentleman she had met. He was a nice fellow, but I really felt that Teri was disregarding my feelings about the whole situation. She didn't think that it was as significant as I did. We stayed in touch for awhile after the trip, but were never really close after our tour—which is too bad, I think. For the most part, we got along remarkably well on the trip and had a lot of fun."

Getting to Los Angeles was a fairly uneventful ending to the ride of June and Teri. They took a train from Las Vegas to Barstow, California, on September 16, arriving there at 2am. The next day they rode for as long as they could in the heat of the desert and then took a ride into Victorville. That evening they went out to the movies and watched *The Rim of Hell*, an appropriately-titled film given June's recent mood. It was as if the movies she watched that summer across America were in some way mirroring her experiences. The title of this movie was as relevant to this moment as *The Best Years of our Lives* had been in Iowa City, Iowa. However, June's scant journal entry for September 17, 1956, describes the movie as being "about a poor old man and his dog. I really had a good cry." In some way this must have been a good film for her to see because it allowed for the emotional release that she so needed at this point.

They rode for awhile out of Victorville the next day, but again, the weather was pretty hot. The traffic was getting pretty busy too, this close to Los Angeles, so they accepted a few final rides into San Marino. They surprised Teri's aunt on their arrival, so there was no great fanfare awaiting them. This was okay with June, who wrote in her journal, "We're here, we've finished, and I'm confused."

This was definitely the end of the line for June. Her idea of getting a flight to Hawaii and maybe even Australia was long gone. She was ready to pack up and head home to the familiarity of her family and friends. She would eventually do that, but she had a few days to kill first.

On Saturday, September 22, 1956, Teri's cousin Neil set her and June up on blind dates. Neil worked at Proctor and Gamble, so he arranged for a couple of engineers to take them out. As that evening approached, the gentleman who was supposed to be June's date couldn't make it, so at the last minute a replacement was lined up. June's memoir recalls the rest:

> Bob Newland was my date and my first thought was that he was a real cutie. He was tall, blonde, and had blue eyes that seemed to reveal a wholesome and genuine personality. He was a real California boy, born and raised in Long Beach, and a graduate of the California Polytechnic Institute.
>
> Teri's date was quiet and she wished that my date had been hers. Bob and I formed an immediate liking for each other. As a matter of fact, we even shared a few kisses before dinner was served.
>
> After a night of dancing, we spent the next day at the beach. Bob took me home to meet his parents and to have a pancake breakfast. His father kissed me at first sight and his mother was sweet and jovial.

I flew home to New York on October 8, 1956, for my mother's birthday. My friends met me at the airport with banners and flowers. Bob packaged and sent my bicycle back on a train. He came to visit me that Christmas and we became engaged.

We were married the next year. And even though we've been married for almost 39 years, I still like to call him "my blind date."

Andrea, Brian, Peggy, and June Celebrate

17

"Each place you stop exists in layers of time, as well as space. The present is merely an intersection of the winding roads of the past."
—Dayton Duncan, *Out West*

Peggy and Brian

The next morning, we set out as soon as light hits the sky, homing pigeons to the western mountains. The land stretches out flat and broken by irrigation streams running in perfect rows. Instead of housing developments, windmills twirl in the distance, reaching out haphazardly for air along the hillsides. We wind and weave through blowing fields until we hit landscape that reminds us of the movie *Out of Africa*. We can see Mount Diablo in the distance as we curve through mounds of faded grass sprinkled with groves of arthritic trees, branches pointing to the sun. Expecting to see lions prowling and elephants swinging their trunks, we instead come upon a riding stable full of tourists on horses. The road sweeps us along the banks of a small canyon and we bob and weave our way west. It's hard to believe that we are only about 30 miles from the Bay Area.

Andrea's friend, Steve Secker, is supposed to meet us in Walnut Creek, a community full of coffeehouses and boutiques selling knickknacks for the homes of upscale suburbia. We're a bit late, but when he finds us he has a huge smile on his face and powerful legs on his racing-cyclist body. We are comforted by the fact that this is a man who knows the roads and can safely lead us to the Promised Land of Andrea's house on the boarder of Oakland and Berkeley.

"There's a lot of stuff brewing back at Andrea's," Steve explains as we stop for a quick lunch. "The crowd is decorating and talking and cooking. We'd better give them a call to tell them where we are. Everyone wants to know—especially your mother, Peg."

We imagine Mom sitting on Andrea's front porch with a cup of coffee and a lit cigarette waving in the wind, watching the road, searching for signs of us nearby. She's probably singing Girl Scout songs and telling anyone that walks past to join in the party for her daughter and son-in-law as they finish their cross-country trip. We're sure that she would add something like, " ... and they were on *The Today Show*. I was too, and I wasn't even nervous, but that's probably just because I had been on before and knew what to expect. You see, I rode my bicycle across the country in 1956, on a three-speed Schwinn. We didn't have any of that fancy stuff that they have now ... " By this time of the day we figure that strangers and neighbors alike probably know the whole story: Mother, daughter, son-in-law, 40-year commemorative ride ...

We picture Dad sitting by the phone waiting for it to ring so he can get the news first. Peggy's brother Paul would be in charge of music; he's probably putting CD after CD of Bob Marley or John Hiatt on the stereo, filling Andrea's house with beats pounding in 4-4 time. We picture Andrea blowing up balloons and dancing around in some Indian print skirt, making sure that everyone is busy and happy. We decide then that the most important thing about our trip is not our accomplishment, but the connection it has to a larger purpose; the connection to family and friends makes our trip whole, complete. Even with the distances, the comings and goings, farewells and arrivals, the connection stays constant.

We talk on the phone to almost everyone, and all their questions are pretty much the same. "Yes, we're almost there ... two hours more ... Yes, we'll be careful ... Yes, we're proud, too ... Yes, we'll be hungry ... " It seems unreal that we are finishing and family is there waiting for us. Our trip seemed small until we got this close; and now it looms large, blanketing us in warmth.

Steve leads us through a maze of city streets, motioning us left and right, telling us where the traffic will come and go, finding secret little bike paths off the main arteries. We free ourselves from the maps, the mileage, the directions, the altitude, the routes, and just follow our trusty escort and throw away all thoughts of maps. Our worries about place and direction have taken leave for the first time on the trip. Then, we hit one final climb. We joke with Steve that he must be some kind of sadist, but then figure that he might just want to see how that altimeter watch of ours really works.

We ride upward on the Skyline Road, through Redwood Regional Park—about a 1,000-foot ascent. Then, near the top, one of the best images of our trip presents itself. Sweet eucalyptus that shreds into vines holds back the full view of San Francisco Bay from us like someone holding a present behind his back. It seems as if we are slowing almost to a crawl, as if we really don't want to see the Bay, the "other" ocean—the ending. Since that very first night four years ago at Paul's place in Chicago, it seems as if our whole life has been about this trip, and here we are, almost finished.

We crest the top and another world spreads before us, teeming with life. Boats are on the bay, cruising in and out under the Golden Gate Bridge, and an aerial show is underway with the Blue Angels flying in formation. We feel as if they are saluting us as we take video and laugh at our shameless comments. Then we ride downhill a few miles to our welcoming committee.

It's over before we even have a chance to hug and kiss at the corner of Andrea's house. Paul runs down the street to greet us and we hear hooting and hollering just about the time Mom rounds the corner with a bouquet of flowers, singing Girl Scout songs. Dad wheels himself down the sidewalk while Paul's wife Rebecca captures us all on film. Andrea rushes out with champagne and her boyfriend Eric takes the video camera and pans the pandemonium. Paul grabs one of our bicycles and rides it around the block while Dad holds one of our helmets in his lap as the other sits cockeyed on his head. He's smiling ear to ear.

"I can't believe you made it—*I'm so proud of you!*" June exclaims. We stand in the middle of the commotion, speechless and sweating. Holding hands, we shake our heads at what we have done and smile at those around us. June wants a photo with us, so we pose with her and the arrangement of sunflowers as we hug. Then, it's just Mom and I, smiling at each other. We're speechless as she raises her arms up in joy.

We head inside Andrea's house, which is all decked out with banners, balloons, streamers, and a big sign that says, "Peggy and Brian: Congratulations on making your dream a reality." Before we can sip the first of the cold beers, we are bulldozed by Andrea's dog, Poppy, and Lyla. With telephone calls to Phil in New York City and Rhoda in Ohio, we are united as one.

Later, we sit around the table, eat pizza and drink beer. Phil has sent a big package of our photos, so we pass the albums around and re-live our trip in pictures, answering questions along the way: "Yeah, we walked our bicycles down Times Square the night before we started—we had to get into the feel of things you know ... Oh, there's Brian all covered in sweat, those first couple of weeks were really rough on him ... See, Canada's roads don't have any shoulder, but they sure have a lot of traffic ... Here's that kind couple that gave us a ride to the ferry across Lake Erie and here we are sitting on the beach watching the sunset with Rhoda and Dutch ... Those are the real Bridges of Madison County—they didn't just build them for the movie, either ... That's our cousin that lives in Nebraska ... That's cousin John's house, and those are the flowers Mom sent for my birthday, and there are those flowers again at the top of the Continental Divide ... Look at us sitting in that Aspen hot tub with all the snow blowing around us ... That one is of Southern Utah near the Escalante-Grand Staircase National Monument ... That's Bryce Canyon and that one is of Zion."

Everyone coaxes June into reading a little bit from her journal. Actually, it doesn't take that much coaxing. She chooses to read about the Fort Des Moines "red carpet" welcoming and the kind people that helped her out in Winterset, Iowa.

Everyone laughs heartily when June mentions getting rides from Winterset to Red Oak in a cement truck, a pickup truck, and a station wagon. "I thought you *rode* your bicycle across the country, Mom," Paul teases. "This sounds more like you hitched and *hauled* your bicycle across the country. You should write a book: 'How I Hauled My Bicycle Across The Country!"

June is laughing so hard by this time that her glasses are about to fall off her head, but she defends her decisions. "We were having gear trouble that day and it was 105 degrees out. You don't say no when someone offers you a ride in 100-degree heat. Besides that, we met a lot of people that way. It was a ball."

Andrea asks how they were able to hitch all those rides and where they put their bicycles when people picked them up.

"How did we get all those rides?" June repeats. "Well, I don't quite remember—it wasn't hard, though. You know, we were two young women on bicycles. You didn't see that much back then, so people would stop and ask us questions. A lot of them would offer rides, so sometimes we'd take them up on their offer, especially in the desert."

"As for where we put our bicycles, it was easy," she continues. "When a truck driver picked us up, we'd just throw them in the back. Sometimes we even rode in the back with them. Some people had station wagons, but mostly, people with cars would just stuff our bikes in the trunk and off we'd go."

"Enough of my stories," June says. "Read something from your journal, Peggy."

"Okay. Des Moines, Iowa: Governor Wilson is here for a conference. We were lucky to get a room; at least that's what the hotel says. No hoopla for us like Mom. The next day I almost have a nervous breakdown on the way to Winterset. Lightning bolts everywhere. Got a hotel room and a Cadillac to see the bridges."

"A Cadillac?" someone asks.

"Oh yeah, these people saw us on the road, bought us lunch, and then gave us their Coupe DeVille to tour the bridges."

"What kind of people would do that for perfect strangers?" someone else asks.

"People from Iowa."

"Read us something from yours, Brian," Andrea says.

"Okay, leaving Winterset for Red Oak we took a ride in a cement truck, a pickup, and a stationwagon ... Oh, sorry, that was yours, wasn't it, June?" More laughter all around.

We sit around the table until all the pizza is gone and we've blown out the candles on the chocolate cake that reads, "Congratulations Peggy and Brian!" We have almost finished off the last beer when Lois, a long-time friend of Tim's from his days at Ohio University, stops in to join in the celebration. We tell her all about our need to stop in Chinese Camp to take photographs. She turns ashen, and her expression is a bit startled. "You know," she says, "Tim was out to visit me about ten years ago and he wanted me to take him to a unique place so he could shoot some photographs—I took him to Chinese Camp. It's amazing that you would stop and take the time yourselves to walk around taking pictures of the place. Tim must have played a part in that."

"Oh, he played a part all right," we respond. "We weren't alone out there. We always felt like we had lots of people watching over us."

Peggy

October 13, 1996. Golden Gate Park is alive with people celebrating life. Rollerbladers boogie to KC and the Sunshine Band as parents jog past with babies in strollers. A soccer game is full of screaming fans lifting beers. Bikers meander across the sidewalks and the closed streets of the park. Today, Brian and I are just a couple of these cyclists out on a Sunday ride, without our helmets, without packs, without any evidence of our 3,000-mile journey across America. We know that once we pass through this park our trip will be finished. We'll see the Pacific Ocean, the shoreline that is the last great sight of our journey. Distance will no longer be based on mileage per day but by how we look at each other, and the memories we hold together.

I almost don't want to see the Bay, the "other" ocean, the ending; I'm content with the fact that our trip is not about endings, but beginnings. I'm beginning to see myself slowing down, beginning to understand that life is a process, a continuation rather than a numerical line of time. Now I see my mother as a comrade, a collaborator on this trip, not a competitor. And I'm also recognizing that I'm beginning to find myself at home within myself.

Perhaps there are many ways to find your home—those hidden places where memories have active heartbeats—but I think the quickest way there is to take time in the palm of your hand and listen slowly to its sounds. By doing this trip I've proven to myself that a bicycle is a great way to make your life slow down to that manageable level—65 miles a day rather than 65 miles an hour.

We linger, stop for a hot dog, and sit on the curb watching others on their routes through the park. We're quiet because there is nothing more to say. We've mapped ourselves together across the miles and the silent markings we carry within our hearts crisscross and intersect.

We coast downhill to where our family is waiting to celebrate with open bottles of wine and champagne. We toast and laugh as the clouds open up from the misty gray to pink, the sun finally out. We circle around my dad as he raises a hand to say a prayer of thanks for our trip.

Pushing and carrying our bikes across the sand we make it to the edge of the ocean. A salty breeze hits us as the surf claps for our success. It's quiet, just Brian and myself. We're alone as we touch the finish line.

"Now, turn around, kids. Get the bikes facing the sunshine so you glow."

We should have known that Mom would follow us out. After all, this is her trip, too. While we spent 52 days riding our bicycles, she was by the phone and in front of her map of the country, waiting for our calls and updates so she could stick another pin into it to mark our progress: New Jersey, Pennsylvania, New York, Ontario, Ohio, the Midwest, the West, and finally, California. Her map is worn and full of pins from her trip across America 40 years ago. I always found it interesting to look at, though, because it is so different from the maps today—fewer roads, no interstates, smaller towns. But that's because so much has changed in 40 years—that is, everything but my mother.

I notice that her flip-flops are starting to sink in the sand as she tries to position us just right for our picture. Her camera is the old kind that requires hard-to-find 110-type film and its battery is constantly dying, but Mom keeps it because she knows how it works. "Now, ready? One ... two ... three ... oh, the green light isn't flashing! Wait just a minute!"

We stand smiling, our backs to the water, when suddenly a wave crashes over our feet, almost up to my mother's knees. It doesn't phase her.

"Oh, that's perfect!" She exclaims as her camera clicks.

Mom's face is full of light and pride, her eyes tearing. Together, we hug and face the oncoming ocean.

Epilogue

Peggy

Tim's scarf rode across the country with me. Not for a cause, not for protection, not for any reason other than I wanted him along with me. I tied the scarf on my handlebars in a square knot, strong enough to stay around yet free enough to enjoy riding with the wind that would hit us each day on the road. The bike, the scarf, and I would stop at places where the light hit leaves in translucent patterns, shadowed on the prairie grasses. Occasionally, I'd take the camera from Brian and, leaning on my handlebars, shoot a wisp of moment, time held silently in the grain of an abandoned barn or a dazzling movement of the sky. When it rained, we were both soaked equally and we'd dry together, dripping by the warmth of a loud old hotel heater turned on high. I watched as the scarf held snow on Independence Pass, layer upon layer of snow hiding the faded pattern of ice skaters on the knotted fabric. In Oakland, I wore the scarf to Andrea's party, a sash around my waist. We all laughed about the icicles in my socks, about singing cartoon jingles in the desert, about birthday dinners and flowers. We groaned about the traffic, the heat, the wind, the sun, the sweat, and the hills.

That night, on the porch at Andrea's, I tightened the scarf with amazement, surrounded by a circle of family and friends.

We all lifted our glasses to those not there—and to those who were.

Thanks

We would like to thank everyone that made our ride and this book possible:

For our friends in Salt Lake that helped with trip preparation: Tim Nelson of Holy Cow! Productions for his contacts with Schwinn; Schwinn Bicycles for providing us with two great bicycles and much of the gear for our trip; Bingham Cyclery, for putting them together and packing them for the flight to New York City; Mark Boyer, for a great sendoff party; Karen Adams, for watching our house and providing support through Nevada and California.

For those that helped during the trip: Philip Goetz, who spent every day with us via the internet, providing updates and developing all our film, and renting "the last car in New York City" to give us support on Days Two and Three; Tracy Goetz for helping with logistics and accomodations in New York; Andy Pollock, for letting us put a bike rack on his brand-new white Honda Accord so he could shuttle us out of New York on Day One; Jane and David Sweet for a great evening in Buffalo full of all those funny June stories; Glenn and Mary Cleveland and their daughter and son-in-law Sue and Jim McCullum for rescuing us in Canada; Rhoda and Dutch Myers for two great days in Port Clinton and a wonderful barbeque in Findlay; Dan Sheaffer for shuttling us to and from Bowling Green to Findlay and for keeping Brian's "webless" mother posted on our progress; Betsy and Francis Disori for sharing touring stories over an Indiana dinner; Patti and Courtney Witt for a great night of Iowa hospitality; Dick and Jeanne Cooper for loaning us their car to tour "the Bridges of Madison County"; Cindy and Denny Done for a great dinner and evening in Lincoln,

Nebraska; Paul and Laura Brannigan, for saving us from a Colorado windstorm; Tom and Jenny Day for a great deck party and meal to ready us to ride the Rockies; John Meyer, for helping us "carbo load" and making sure we made it up and over the Continental Divide; Janet Brown, for another great pasta dinner in St. George, Utah; Hal, owner of the Railtown Motel, for our lucky "Silver Bullets"; Paul Secker, for guiding us those last 30 miles into Oakland (we took literary license with Paul's name, changing it to "Steve" so readers wouldn't confuse him with Paul Newland, Peggy's brother); Andrea Goetz, for making the end of our trip such a celebration; Paul and Rebecca Newland, for coming out and celebrating with us; Bob and June Newland for being there, too; Silver Springs Water Company in Park City, Utah, and its owner, Bob Larsen, and the University of Utah for allowing us the time to take this trip.

And we are in debt to those that read numerous drafts of this book and gave us guidance and constructive criticism: Debbie Bird, Brooke Williams, Rhoda Myers, Adelaide Sanders, Rachael Jahn, and most of all, our biggest supporter in this literary journey, John Weiss of Cycling Classics.

We are most grateful to our publisher, Albert Knight, and our editor, Christian Glazar, at Anacus Press for being so good to work with throughout this project.

And thanks to all of our family and friends not mentioned for their interest, words of encouragement, concern, prayers, inspiration, and general good thoughts coming our way during our adventure.

Last, but not least, thanks to Saint Rita. This trip never seemed "impossible" to us, however, at times it was "nearly impossible."

If you haven't had enough already, you can read more about both trips at: **www.TheAdventureBook.com**